Collection Editor: Jennifer Grünwald
Editorial Assistants: James Emmett & Joe Hochstein
Assistant Editors: Alex Starbuck & Nelson Ribeiro
Editor, Special Projects: Mark D. Beazley
Senior Editor, Special Projects: Jeff Youngquist
Vice President of Sales: David Gabriel
SVP of Brand Planning & Communications: Michael Pasciullo
Book Design: Jeff Powell

Editor in Chief: Axel Alonso
Chief Creative Officer: Joe Quesada
Publisher: Dan Buckley
Executive Producer: Alan Fine

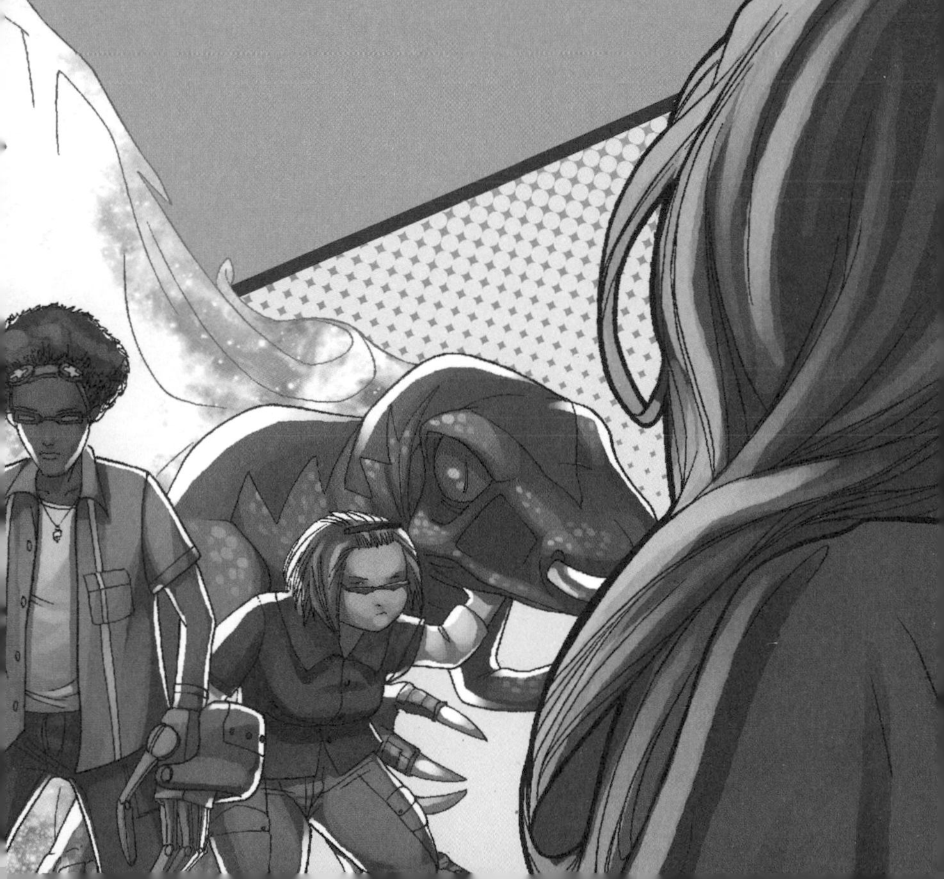

KAROLINA DEAN

ALEX WILDER

MOLLY HAYES

Teenager Alex Wilder and five other only children always thought that their parents were boring Los Angeles socialites, until the kids witness the adults murder a young girl in some kind of dark sacrificial ritual. The teens soon learn that their parents are part of a secret organization called The Pride, a collection of crime bosses, time-traveling despots, alien overlords, mad scientists, evil mutants, and dark wizards.

After stealing weapons and resources from these villainous adults (including an encrypted book about The Pride, a mystical decoder ring, and a psychic velociraptor named Old Lace), the kids run away from home and vow to bring their parents to justice. But with the help of operatives in the LAPD, The Pride frames their children for the murder they committed, and the fugitive Runaways are forced to retreat to a subterranean hideout. Using the diverse powers and skills they inherited, the kids now hope to atone for their parents' crimes by helping those in need.

But The Pride has other plans for their children...

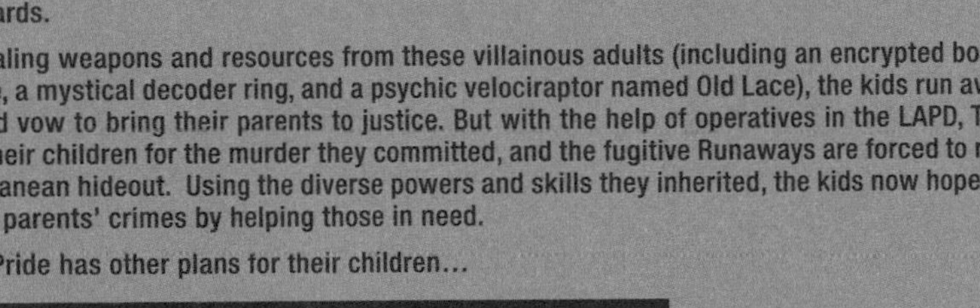

NICO MINORU

GERTRUDE YORKES

CHASE STEIN

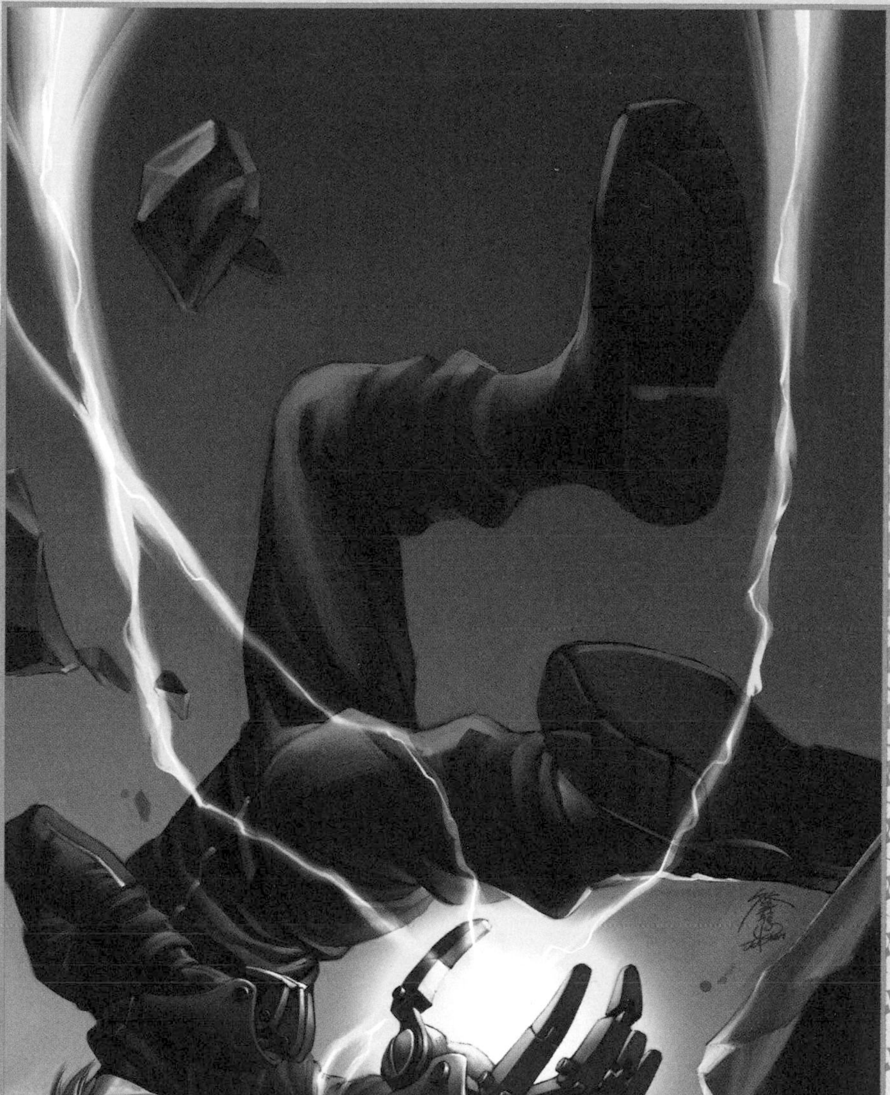

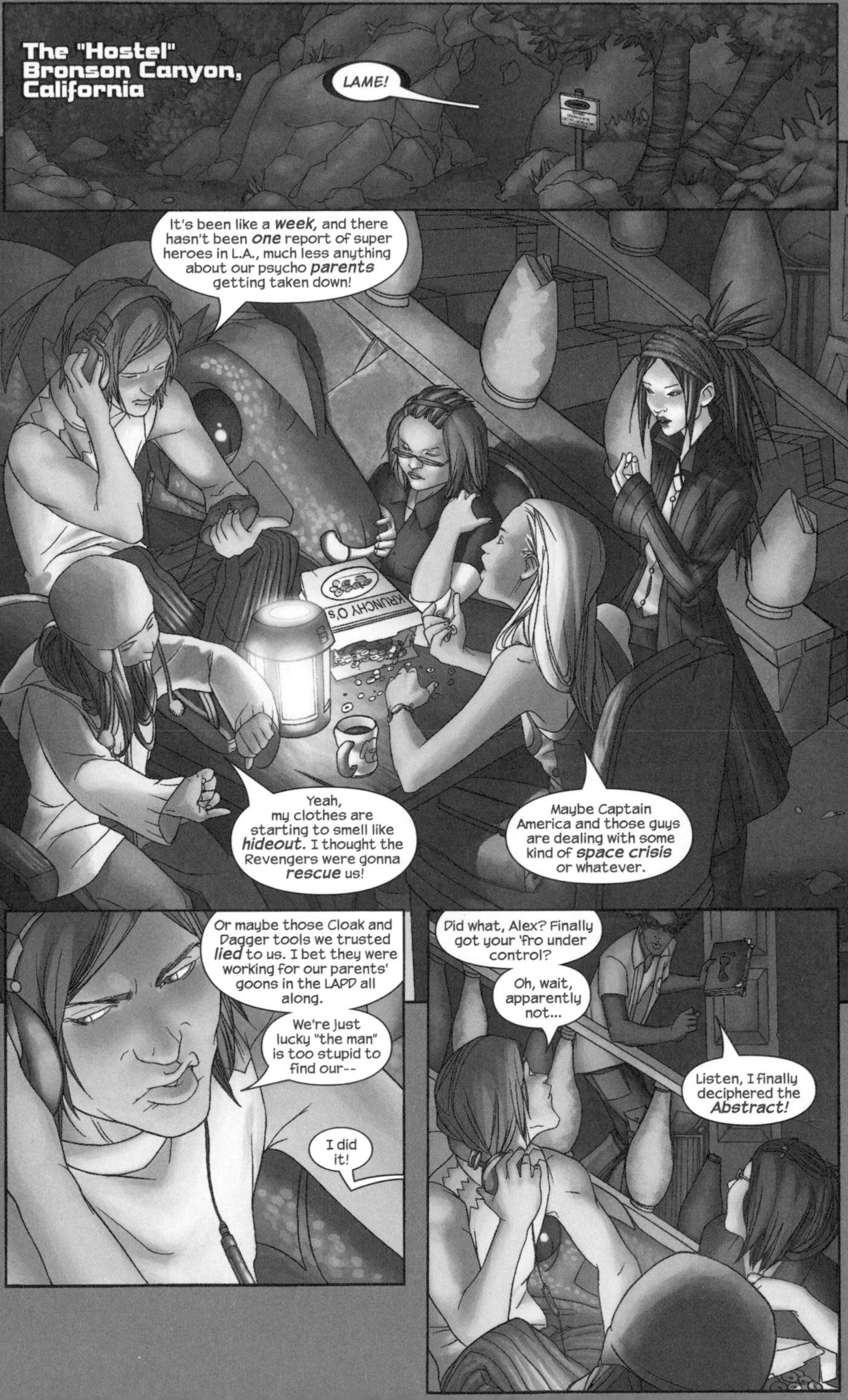
The "Hostel"
Bronson Canyon, California
LAME!
It's been like a *week*, and there hasn't been *one* report of super heroes in L.A., much less anything about our psycho *parents* getting taken down!
KRUNCHY O's
Yeah, my clothes are starting to smell like *hideout.* I thought the Revengers were gonna *rescue* us!
Maybe Captain America and those guys are dealing with some kind of *space crisis* or whatever.
Or maybe those Cloak and Dagger tools we trusted *lied* to us. I bet they were working for our parents' goons in the LAPD all along.
We're just lucky "the man" is too stupid to find our--
I did it!
Did what, Alex? Finally got your 'fro under control?
Oh, wait, apparently not...
Listen, I finally deciphered the *Abstract!*

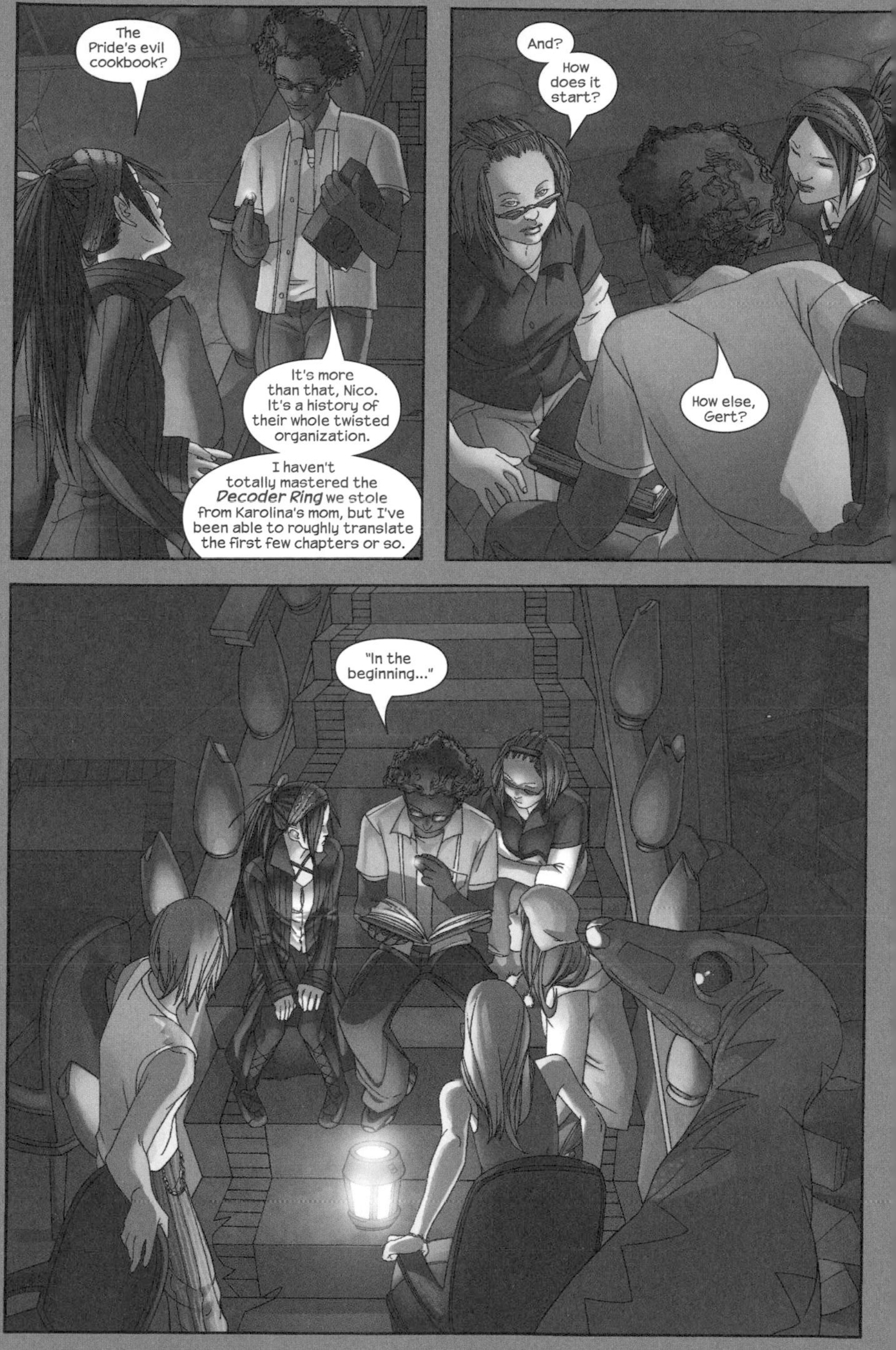
The Pride's evil cookbook?
It's more than that, Nico. It's a history of their whole twisted organization.
I haven't totally mastered the *Decoder Ring* we stole from Karolina's mom, but I've been able to roughly translate the first few chapters or so.
And?
How does it start?
How else, Gert?
"In the beginning..."

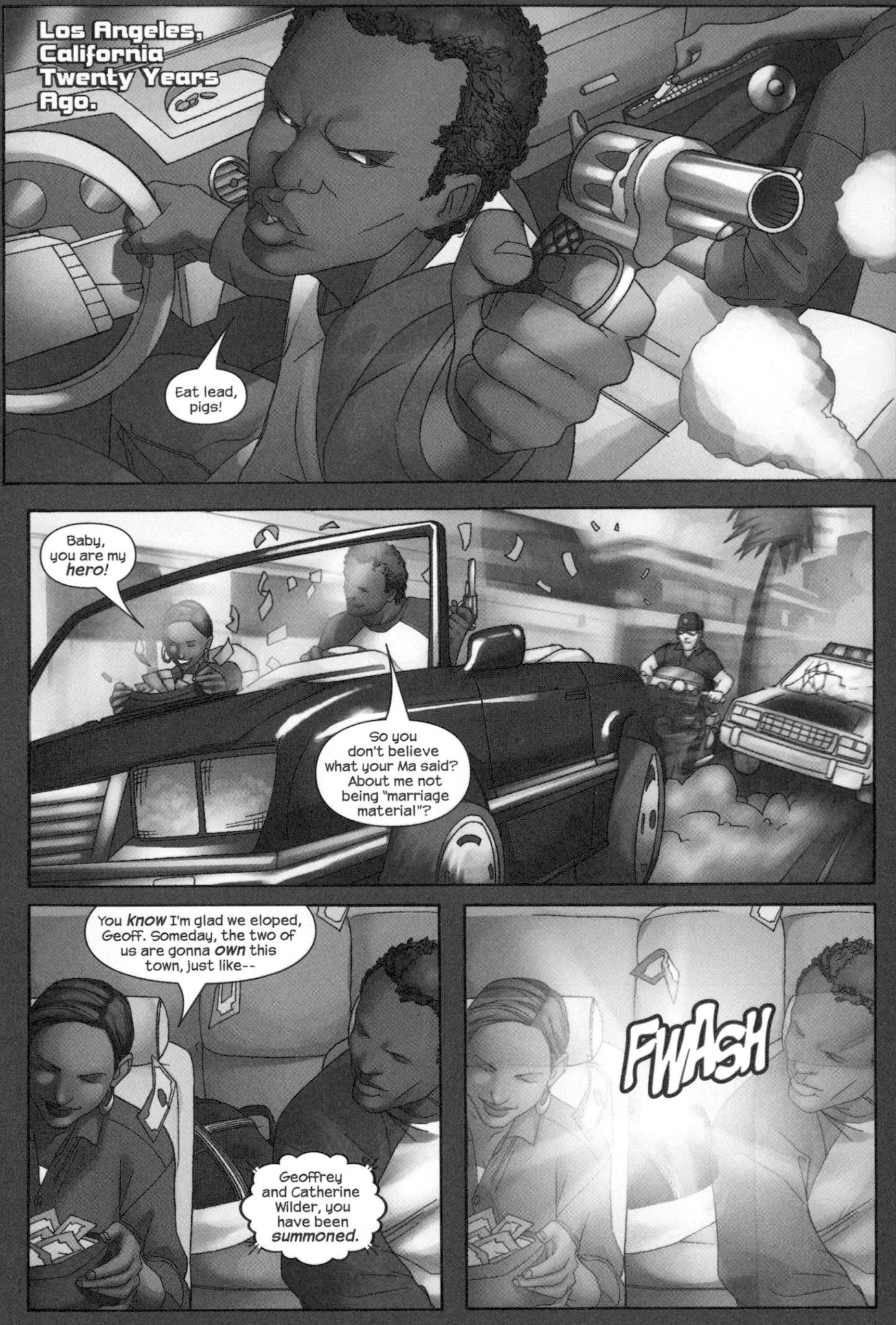

Los Angeles, California Twenty Years Ago.
Eat lead, pigs!
Baby, you are my *hero!*
So you don't believe what your Ma said? About me not being "marriage material"?
You *KNOW* I'm glad we eloped, Geoff. Someday, the two of us are gonna *OWN* this town, just like--
Geoffrey and Catherine Wilder, you have been *summoned.*
FWASH

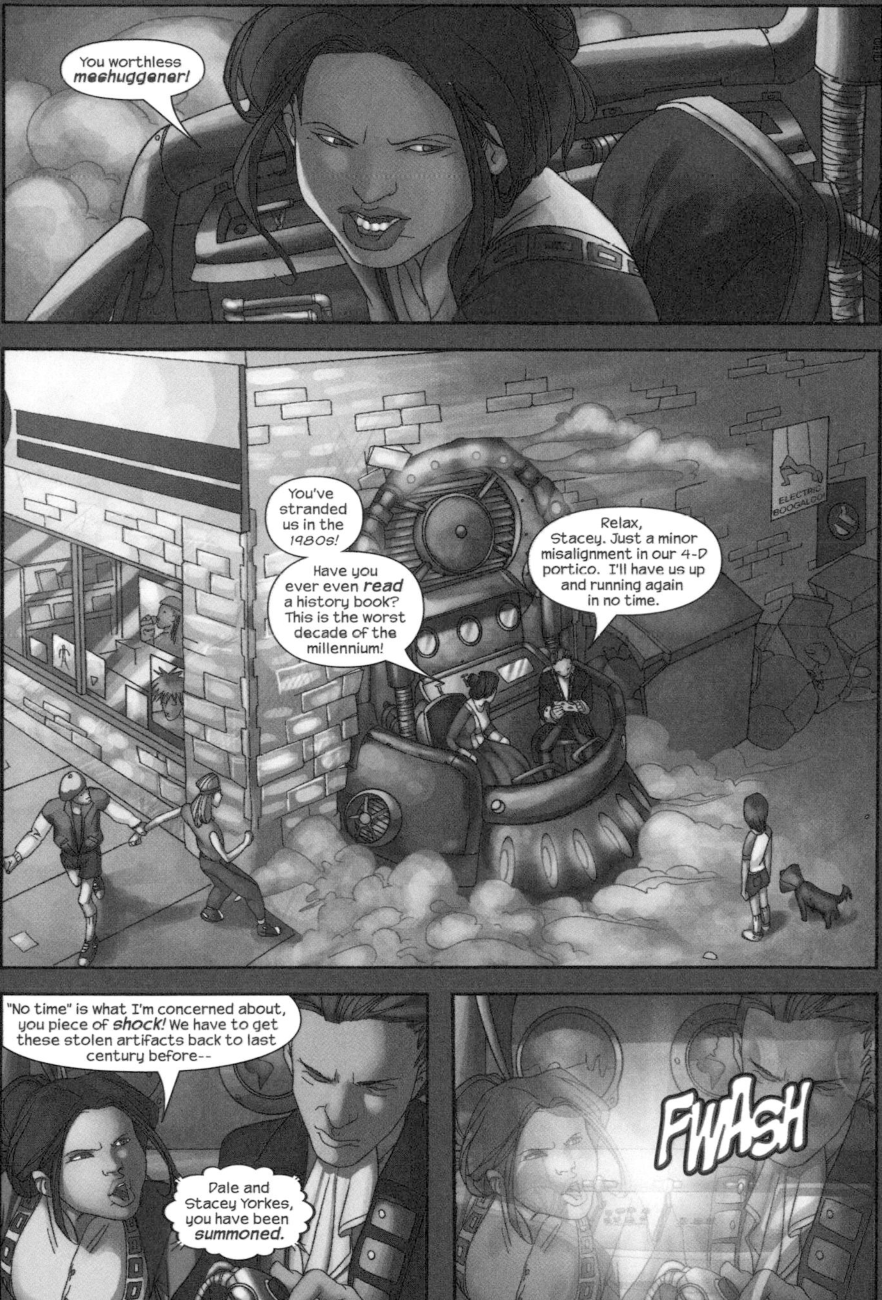

You worthless *meshuggener!*
You've stranded us in the *1980s!*
Have you ever even ***read*** a history book? This is the worst decade of the millennium!
Relax, Stacey. Just a minor misalignment in our 4-D portico. I'll have us up and running again in no time.
ELECTRIC BOOGALOO
"No time" is what I'm concerned about, you piece of ***shock!*** We have to get these stolen artifacts back to last century before--
Dale and Stacey Yorkes, you have been ***summoned.***
FWASH

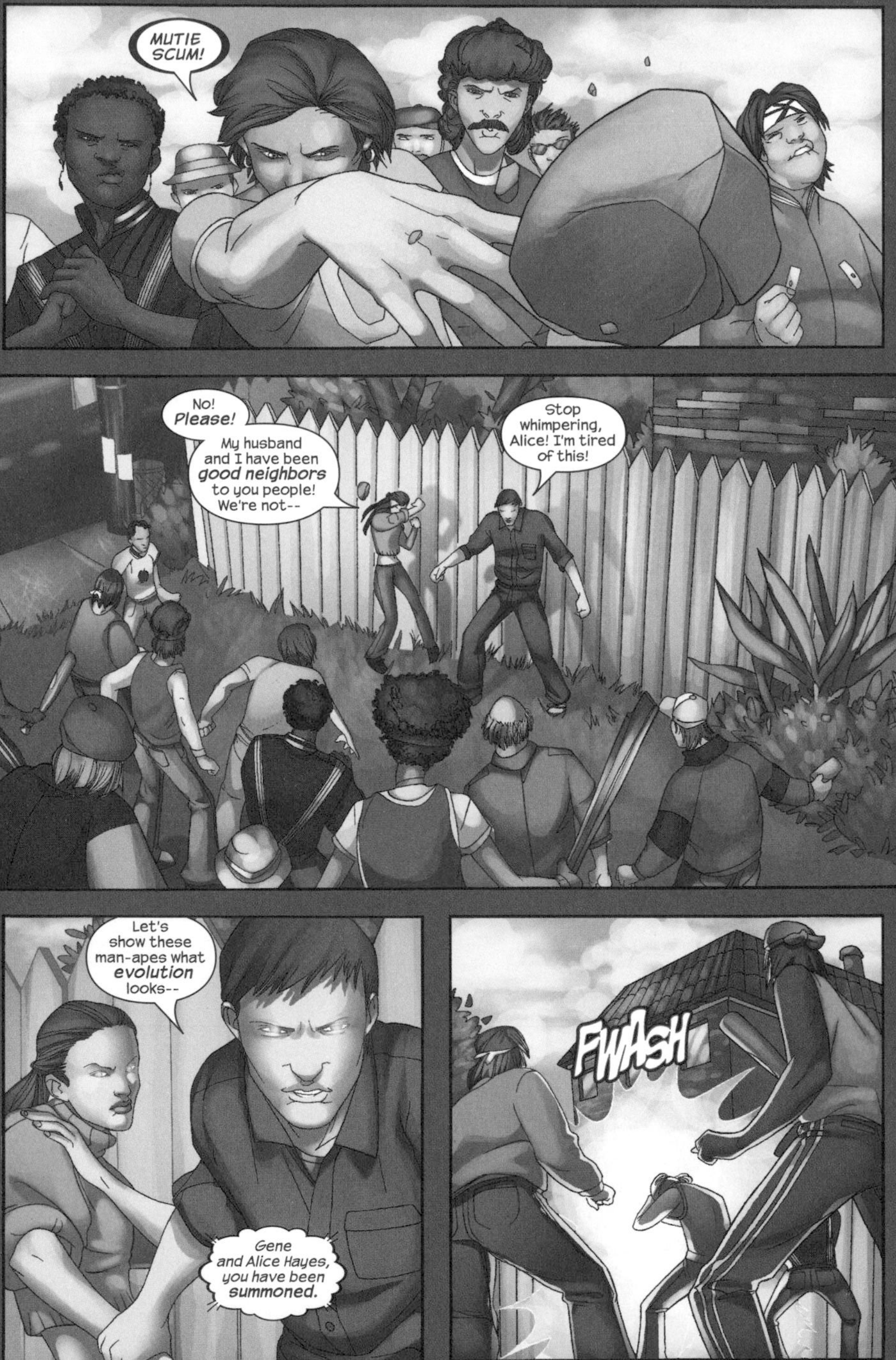
MUTIE SCUM!
No! Please!
My husband and I have been good neighbors to you people! We're not--
Stop whimpering, Alice! I'm tired of this!
Let's show these man-apes what evolution looks--
Gene and Alice Hayes, you have been summoned.
FWASH

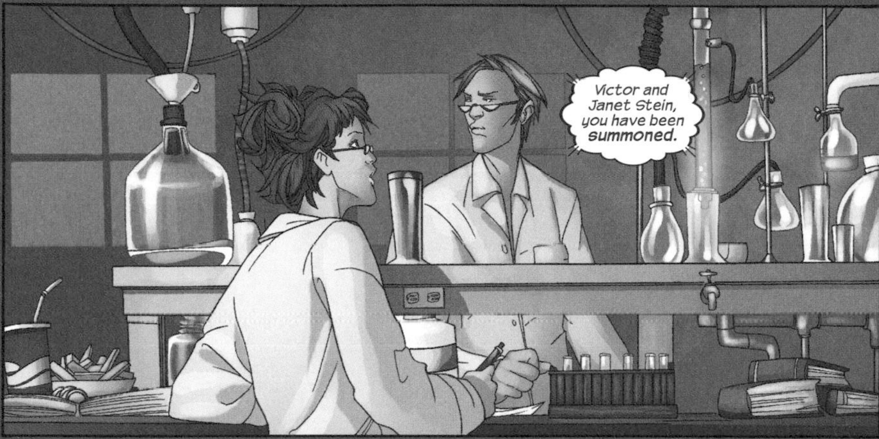
Victor and Janet Stein, you have been **summoned**.

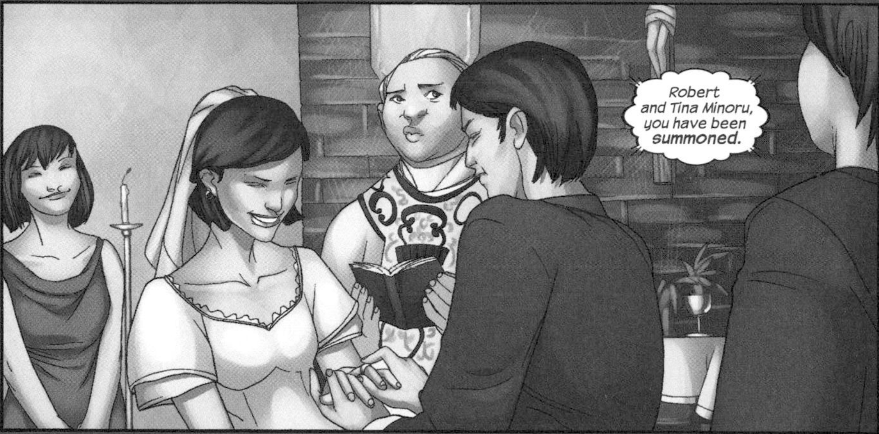
Robert and Tina Minoru, you have been **summoned**.

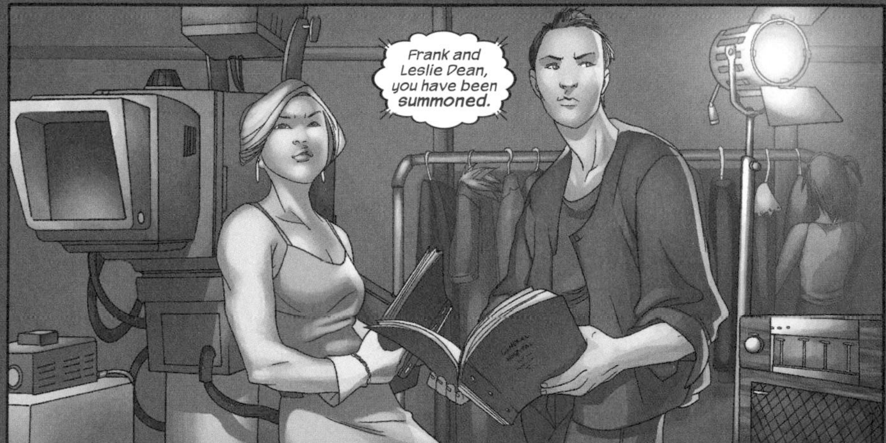
Frank and Leslie Dean, you have been **summoned**.

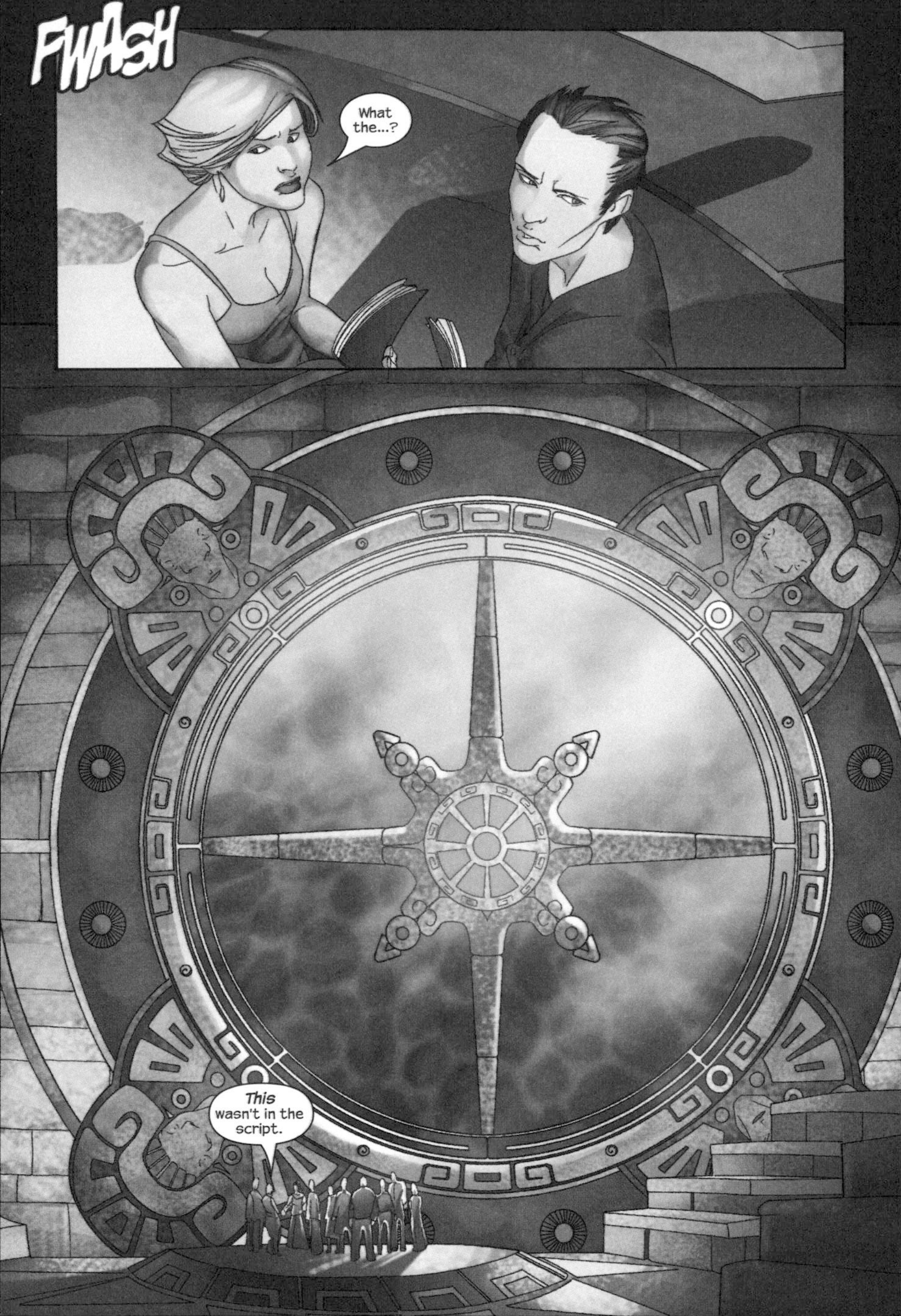
FWASH
What the...?
This wasn't in the script.

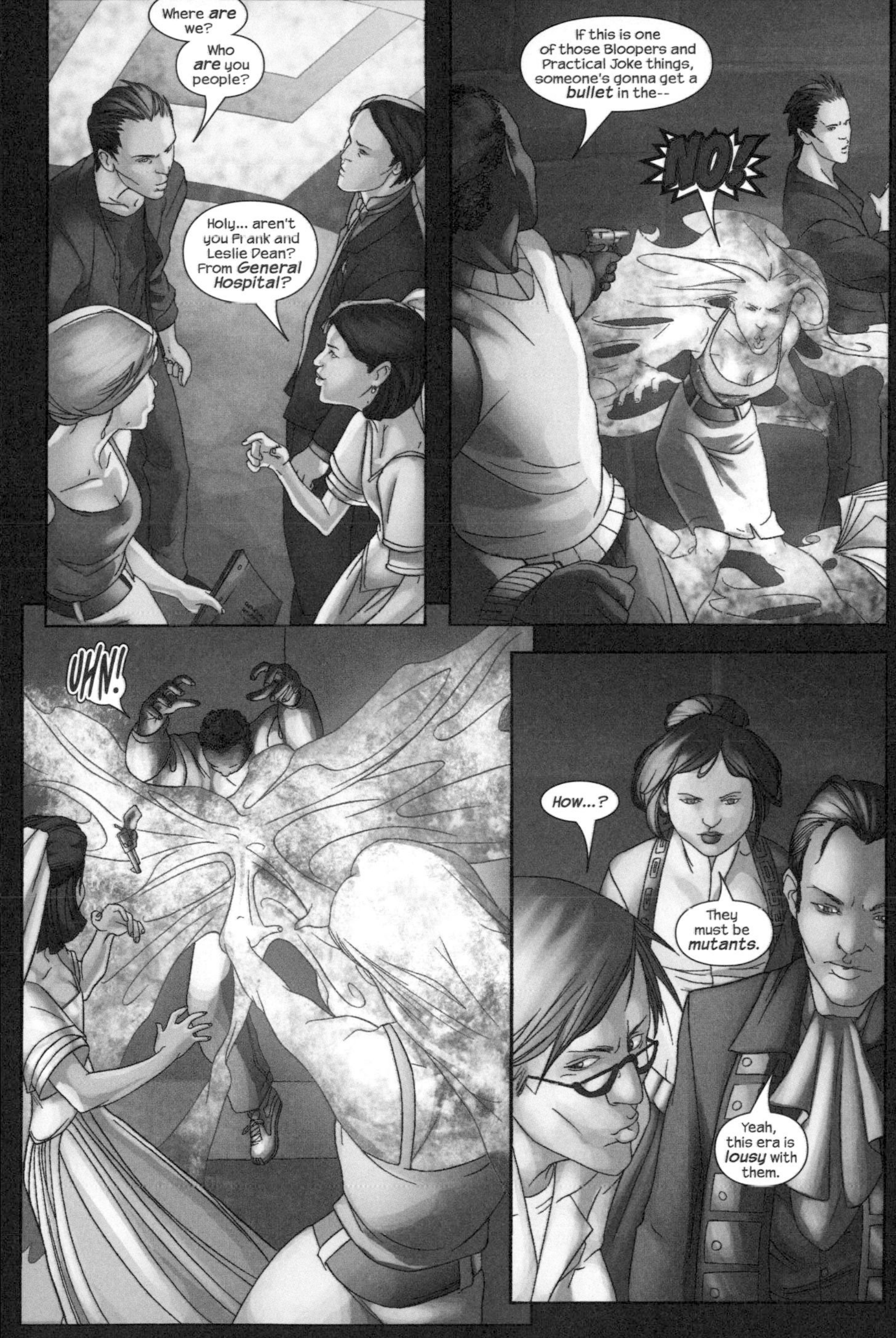
Where *are* we?
Who *are* you people?
Holy... aren't you Frank and Leslie Dean? From *General Hospital?*
If this is one of those Bloopers and Practical Joke things, someone's gonna get a *bullet* in the--
NO!
UHN!
How...?
They must be *mutants.*
Yeah, this era is *lousy* with them.

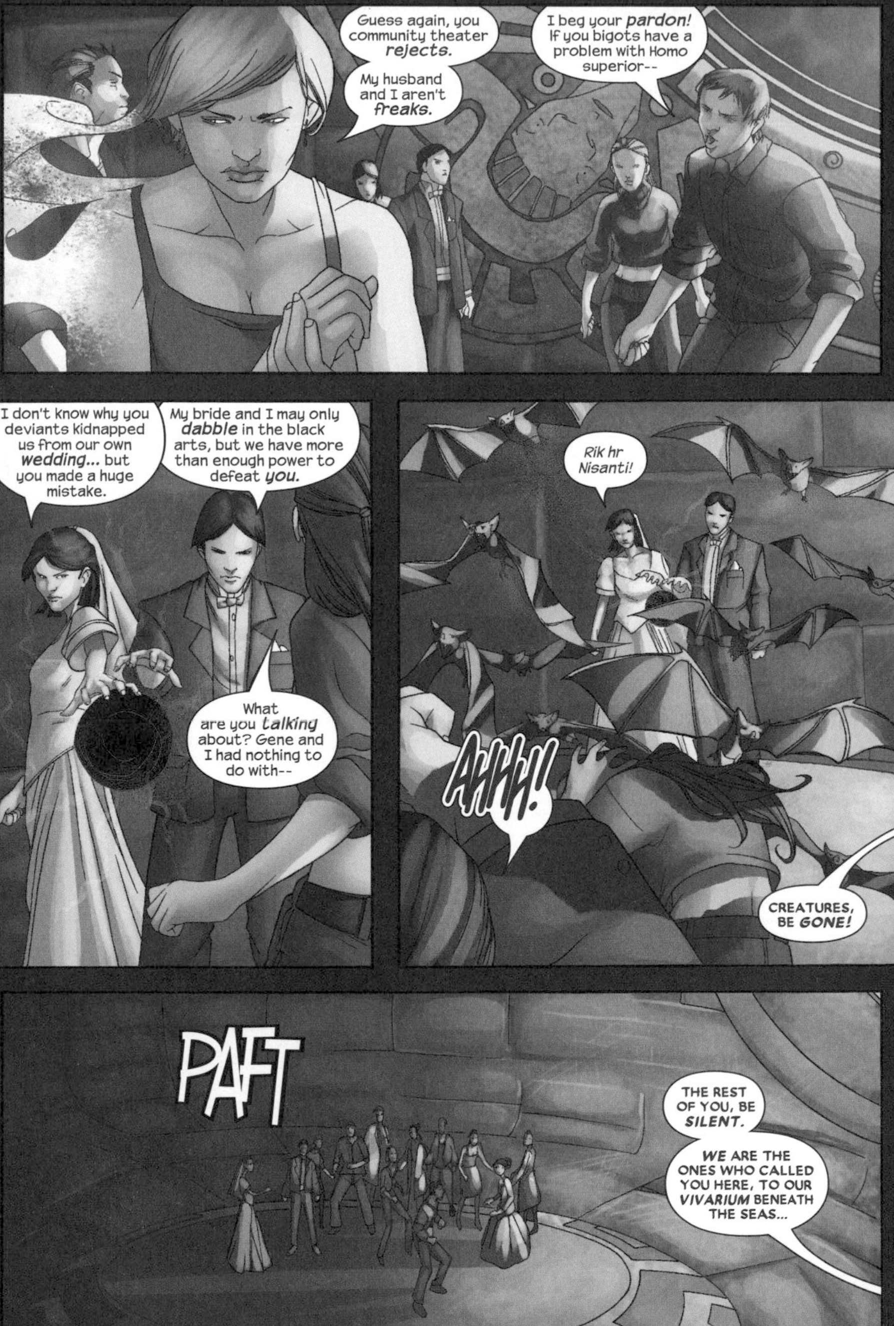

Guess again, you community theater rejects.
My husband and I aren't freaks.
I beg your pardon! If you bigots have a problem with Homo superior--
I don't know why you deviants kidnapped us from our own wedding... but you made a huge mistake.
My bride and I may only dabble in the black arts, but we have more than enough power to defeat you.
What are you talking about? Gene and I had nothing to do with--
Rik hr Nisanti!
AHHH!
CREATURES, BE GONE!
PAFT
THE REST OF YOU, BE SILENT.
WE ARE THE ONES WHO CALLED YOU HERE, TO OUR VIVARIUM BENEATH THE SEAS...

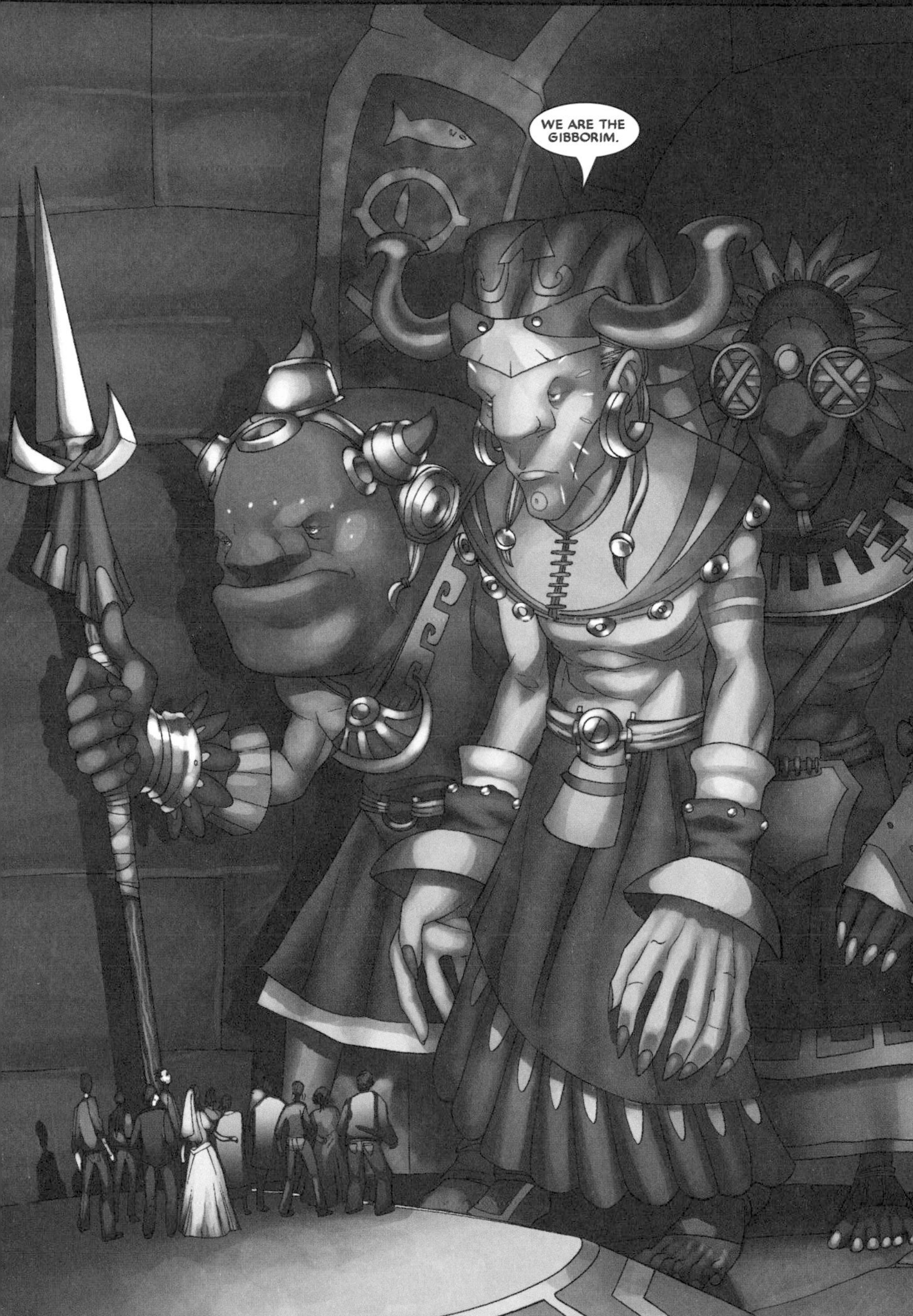
WE ARE THE GIBBORIM.

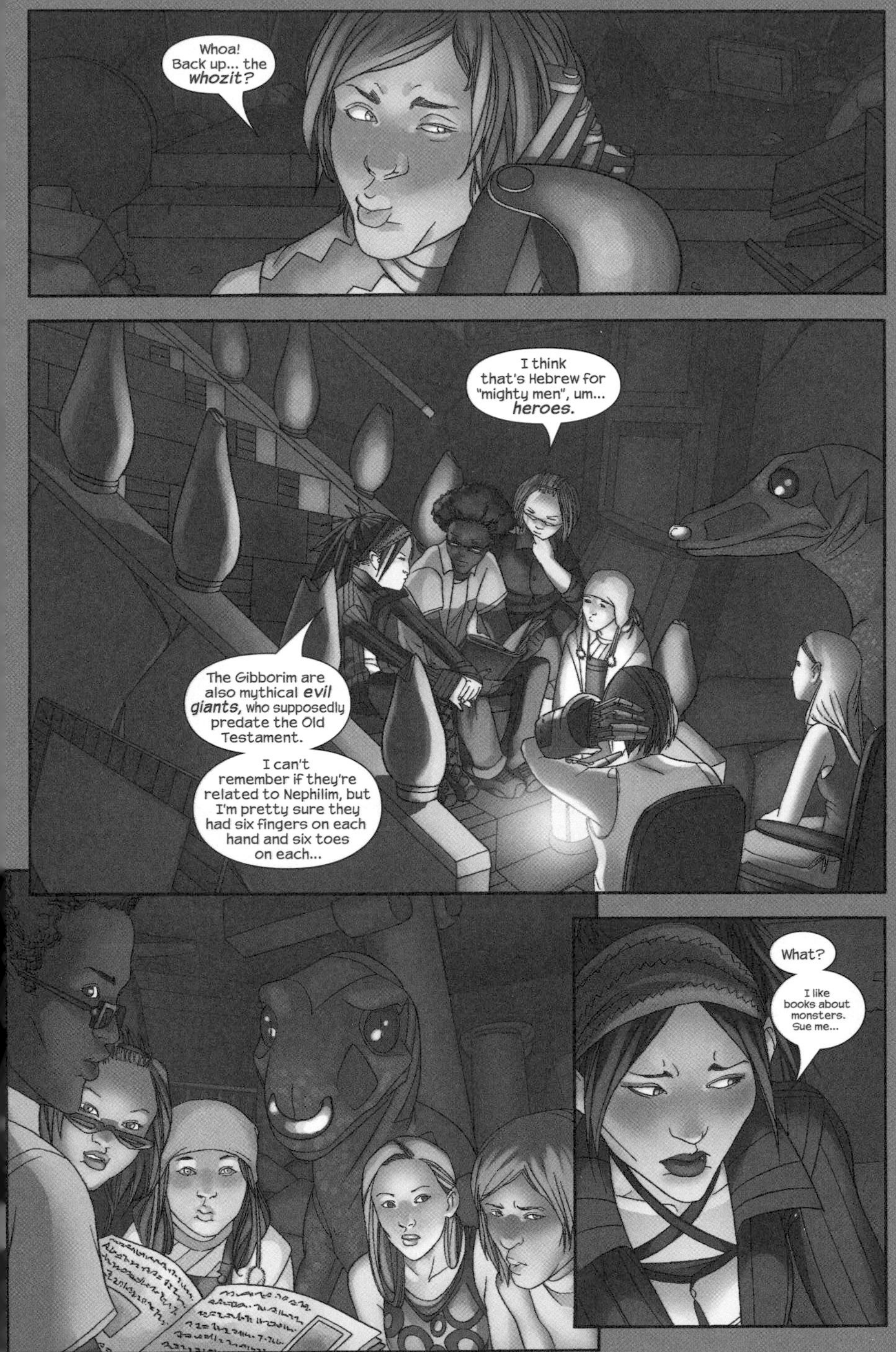
Whoa! Back up... the *whozit?*
I think that's Hebrew for "mighty men", um... *heroes.*
The Gibborim are also mythical *evil giants,* who supposedly predate the Old Testament.
I can't remember if they're related to Nephilim, but I'm pretty sure they had six fingers on each hand and six toes on each...
What?
I like books about monsters. Sue me...

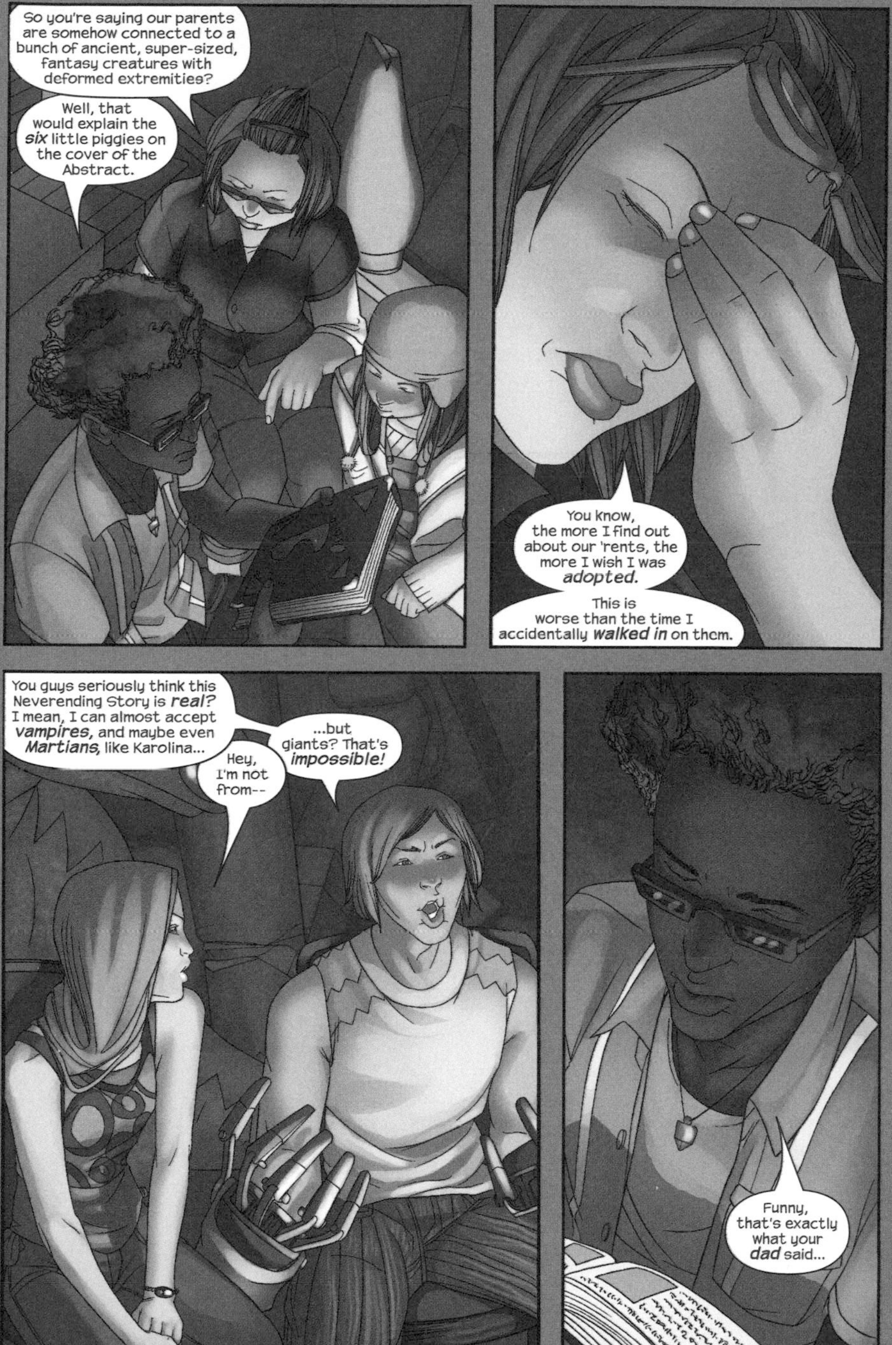

So you're saying our parents are somehow connected to a bunch of ancient, super-sized, fantasy creatures with deformed extremities?
Well, that would explain the *six* little piggies on the cover of the Abstract.
You know, the more I find out about our 'rents, the more I wish I was *adopted.*
This is worse than the time I accidentally *walked in* on them.
You guys seriously think this Neverending Story is *real?* I mean, I can almost accept *vampires,* and maybe even *Martians,* like Karolina...
Hey, I'm not from--
...but giants? That's *impossible!*
Funny, that's exactly what your *dad* said...

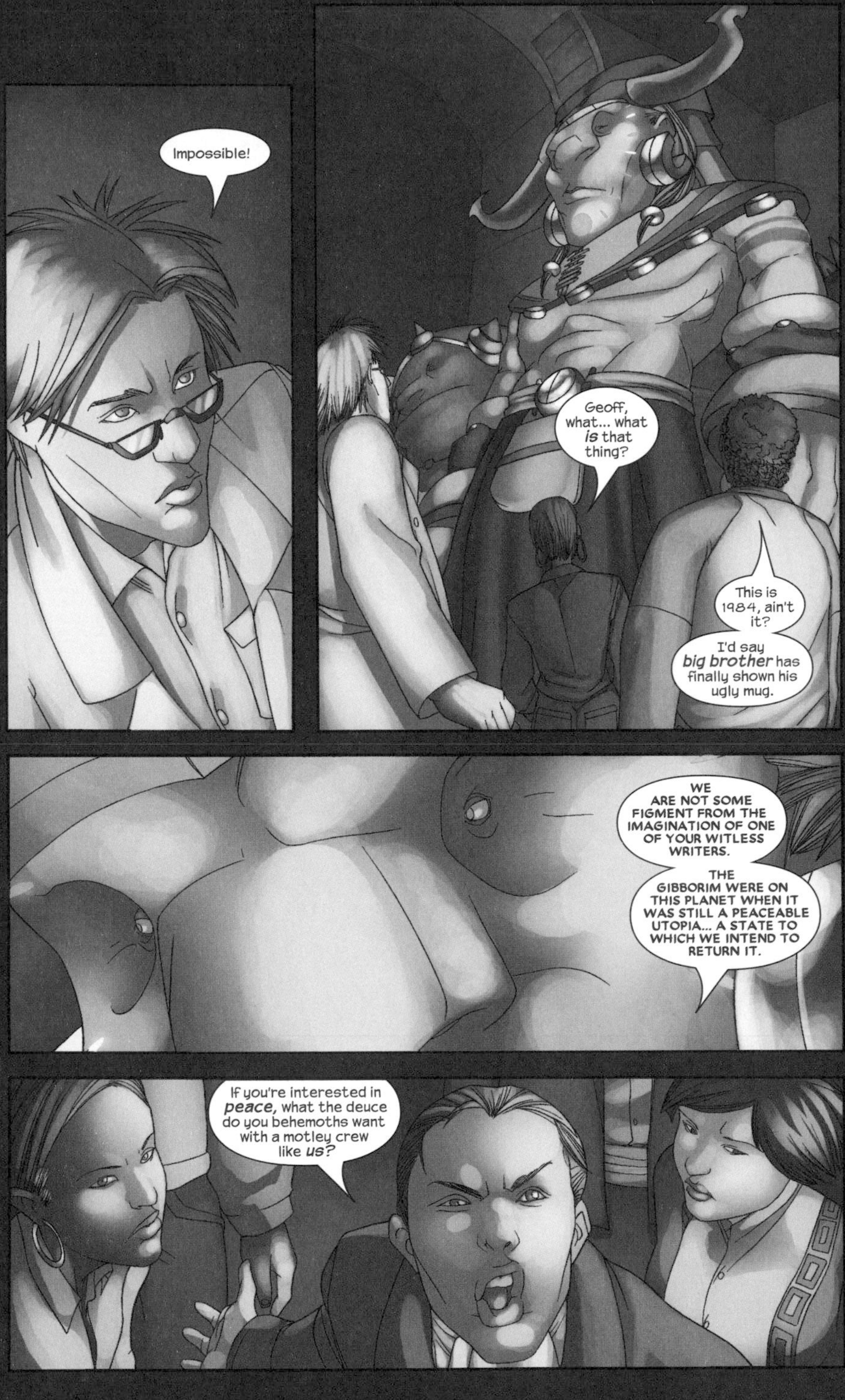
Impossible!
Geoff, what... what *is* that thing?
This is 1984, ain't it?
I'd say **big brother** has finally shown his ugly mug.
WE ARE NOT SOME FIGMENT FROM THE IMAGINATION OF ONE OF YOUR WITLESS WRITERS.
THE GIBBORIM WERE ON THIS PLANET WHEN IT WAS STILL A PEACEABLE UTOPIA... A STATE TO WHICH WE INTEND TO RETURN IT.
If you're interested in ***peace,*** what the deuce do you behemoths want with a motley crew like ***us?***

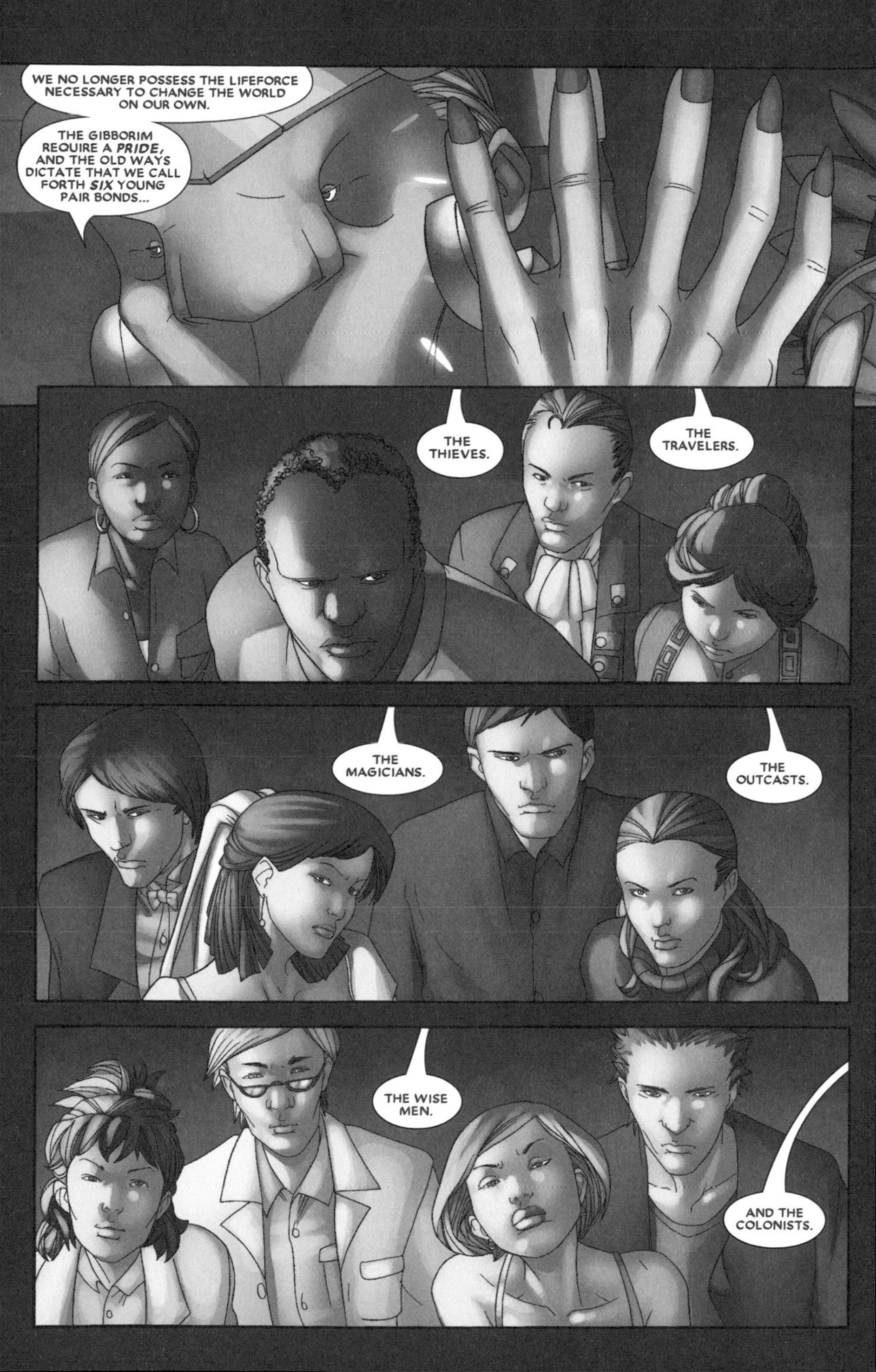
WE NO LONGER POSSESS THE LIFEFORCE NECESSARY TO CHANGE THE WORLD ON OUR OWN.
THE GIBBORIM REQUIRE A *PRIDE*, AND THE OLD WAYS DICTATE THAT WE CALL FORTH *SIX* YOUNG PAIR BONDS...
THE THIEVES.
THE TRAVELERS.
THE MAGICIANS.
THE OUTCASTS.
THE WISE MEN.
AND THE COLONISTS.

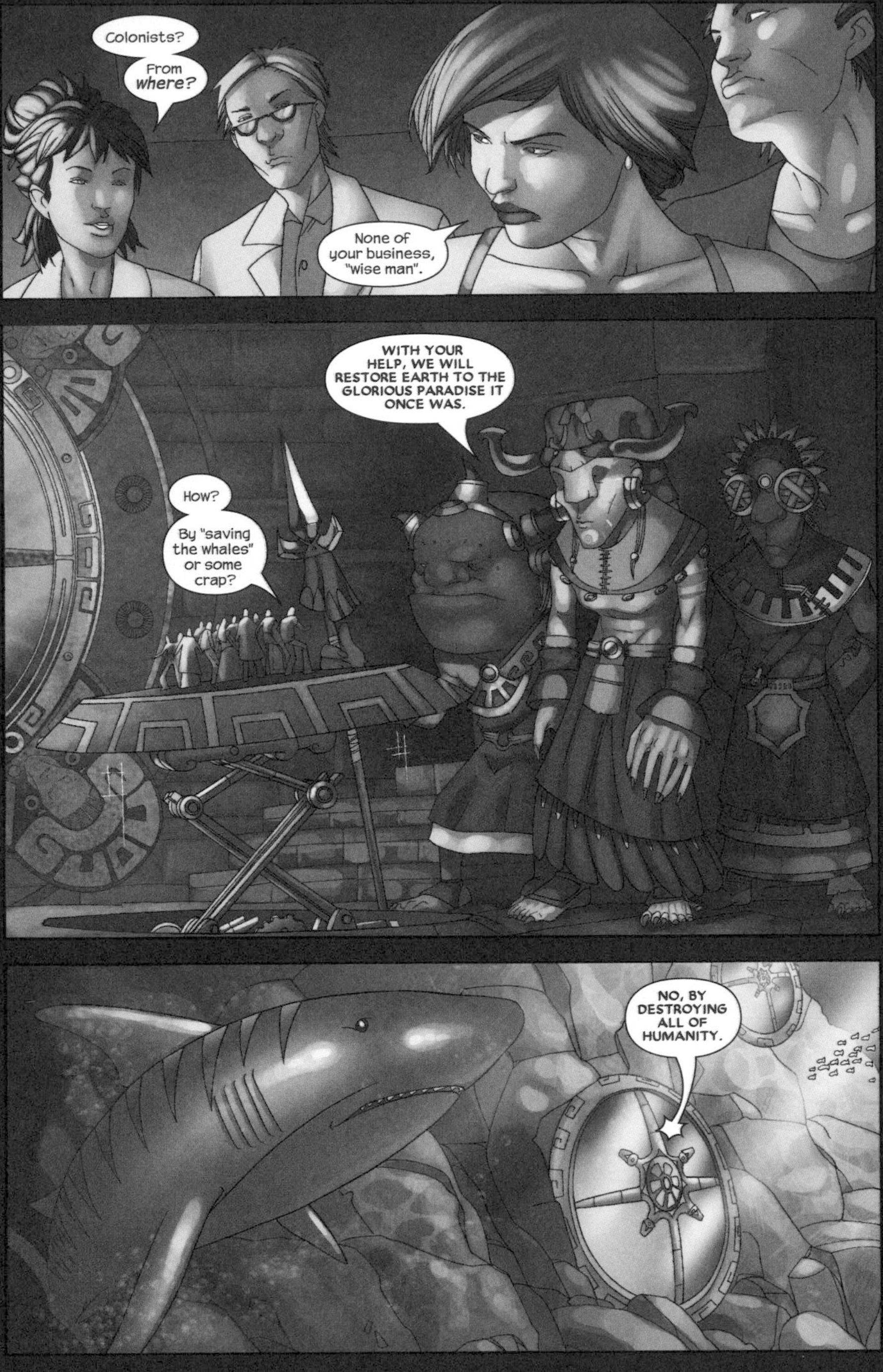
Colonists?
From where?
None of your business, "wise man".
WITH YOUR HELP, WE WILL RESTORE EARTH TO THE GLORIOUS PARADISE IT ONCE WAS.
How?
By "saving the whales" or some crap?
NO, BY DESTROYING ALL OF HUMANITY.

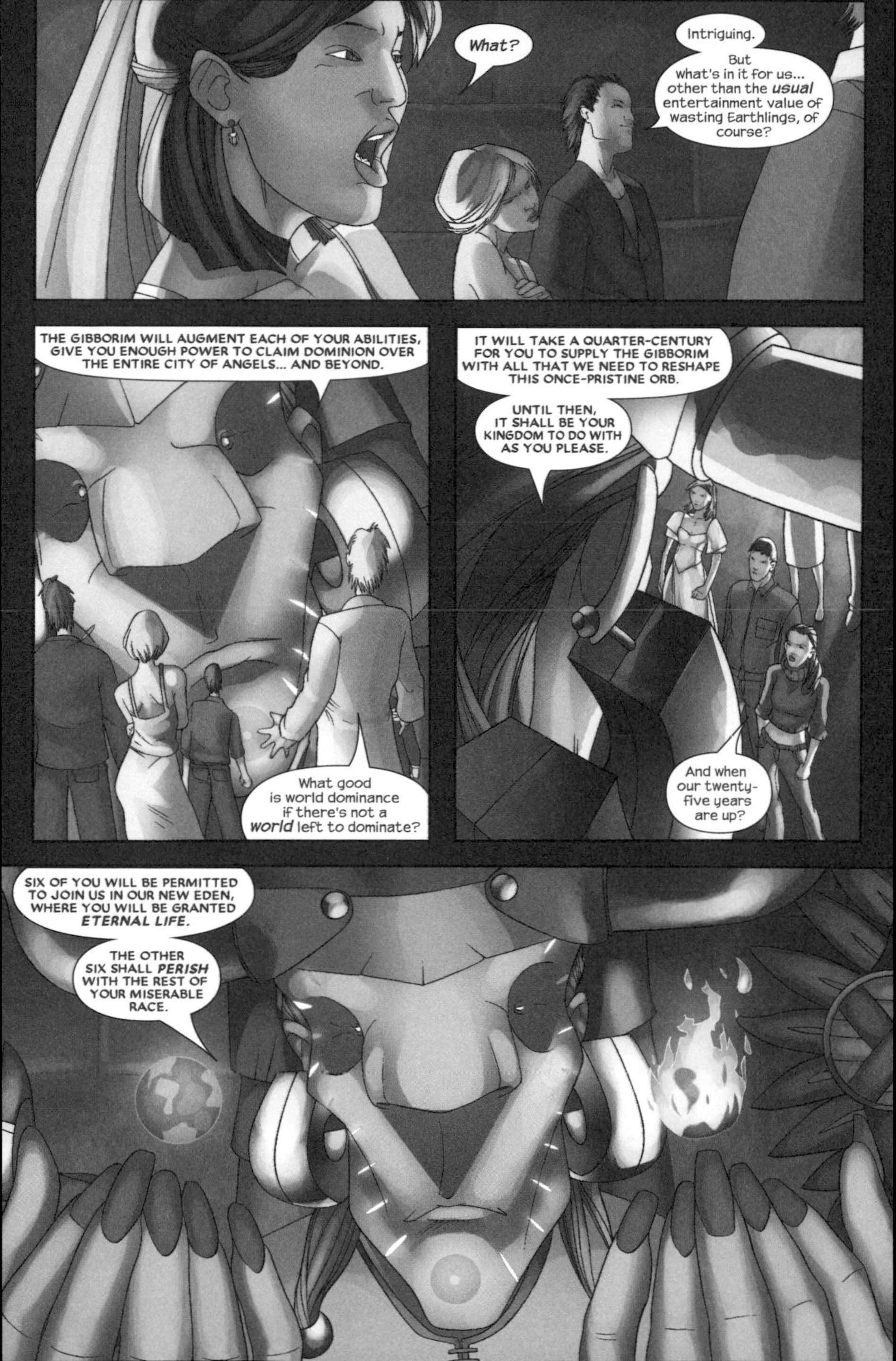

What?
Intriguing.
But what's in it for us... other than the usual entertainment value of wasting Earthlings, of course?
THE GIBBORIM WILL AUGMENT EACH OF YOUR ABILITIES, GIVE YOU ENOUGH POWER TO CLAIM DOMINION OVER THE ENTIRE CITY OF ANGELS... AND BEYOND.
What good is world dominance if there's not a world left to dominate?
IT WILL TAKE A QUARTER-CENTURY FOR YOU TO SUPPLY THE GIBBORIM WITH ALL THAT WE NEED TO RESHAPE THIS ONCE-PRISTINE ORB.
UNTIL THEN, IT SHALL BE YOUR KINGDOM TO DO WITH AS YOU PLEASE.
And when our twenty-five years are up?
SIX OF YOU WILL BE PERMITTED TO JOIN US IN OUR NEW EDEN, WHERE YOU WILL BE GRANTED ETERNAL LIFE.
THE OTHER SIX SHALL PERISH WITH THE REST OF YOUR MISERABLE RACE.

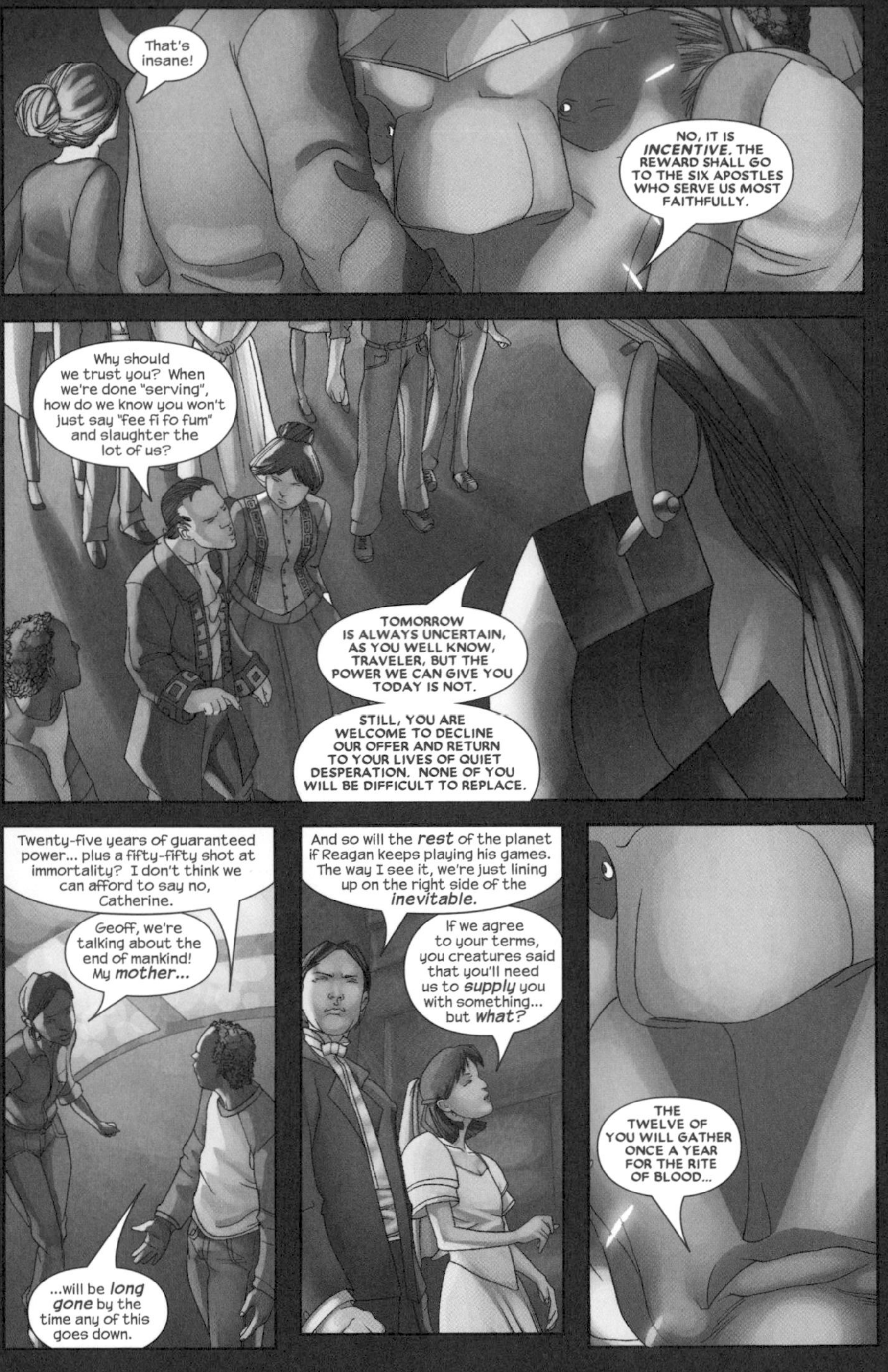
That's insane!
NO, IT IS INCENTIVE. THE REWARD SHALL GO TO THE SIX APOSTLES WHO SERVE US MOST FAITHFULLY.
Why should we trust you? When we're done "serving", how do we know you won't just say "fee fi fo fum" and slaughter the lot of us?
TOMORROW IS ALWAYS UNCERTAIN, AS YOU WELL KNOW, TRAVELER, BUT THE POWER WE CAN GIVE YOU TODAY IS NOT.
STILL, YOU ARE WELCOME TO DECLINE OUR OFFER AND RETURN TO YOUR LIVES OF QUIET DESPERATION. NONE OF YOU WILL BE DIFFICULT TO REPLACE.
Twenty-five years of guaranteed power... plus a fifty-fifty shot at immortality? I don't think we can afford to say no, Catherine.
Geoff, we're talking about the end of mankind! My mother...
...will be long gone by the time any of this goes down.
And so will the rest of the planet if Reagan keeps playing his games. The way I see it, we're just lining up on the right side of the inevitable.
If we agree to your terms, you creatures said that you'll need us to supply you with something... but what?
THE TWELVE OF YOU WILL GATHER ONCE A YEAR FOR THE RITE OF BLOOD...

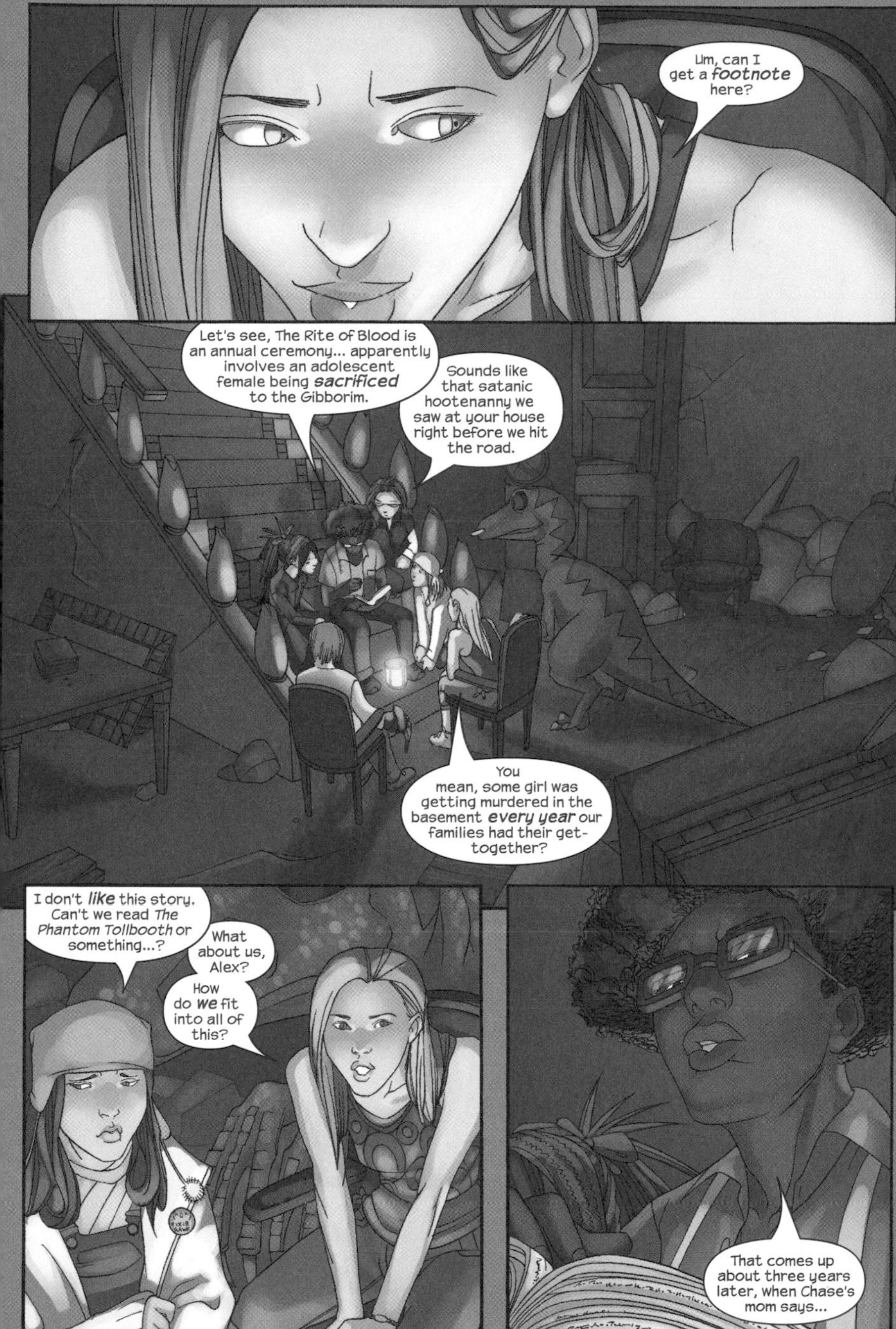
Um, can I get a *footnote* here?
Let's see, The Rite of Blood is an annual ceremony... apparently involves an adolescent female being *sacrificed* to the Gibborim.
Sounds like that satanic hootenanny we saw at your house right before we hit the road.
You mean, some girl was getting murdered in the basement *every year* our families had their get-together?
I don't *like* this story. Can't we read *The Phantom Tollbooth* or something...?
What about us, Alex?
How do *we* fit into all of this?
That comes up about three years later, when Chase's mom says...

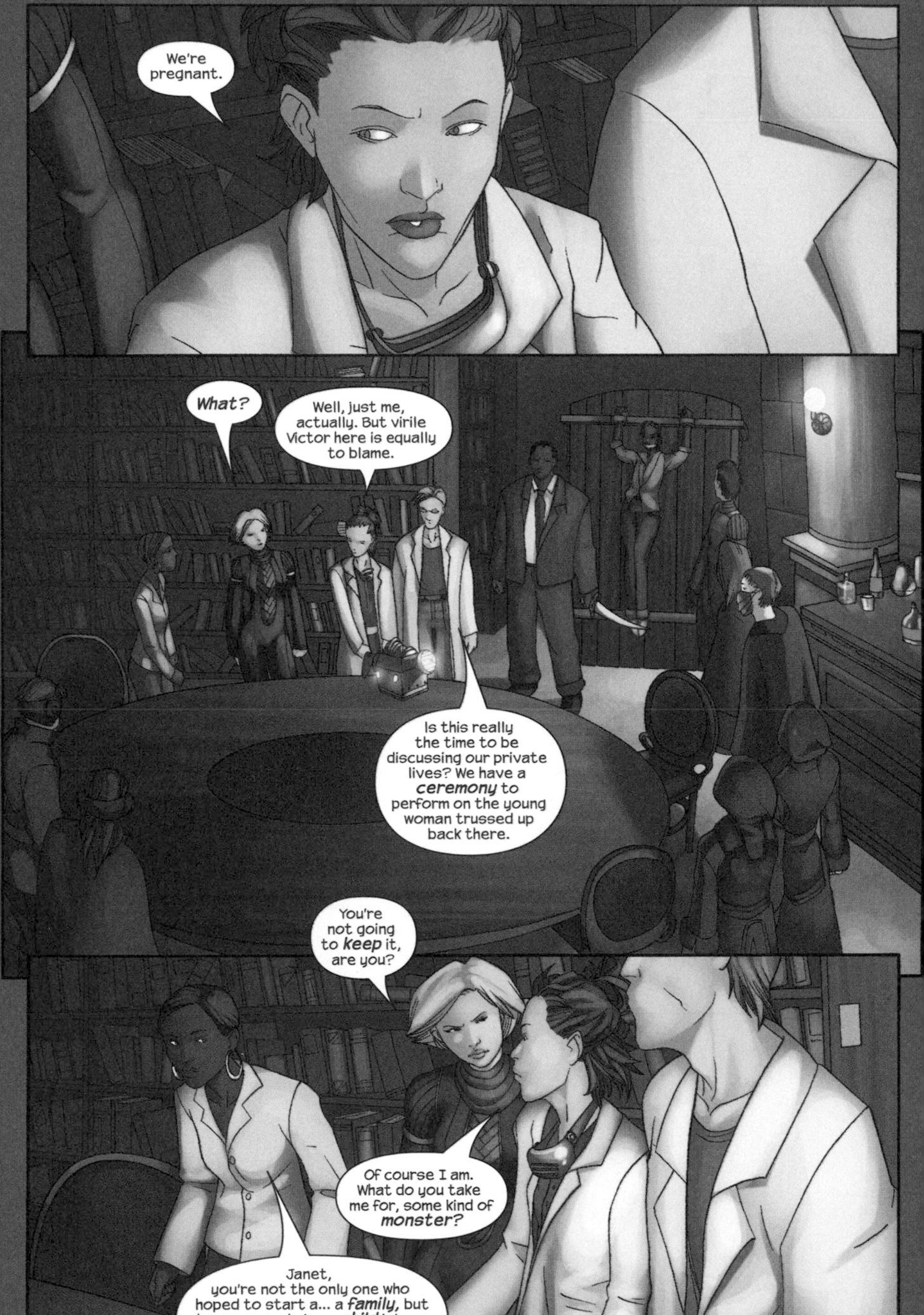

We're pregnant.
What?
Well, just me, actually. But virile Victor here is equally to blame.
Is this really the time to be discussing our private lives? We have a ceremony to perform on the young woman trussed up back there.
You're not going to keep it, are you?
Of course I am. What do you take me for, some kind of monster?
Janet, you're not the only one who hoped to start a... a family, but how can you bring a child into a world we're helping to destroy?

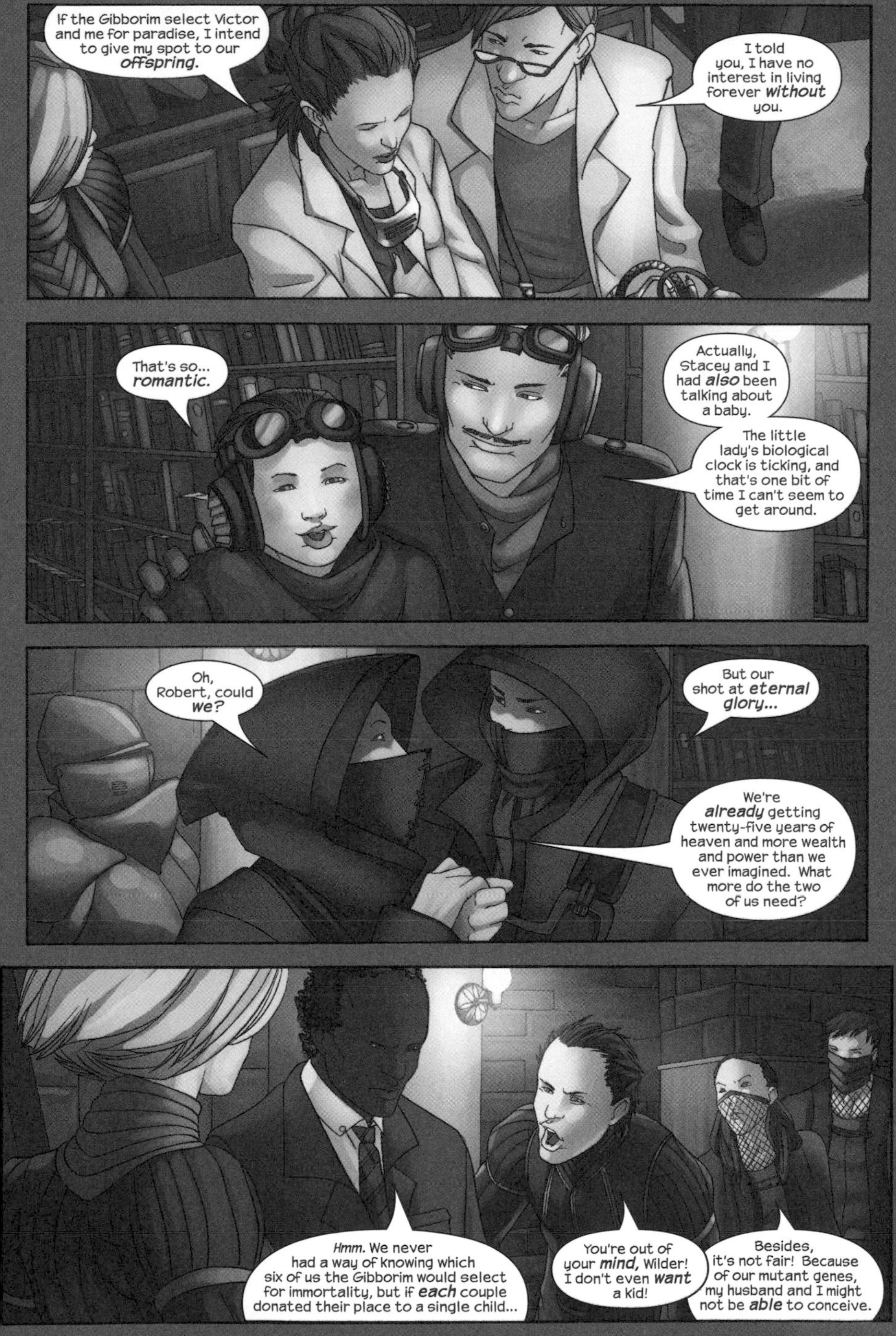
If the Gibborim select Victor and me for paradise, I intend to give my spot to our *offspring.*
I told you, I have no interest in living forever *without* you.
That's so... *romantic.*
Actually, Stacey and I had *also* been talking about a baby.
The little lady's biological clock is ticking, and that's one bit of time I can't seem to get around.
Oh, Robert, could *we?*
But our shot at *eternal glory...*
We're *already* getting twenty-five years of heaven and more wealth and power than we ever imagined. What more do the two of us need?
Hmm. We never had a way of knowing which six of us the Gibborim would select for immortality, but if *each* couple donated their place to a single child...
You're out of your *mind,* Wilder! I don't even *want* a kid!
Besides, it's not fair! Because of our mutant genes, my husband and I might not be *able* to conceive.

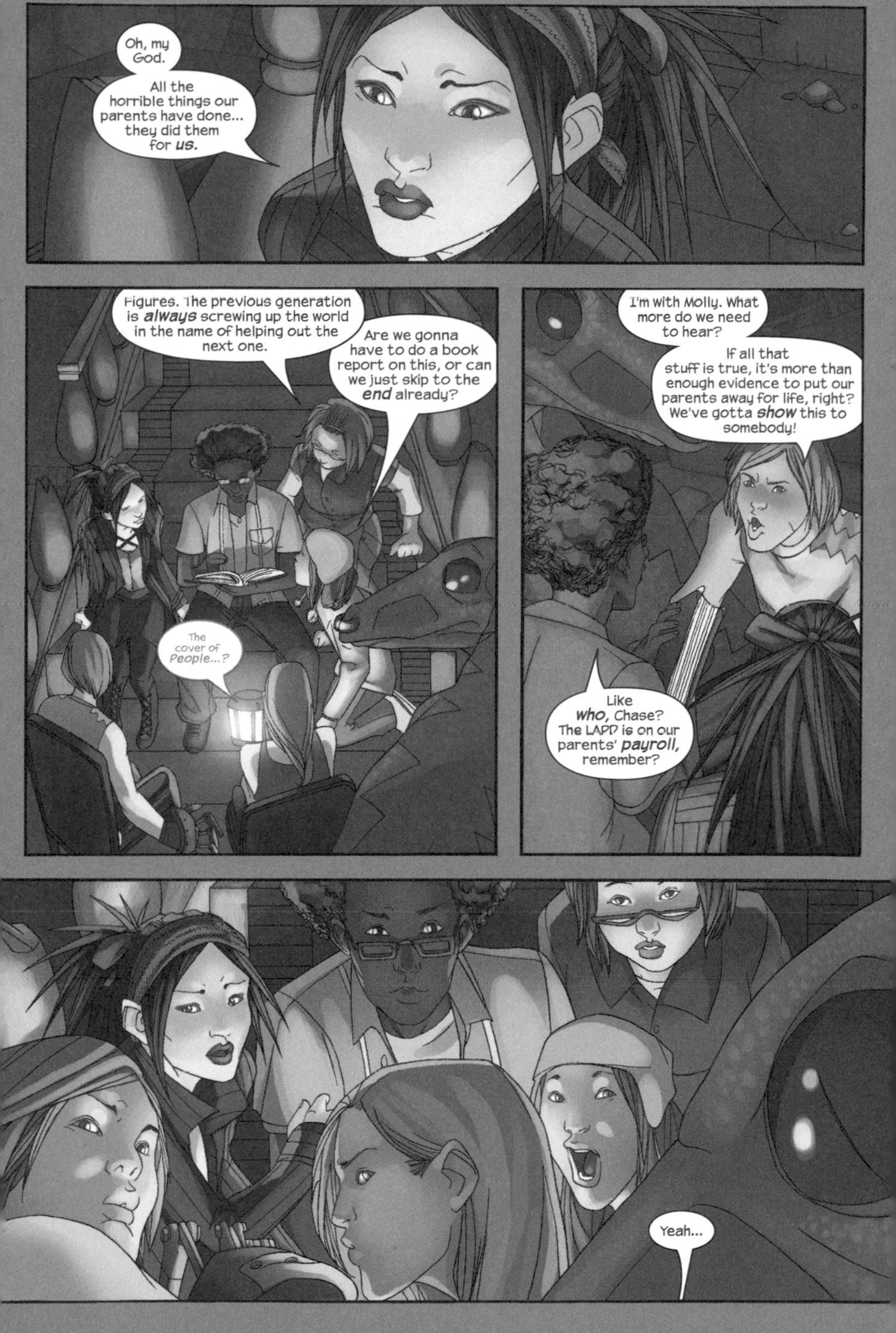

Oh, my God.
All the horrible things our parents have done... they did them for *us.*
Figures. The previous generation is *always* screwing up the world in the name of helping out the next one.
Are we gonna have to do a book report on this, or can we just skip to the *end* already?
The cover of *People*...?
I'm with Molly. What more do we need to hear?
If all that stuff is true, it's more than enough evidence to put our parents away for life, right? We've gotta *show* this to somebody!
Like *who,* Chase? The LAPD is on our parents' *payroll,* remember?
Yeah...

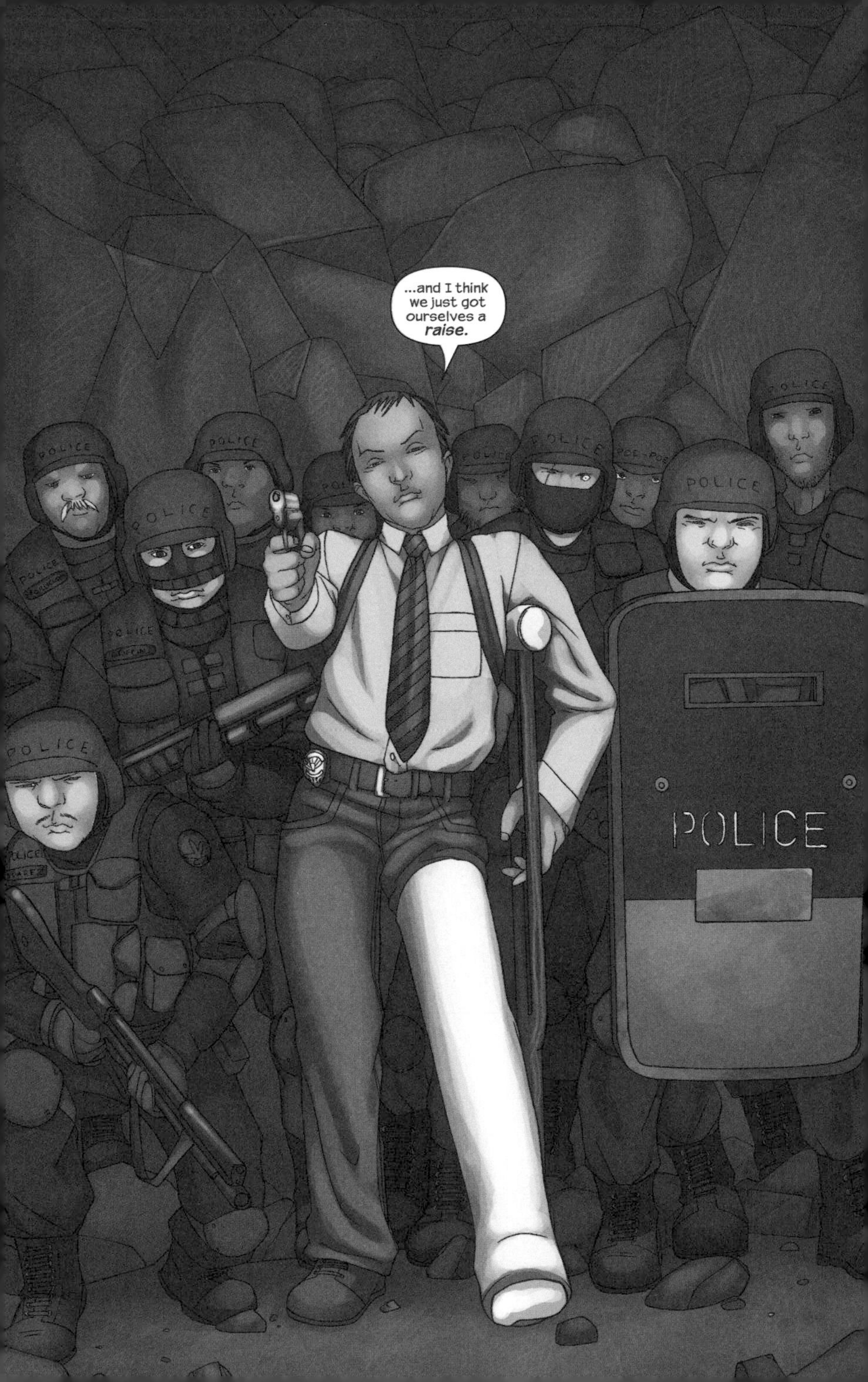
...and I think we just got ourselves a *raise.*
POLICE

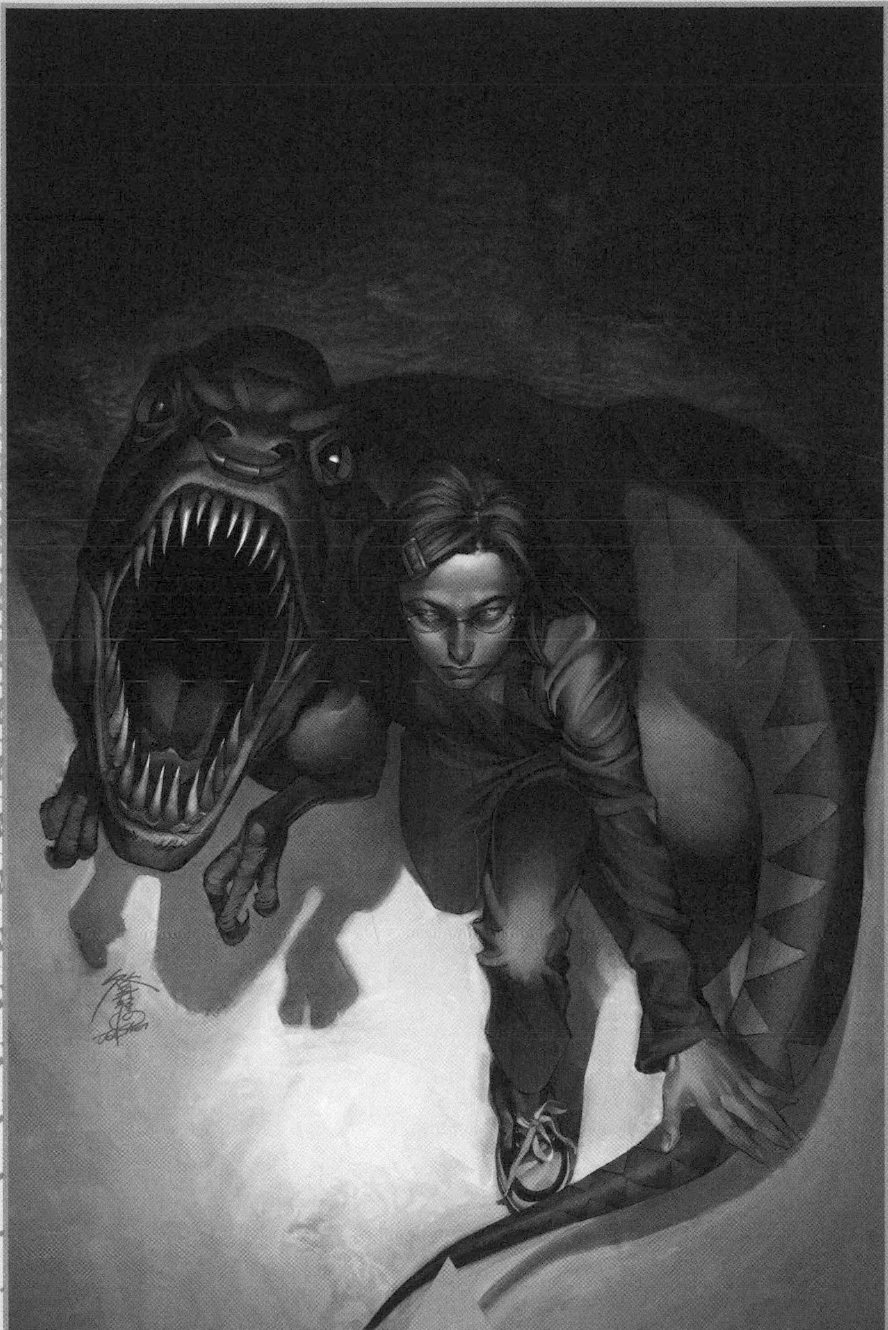

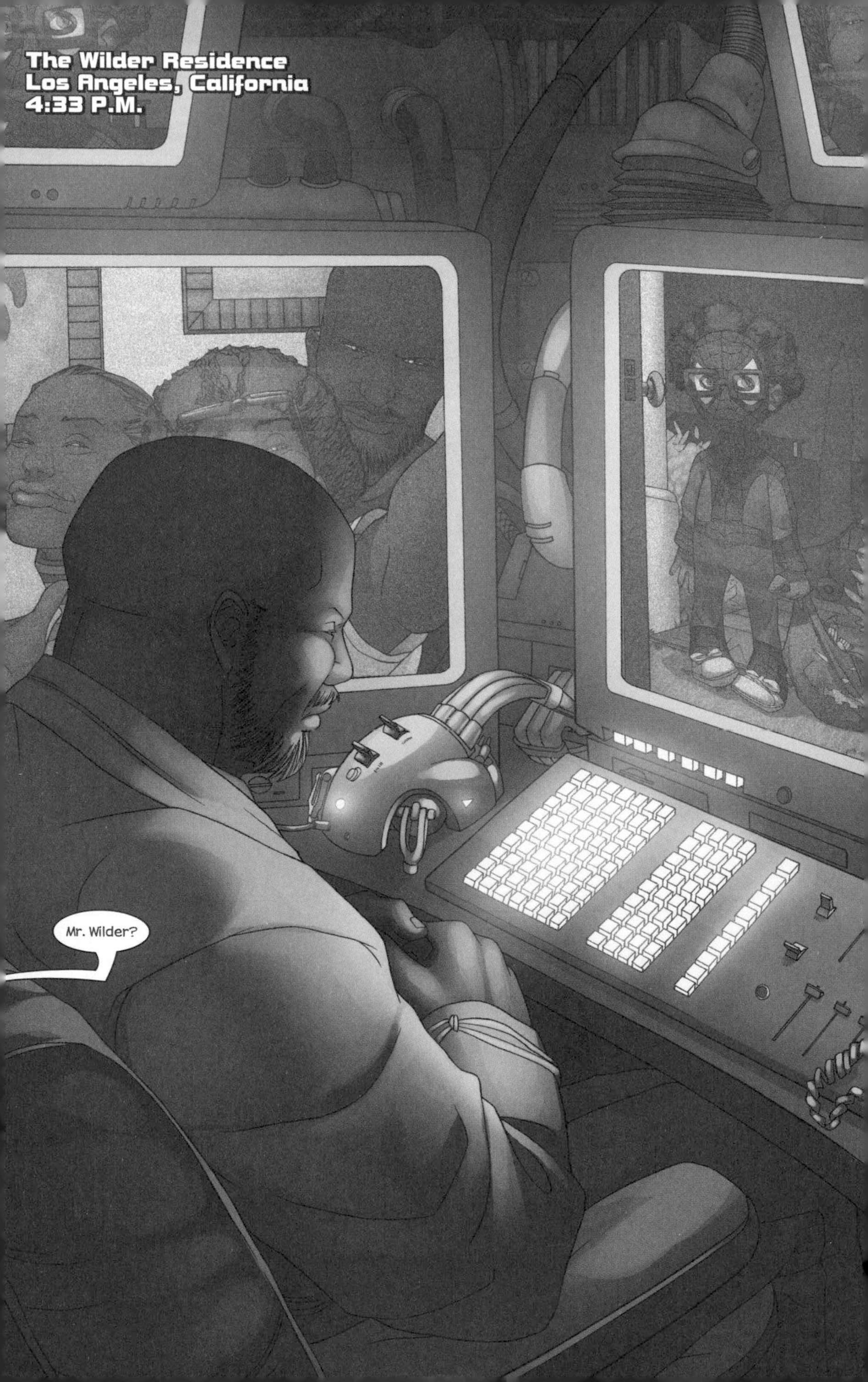

The Wilder Residence
Los Angeles, California
4:33 P.M.
Mr. Wilder?

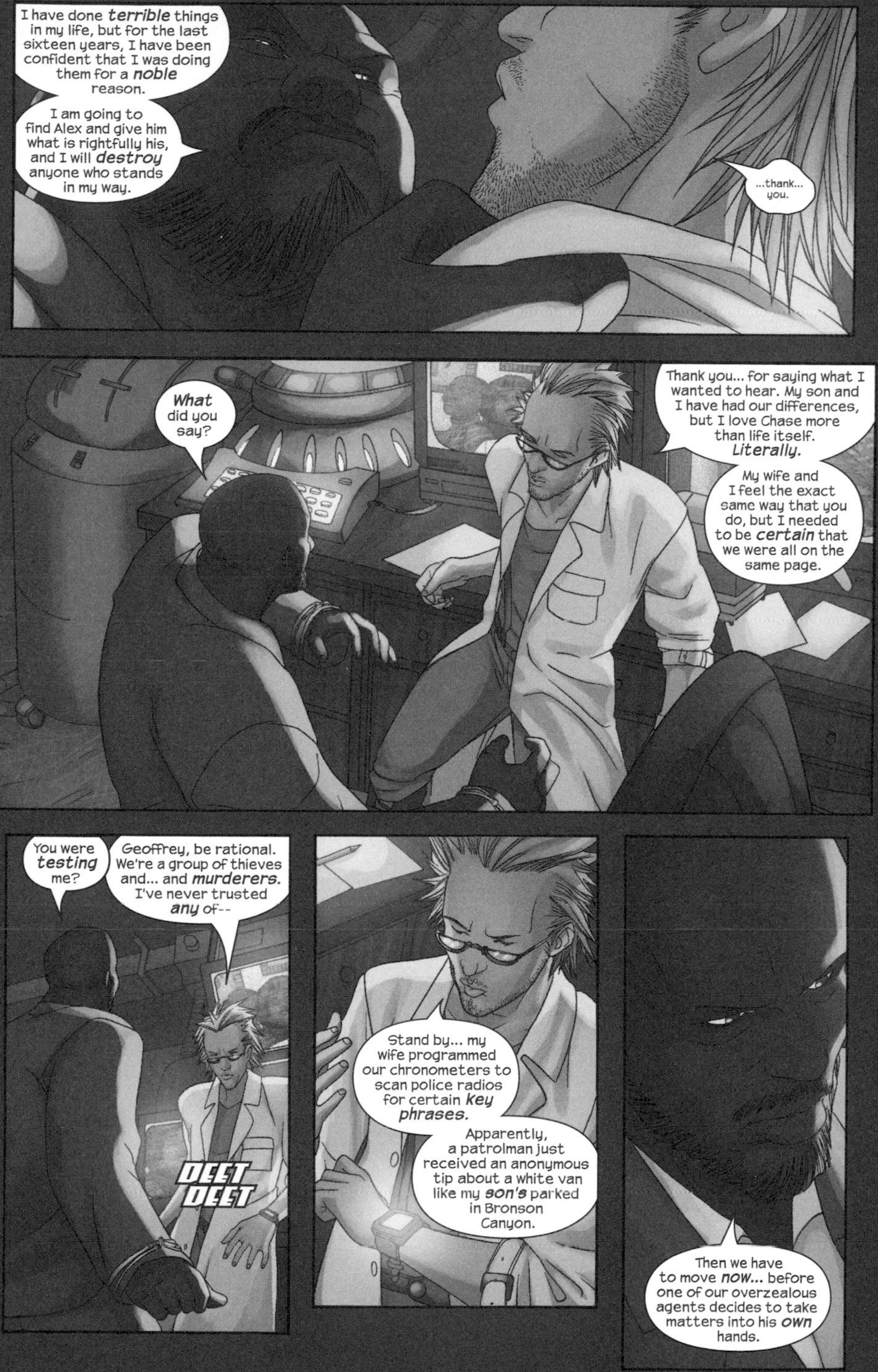

I have done terrible things in my life, but for the last sixteen years, I have been confident that I was doing them for a noble reason.
I am going to find Alex and give him what is rightfully his, and I will destroy anyone who stands in my way.
...thank... you.
What did you say?
Thank you... for saying what I wanted to hear. My son and I have had our differences, but I love Chase more than life itself. Literally.
My wife and I feel the exact same way that you do, but I needed to be certain that we were all on the same page.
You were testing me?
Geoffrey, be rational. We're a group of thieves and... and murderers. I've never trusted any of--
DEET DEET
Stand by... my wife programmed our chronometers to scan police radios for certain key phrases.
Apparently, a patrolman just received an anonymous tip about a white van like my son's parked in Bronson Canyon.
Then we have to move now... before one of our overzealous agents decides to take matters into his own hands.

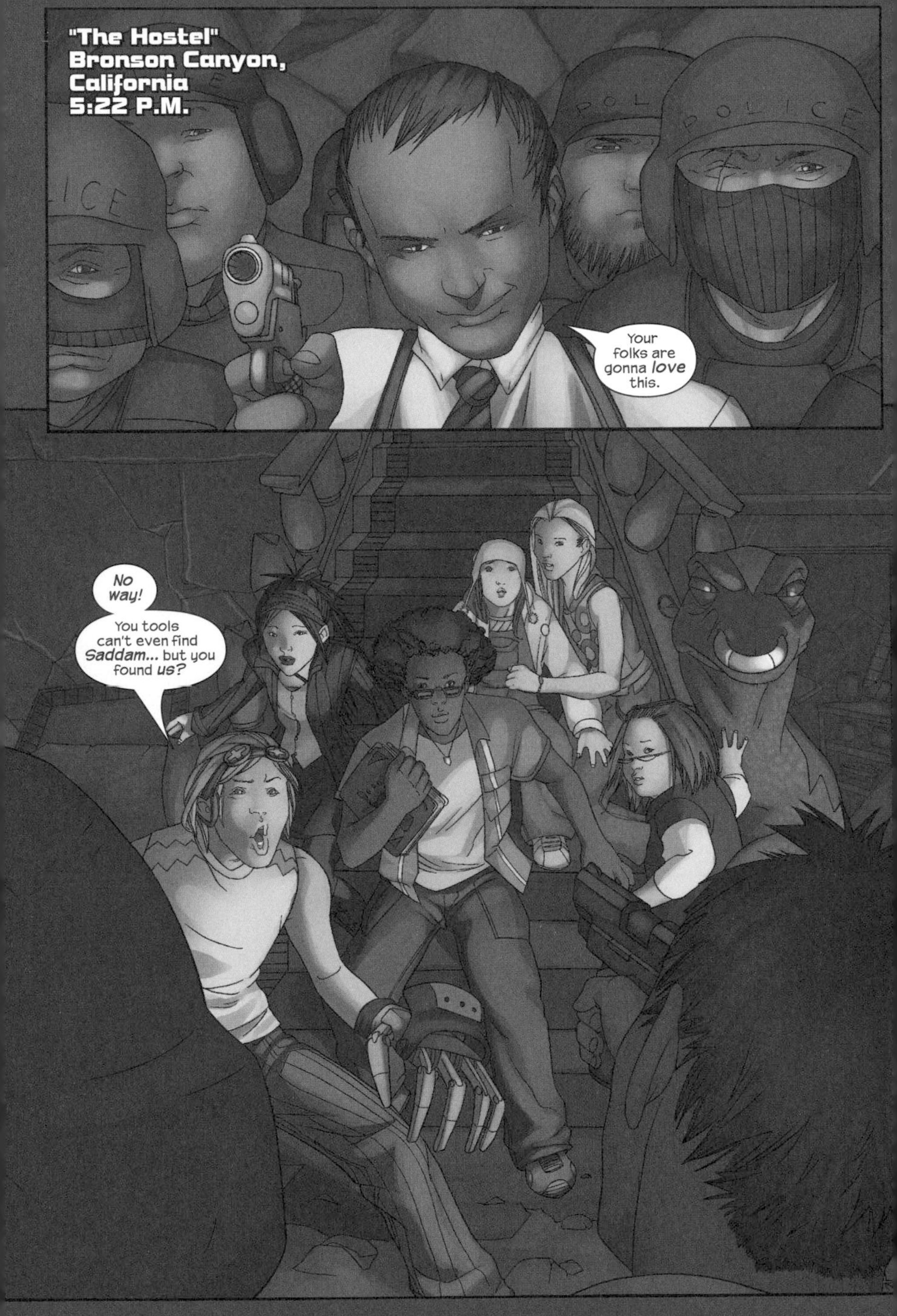
"The Hostel"
Bronson Canyon,
California
5:22 P.M.
Your folks are gonna love this.
No way!
You tools can't even find Saddam... but you found us?

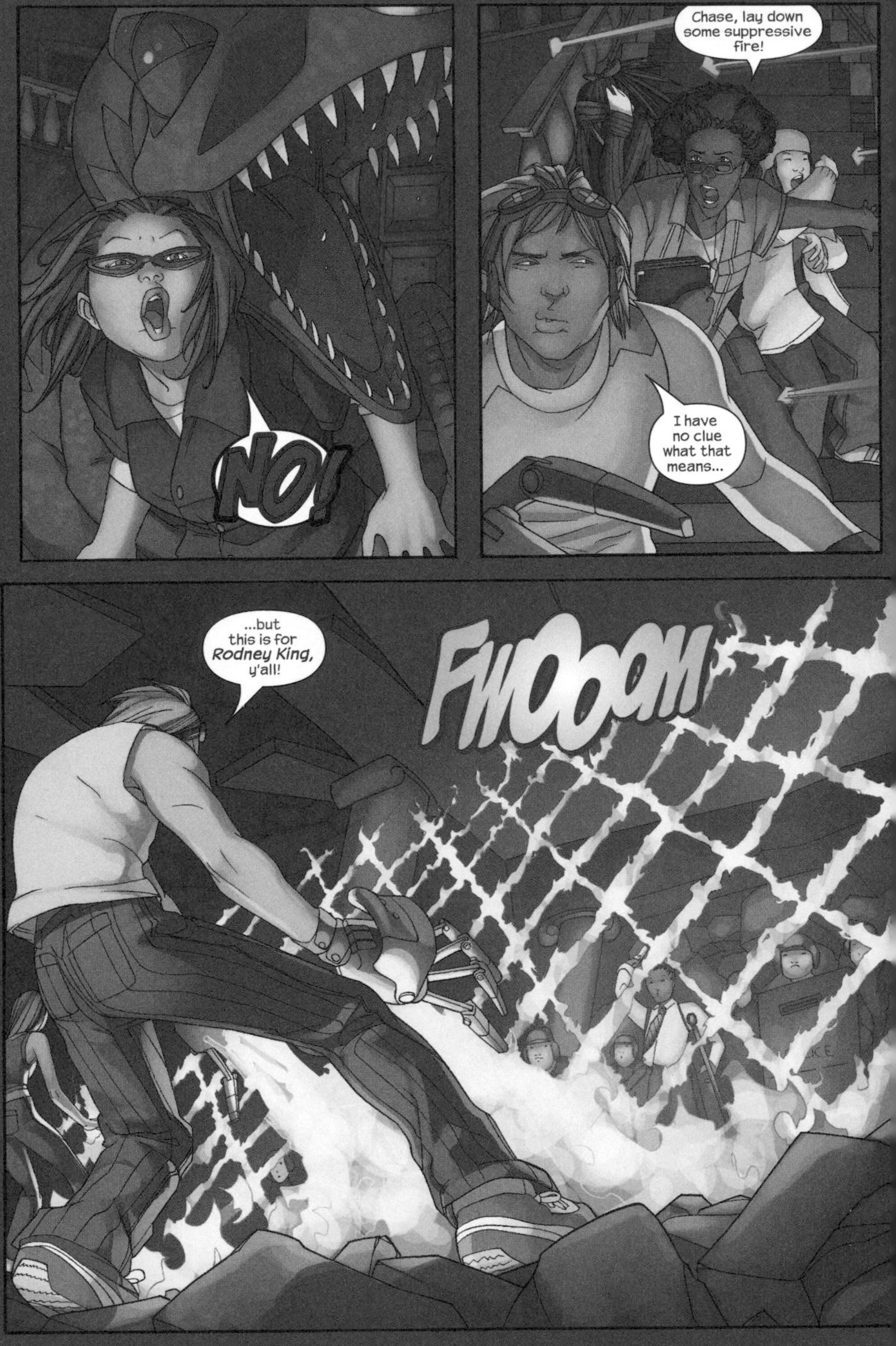
NO!
Chase, lay down some suppressive fire!
I have no clue what that means...
...but this is for Rodney King, y'all!
FWOOOM

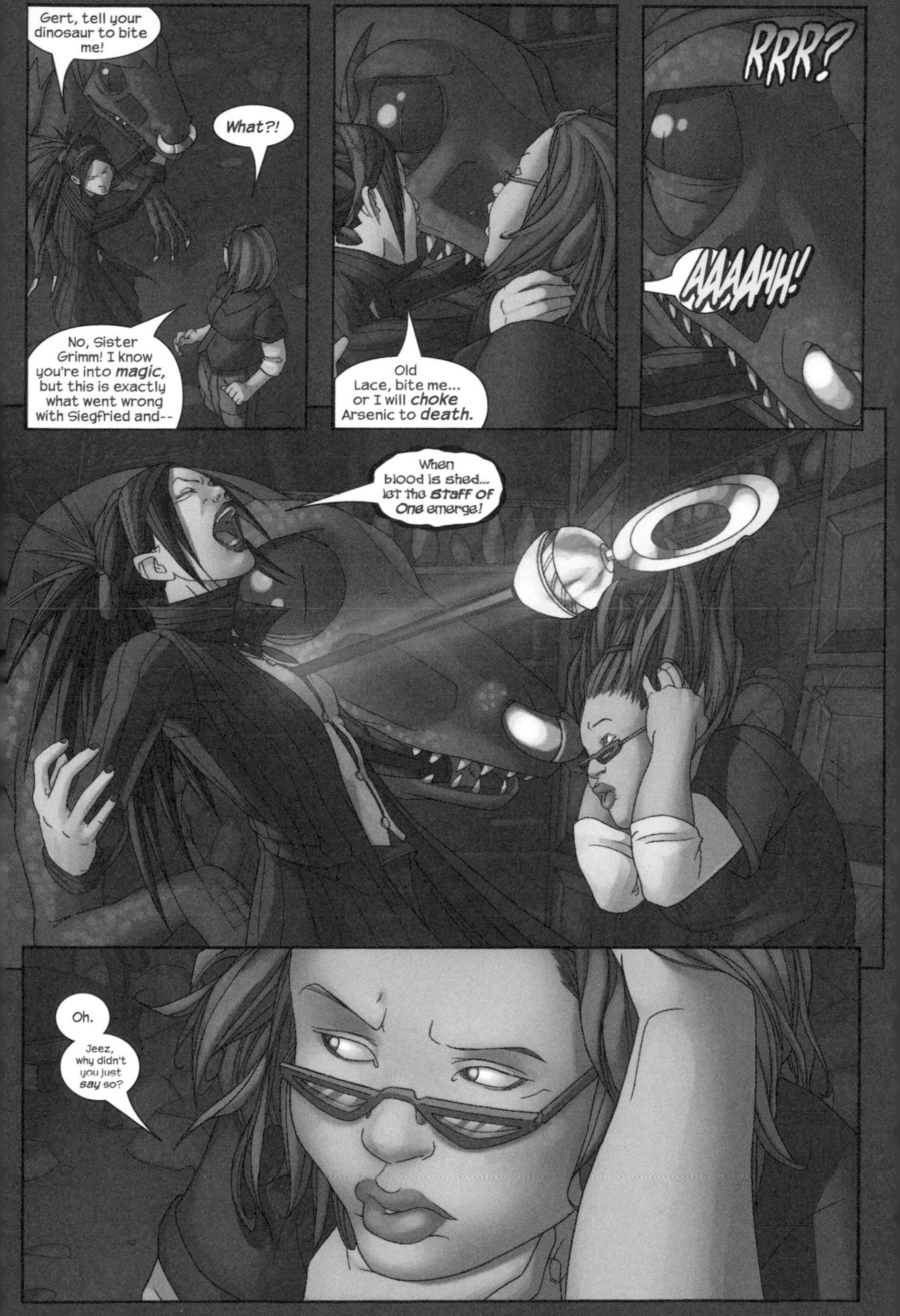
Gert, tell your dinosaur to bite me!
What?!
No, Sister Grimm! I know you're into *magic,* but this is exactly what went wrong with Siegfried and--
Old Lace, bite me... or I will *choke* Arsenic to *death.*
RRR?
AAAAHH!
When blood is shed... let the *Staff of One* emerge!
Oh.
Jeez, why didn't you just *say* so?

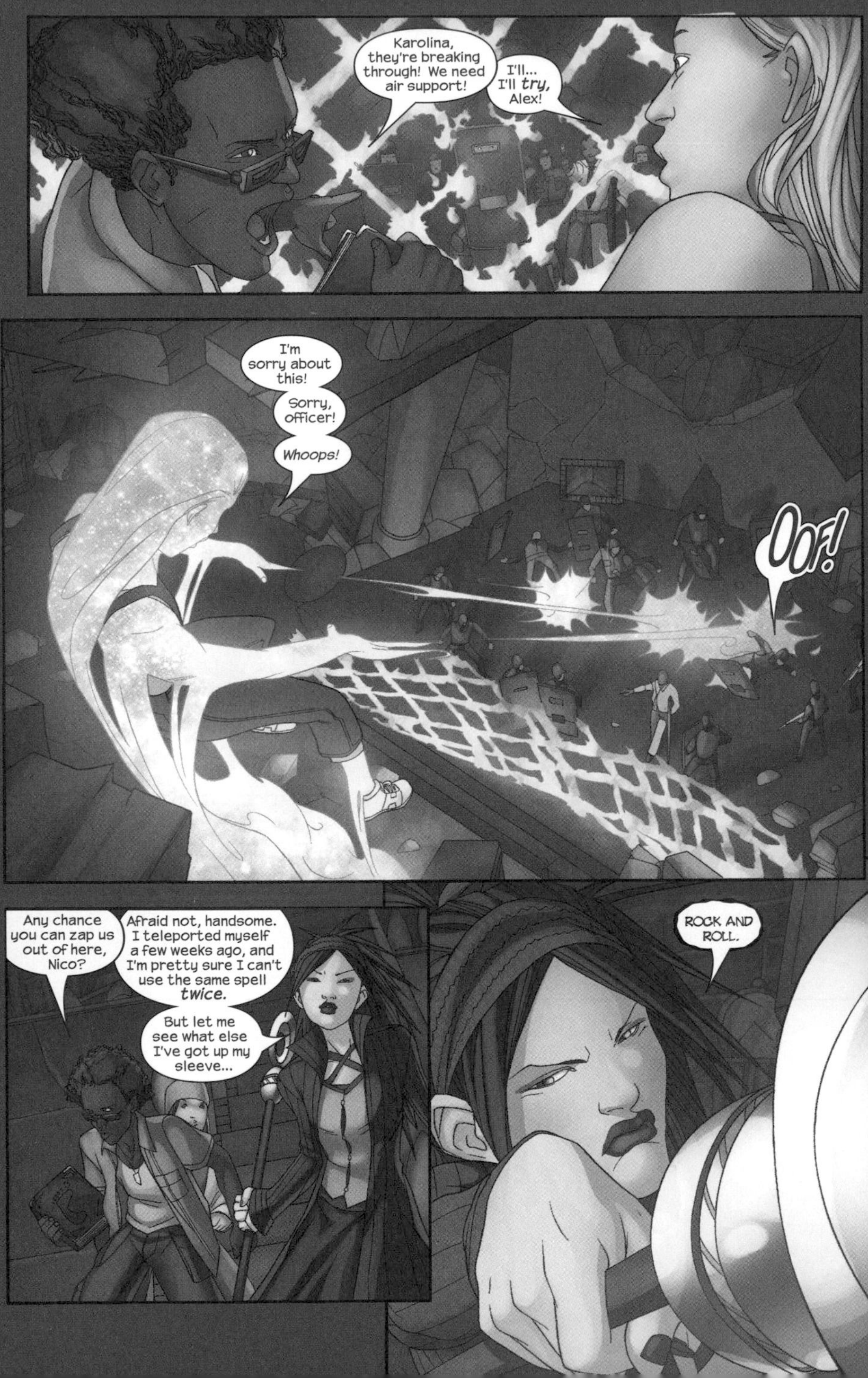

Karolina, they're breaking through! We need air support!
I'll... I'll *try,* Alex!
I'm sorry about this!
Sorry, officer!
Whoops!
OOF!
Any chance you can zap us out of here, Nico?
Afraid not, handsome. I teleported myself a few weeks ago, and I'm pretty sure I can't use the same spell **twice.**
But let me see what else I've got up my sleeve...
ROCK AND ROLL.

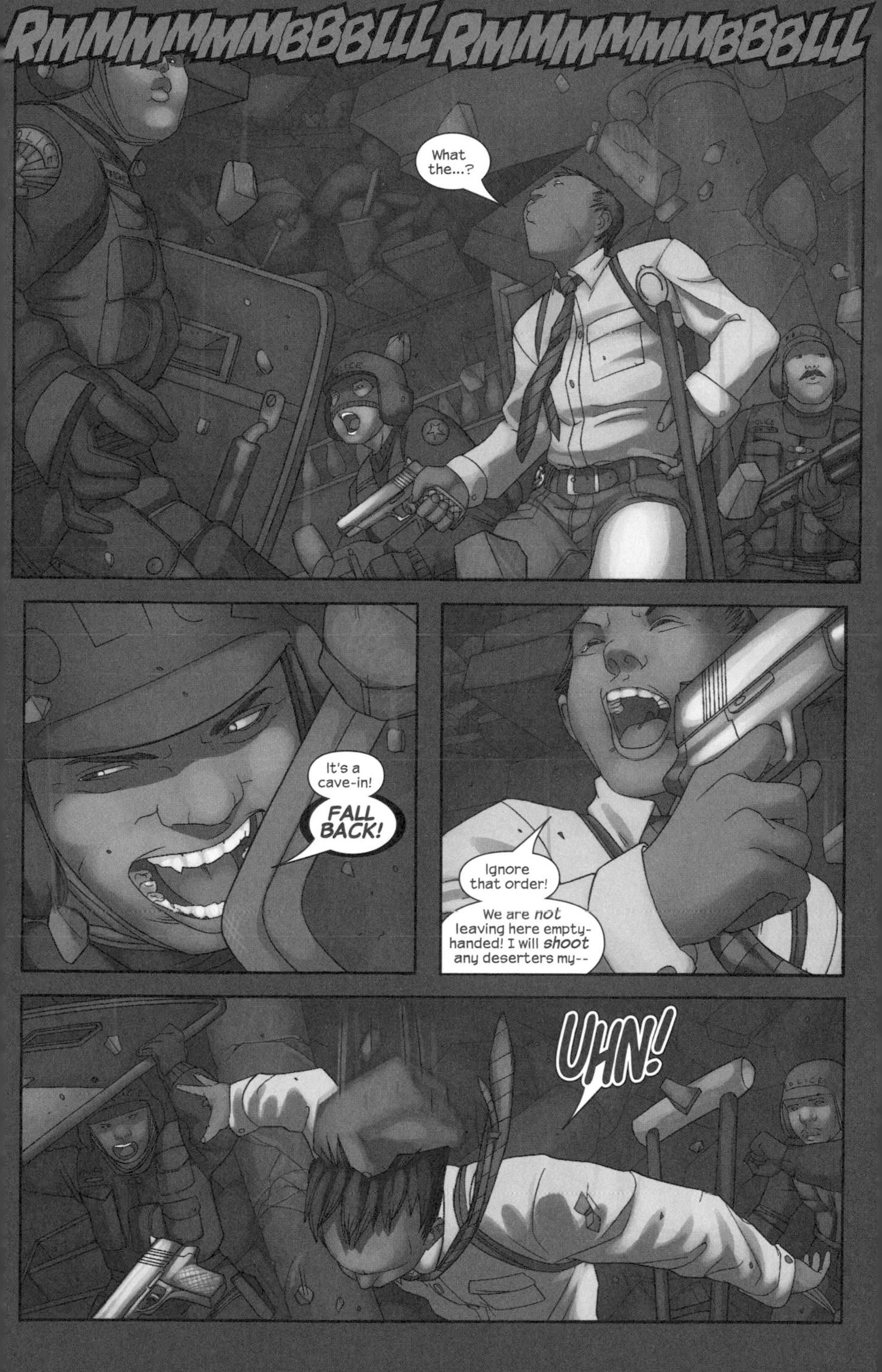
RMMMMMMMBBBLLL RMMMMMMMMBBBLLL
What the...?
It's a cave-in!
FALL BACK!
Ignore that order!
We are *not* leaving here empty-handed! I will *shoot* any deserters my--
UHN!

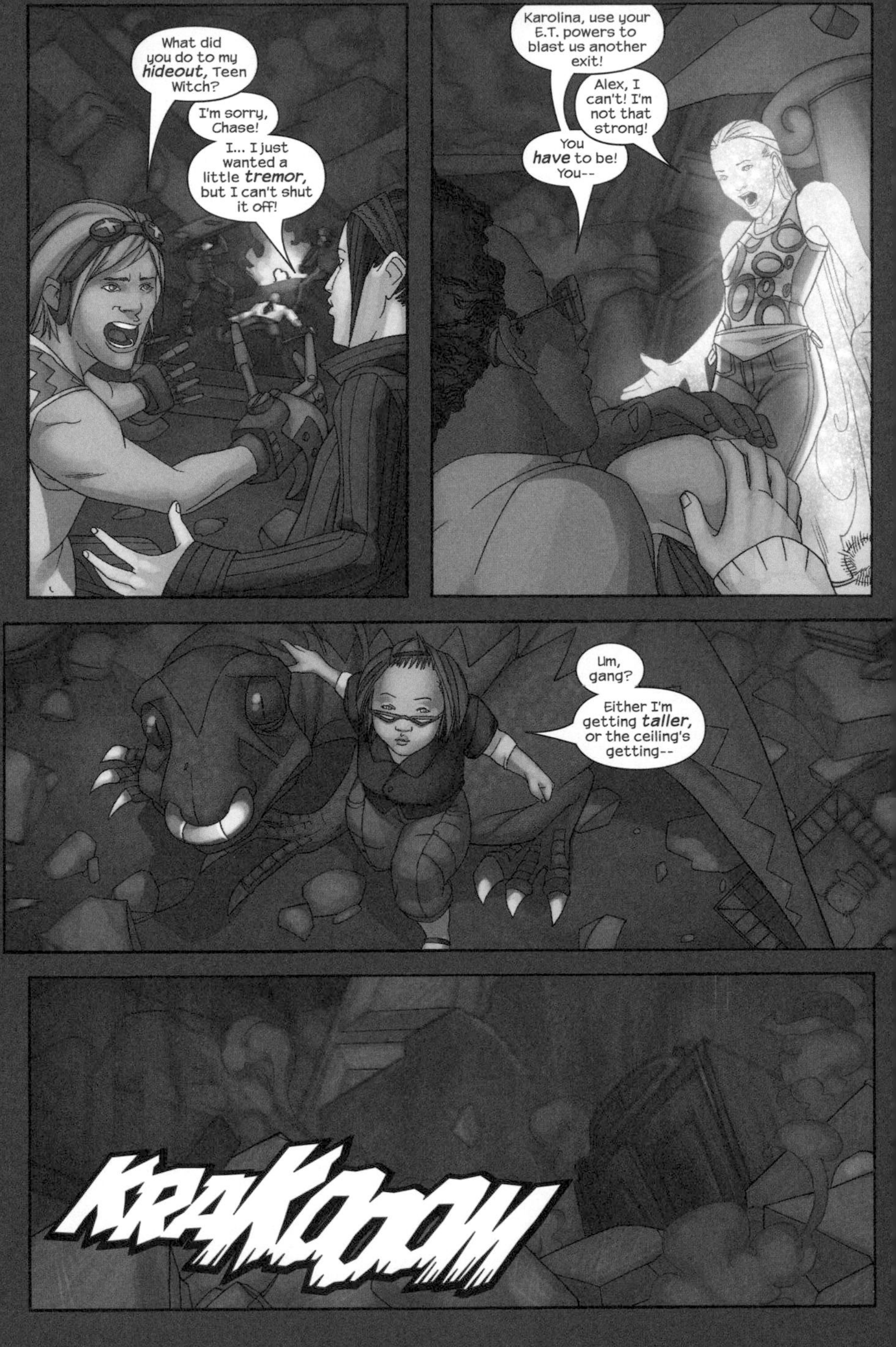
What did you do to my *hideout,* Teen Witch?
I'm sorry, Chase!
I... I just wanted a little *tremor,* but I can't shut it off!
Karolina, use your E.T. powers to blast us another exit!
Alex, I can't! I'm not that strong!
You *have* to be! You--
Um, gang?
Either I'm getting *taller,* or the ceiling's getting--
KRAKOOOM

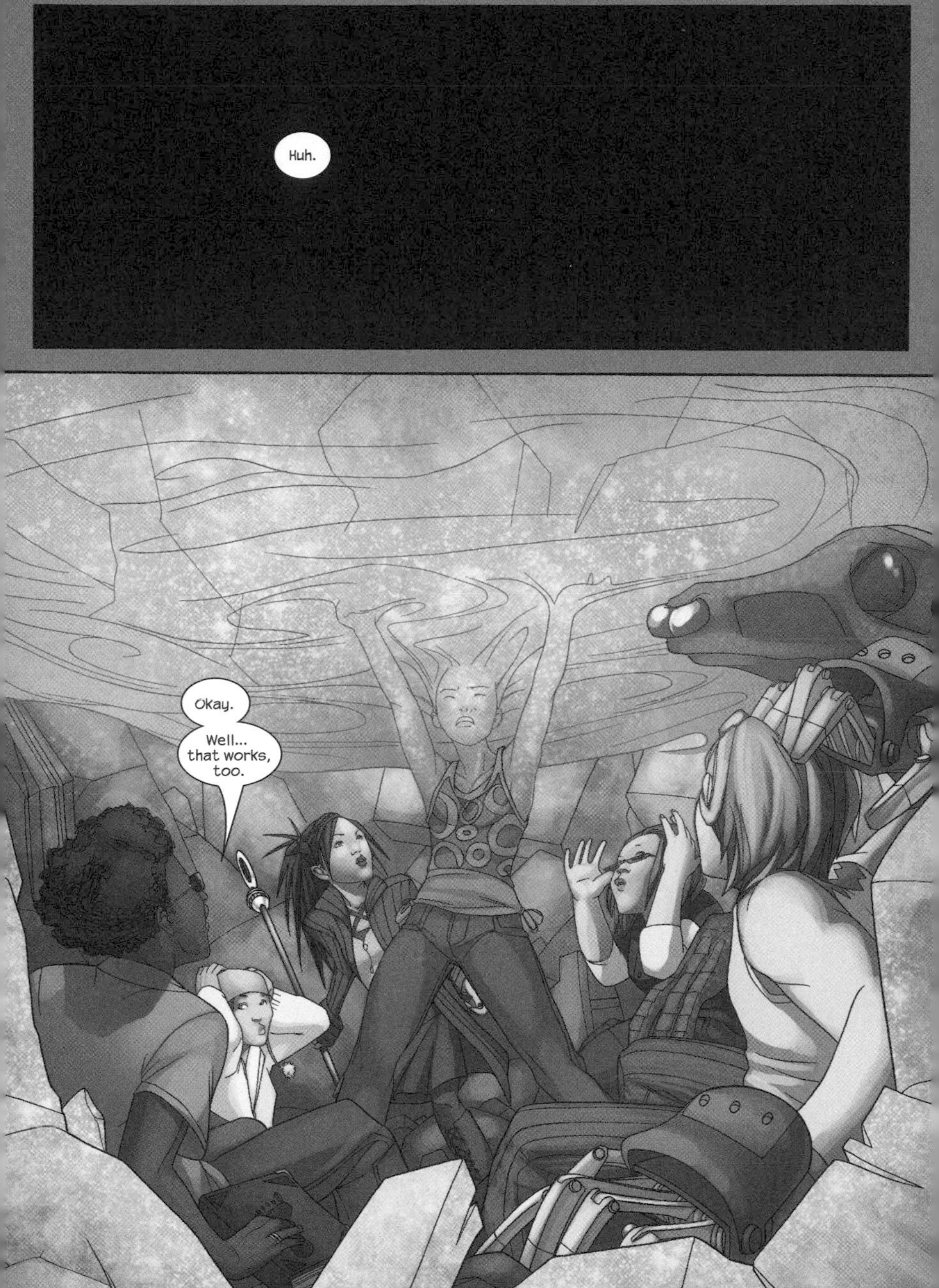
Huh.
Okay.
Well... that works, too.

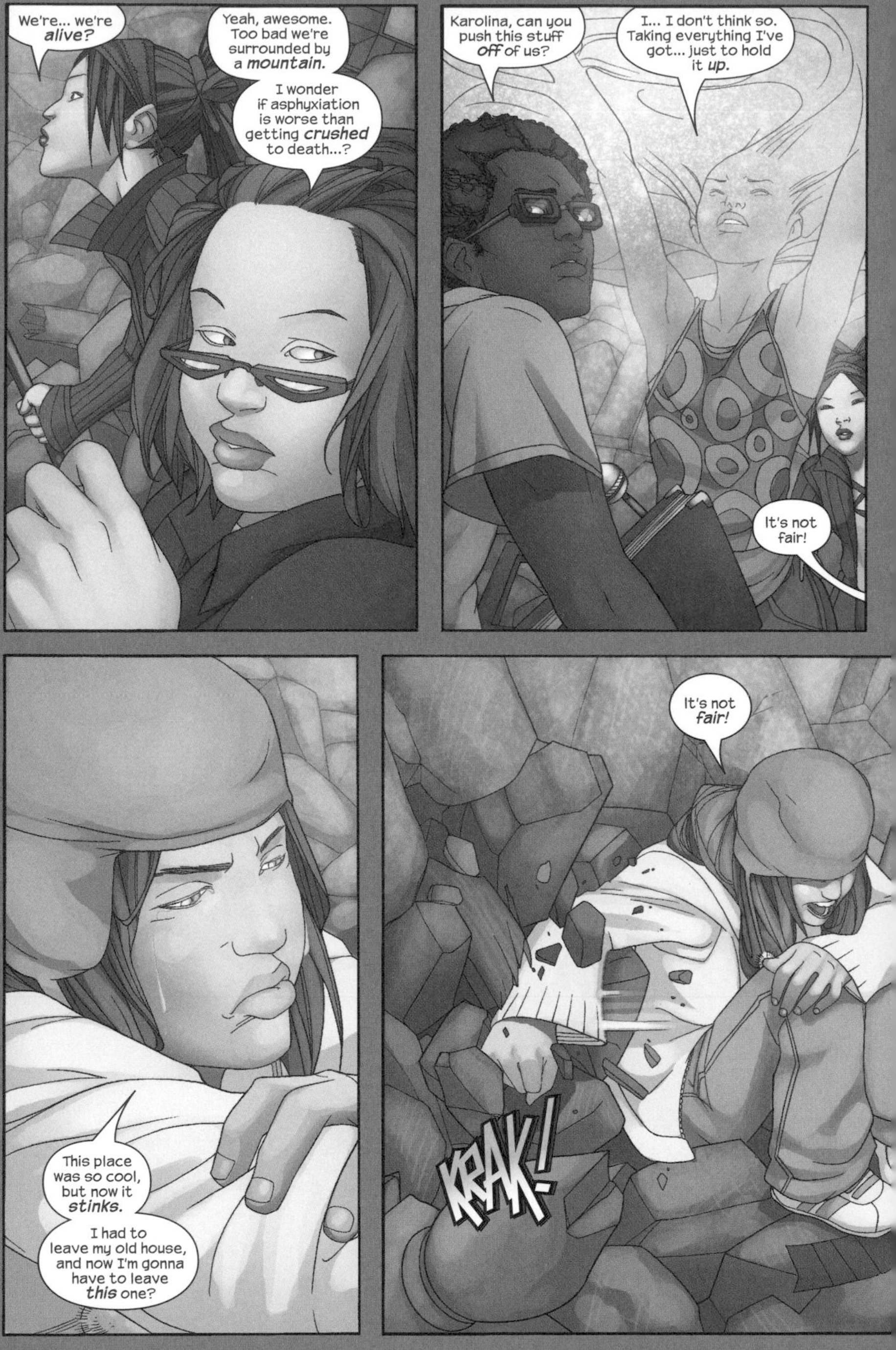

We're... we're *alive?*
Yeah, awesome. Too bad we're surrounded by a **mountain.**
I wonder if asphyxiation is worse than getting *crushed* to death...?
Karolina, can you push this stuff *off* of us?
I... I don't think so. Taking everything I've got... just to hold it *up.*
It's not fair!
This place was so cool, but now it **stinks.**
I had to leave my old house, and now I'm gonna have to leave *this* one?
It's not *fair!*
KRAK!

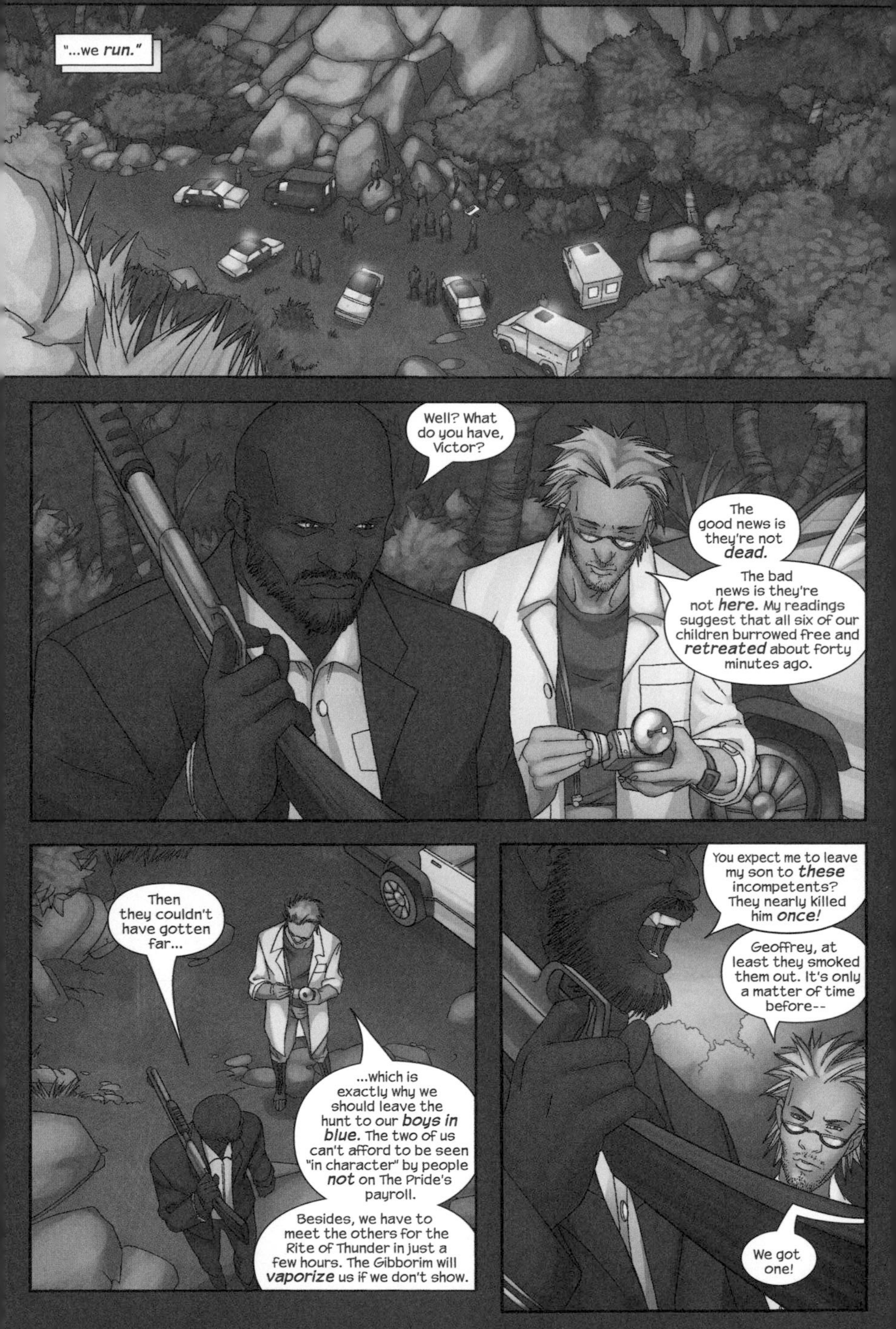
"...we run."
Well? What do you have, Victor?
The good news is they're not dead.
The bad news is they're not here. My readings suggest that all six of our children burrowed free and retreated about forty minutes ago.
Then they couldn't have gotten far...
...which is exactly why we should leave the hunt to our boys in blue. The two of us can't afford to be seen "in character" by people not on The Pride's payroll.
Besides, we have to meet the others for the Rite of Thunder in just a few hours. The Gibborim will vaporize us if we don't show.
You expect me to leave my son to these incompetents? They nearly killed him once!
Geoffrey, at least they smoked them out. It's only a matter of time before--
We got one!

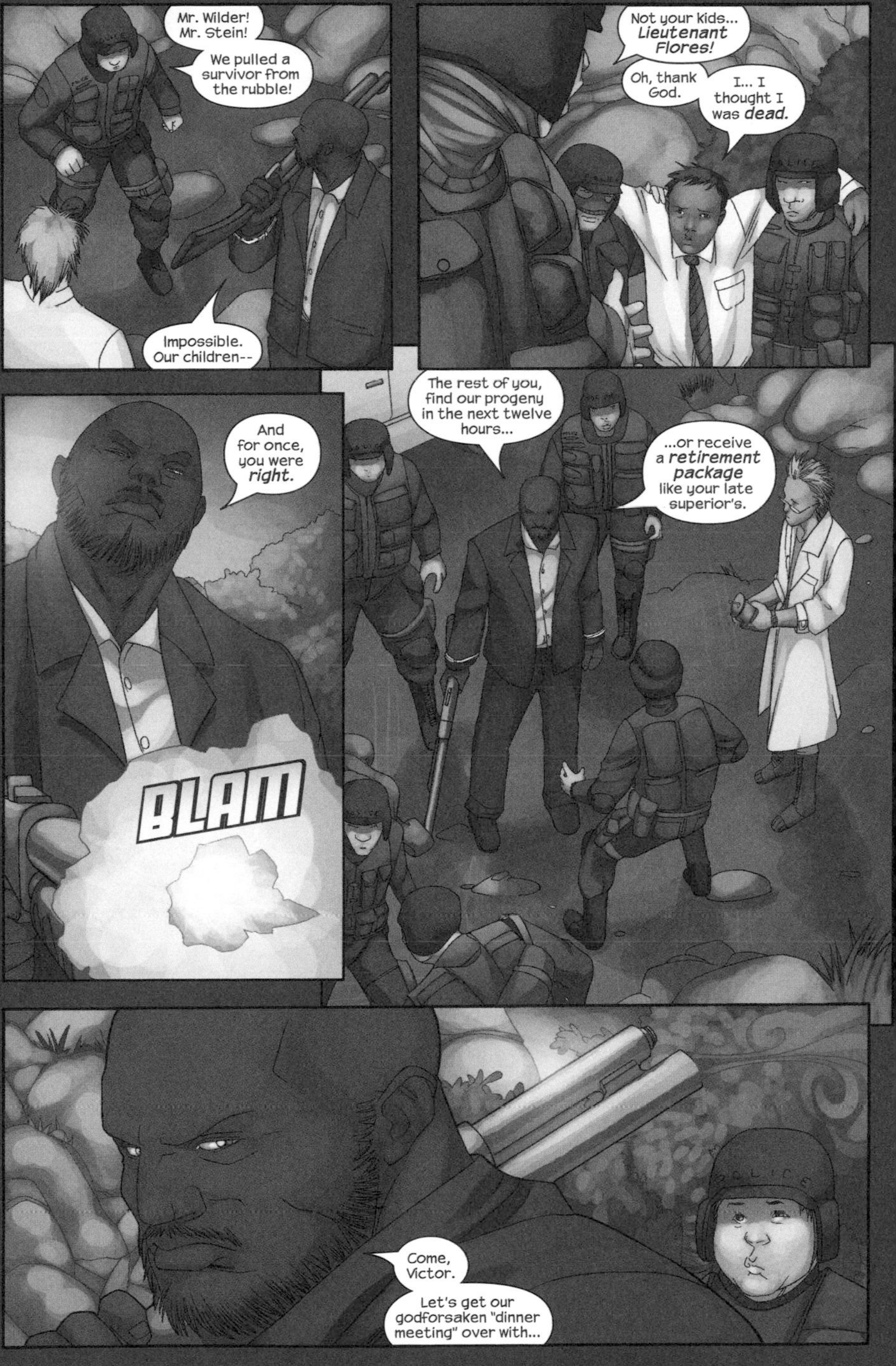
Mr. Wilder! Mr. Stein!
We pulled a survivor from the rubble!
Impossible. Our children--
Not your kids... Lieutenant Flores!
Oh, thank God.
I... I thought I was dead.
And for once, you were right.
BLAM
The rest of you, find our progeny in the next twelve hours...
...or receive a retirement package like your late superior's.
Come, Victor.
Let's get our godforsaken "dinner meeting" over with...

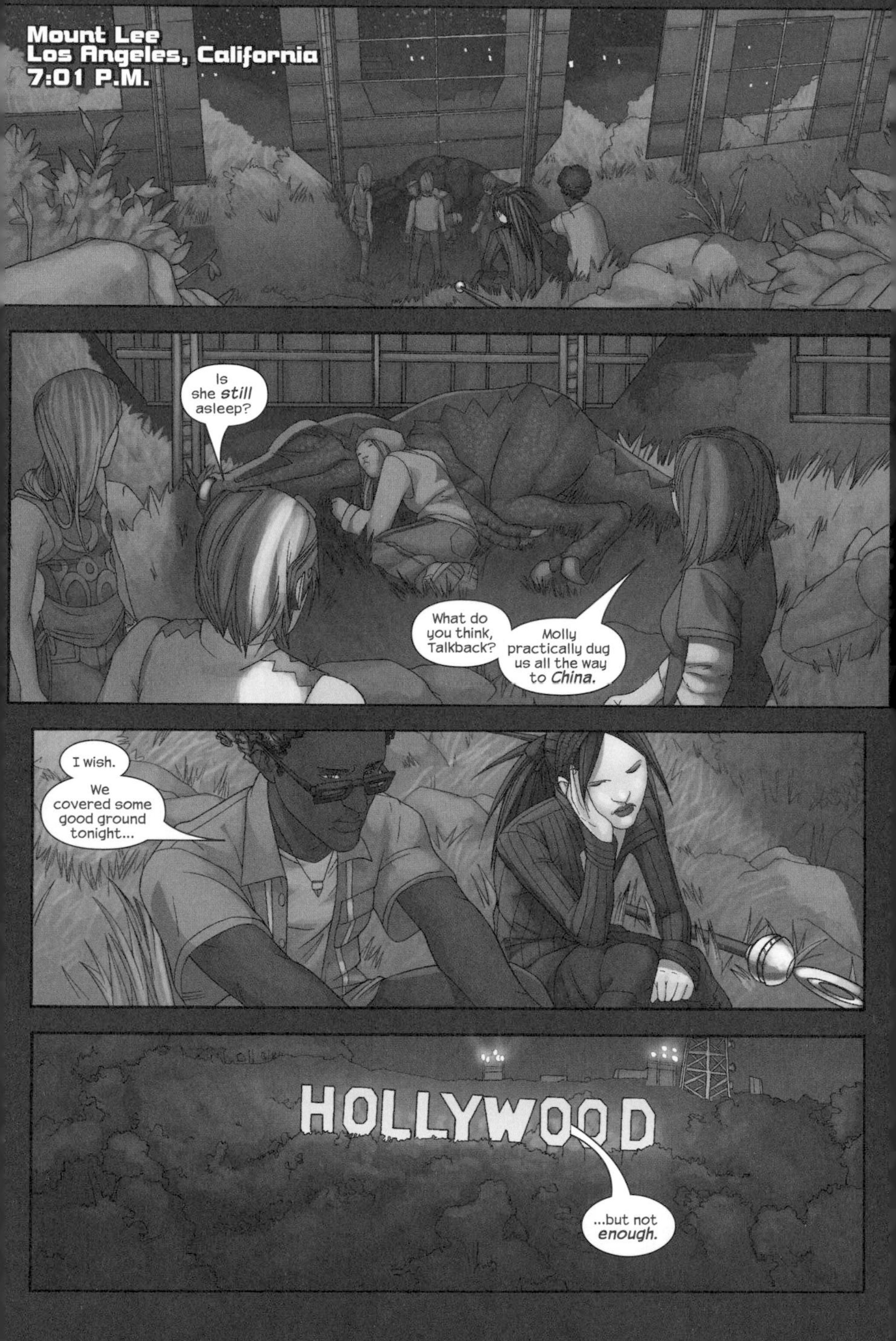
Mount Lee
Los Angeles, California
7:01 P.M.
Is she *still* asleep?
What do you think, Talkback?
Molly practically dug us all the way to *China.*
I wish.
We covered some good ground tonight...
HOLLYWOOD
...but not *enough.*

The Dean Residence
7:30 P.M.

IDIOTS!

Wilder and Stein *had* them, and they let our children *slip away!*

Use your inside voice, dear. You heard what Victor said, they were tipped off by whichever child is our *mole.*

It's only a matter of time before he or she alerts us to their *new* whereabouts.

Indeed. I trust we'll hear from *Molly* again soon enough.

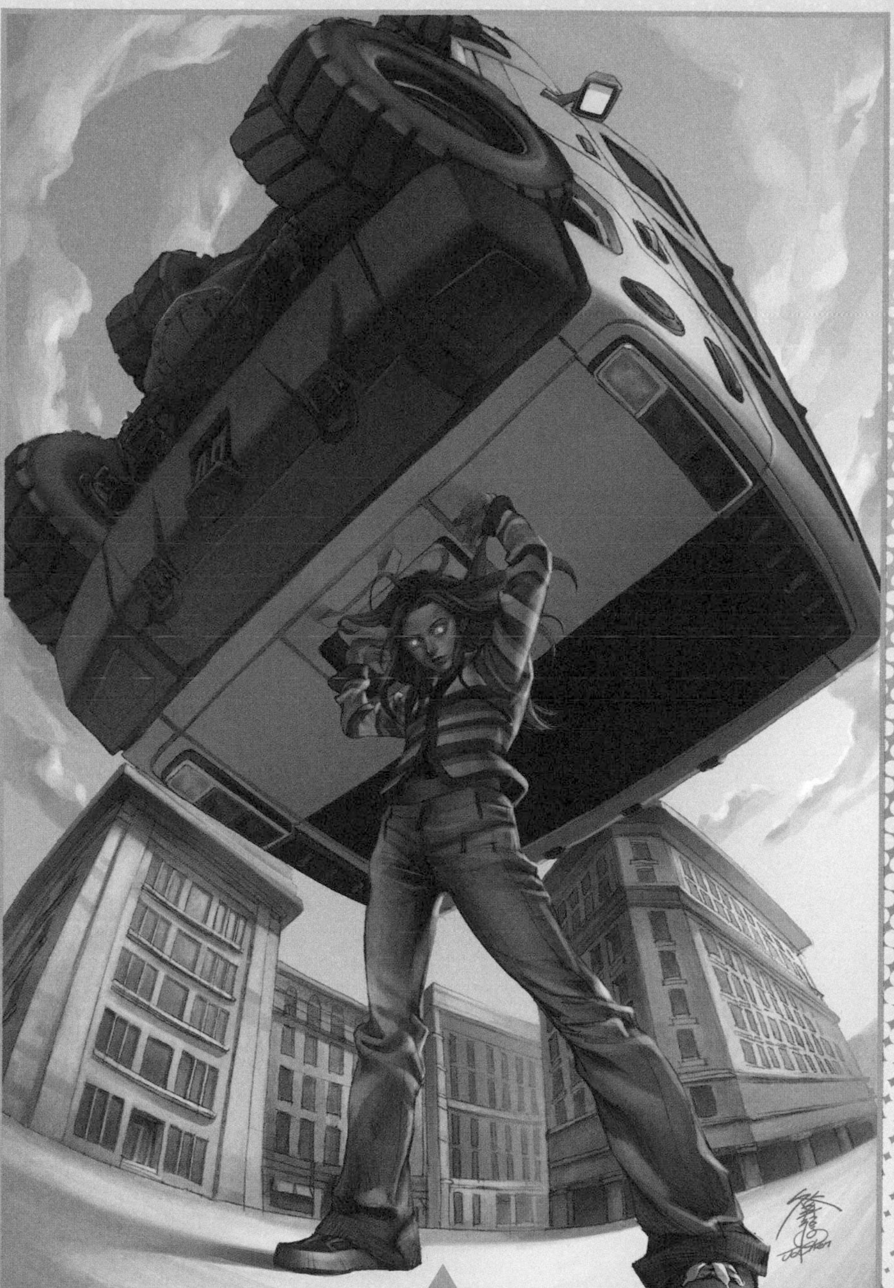

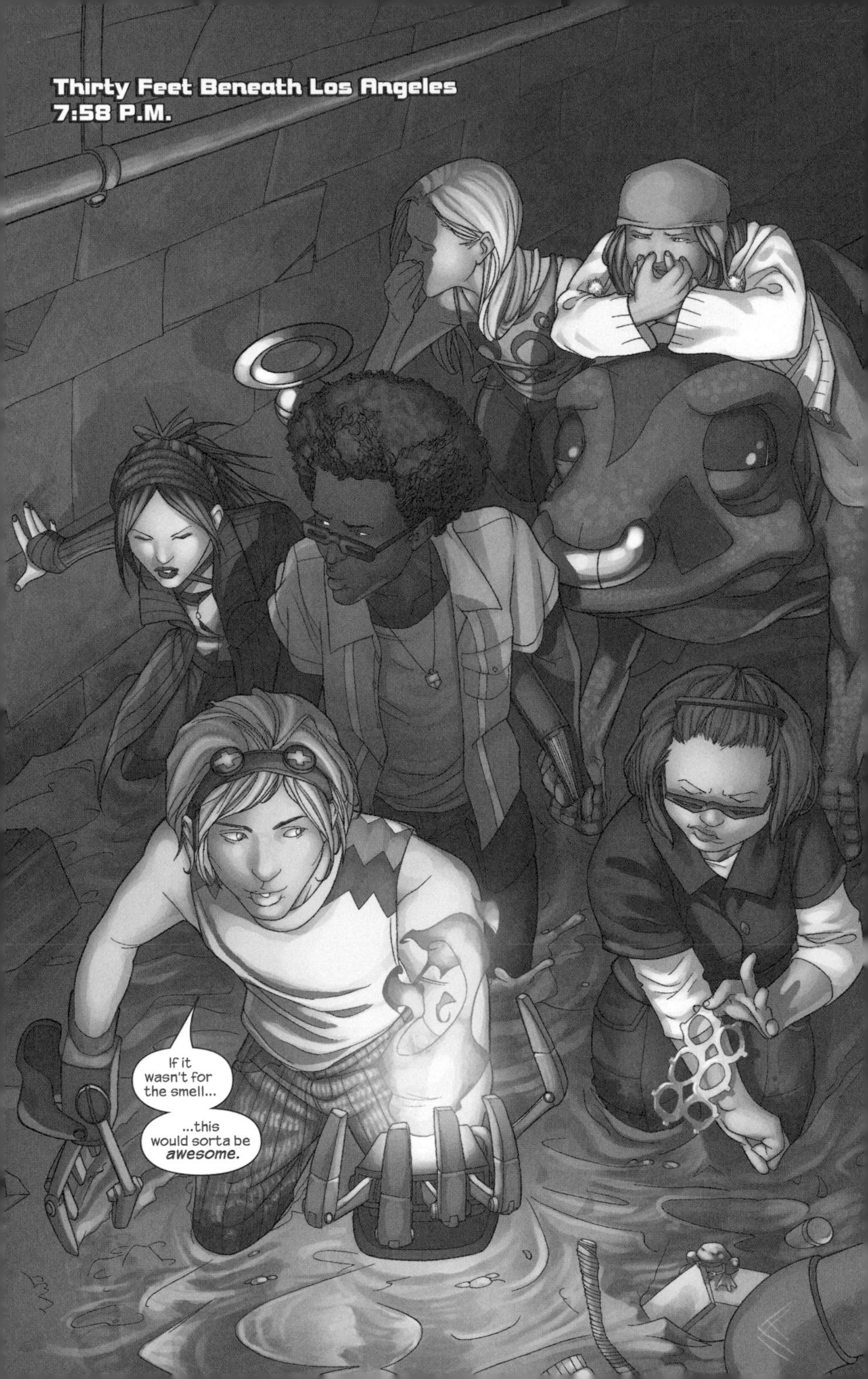
Thirty Feet Beneath Los Angeles
7:58 P.M.
If it wasn't for the smell...
...this would sorta be *awesome.*

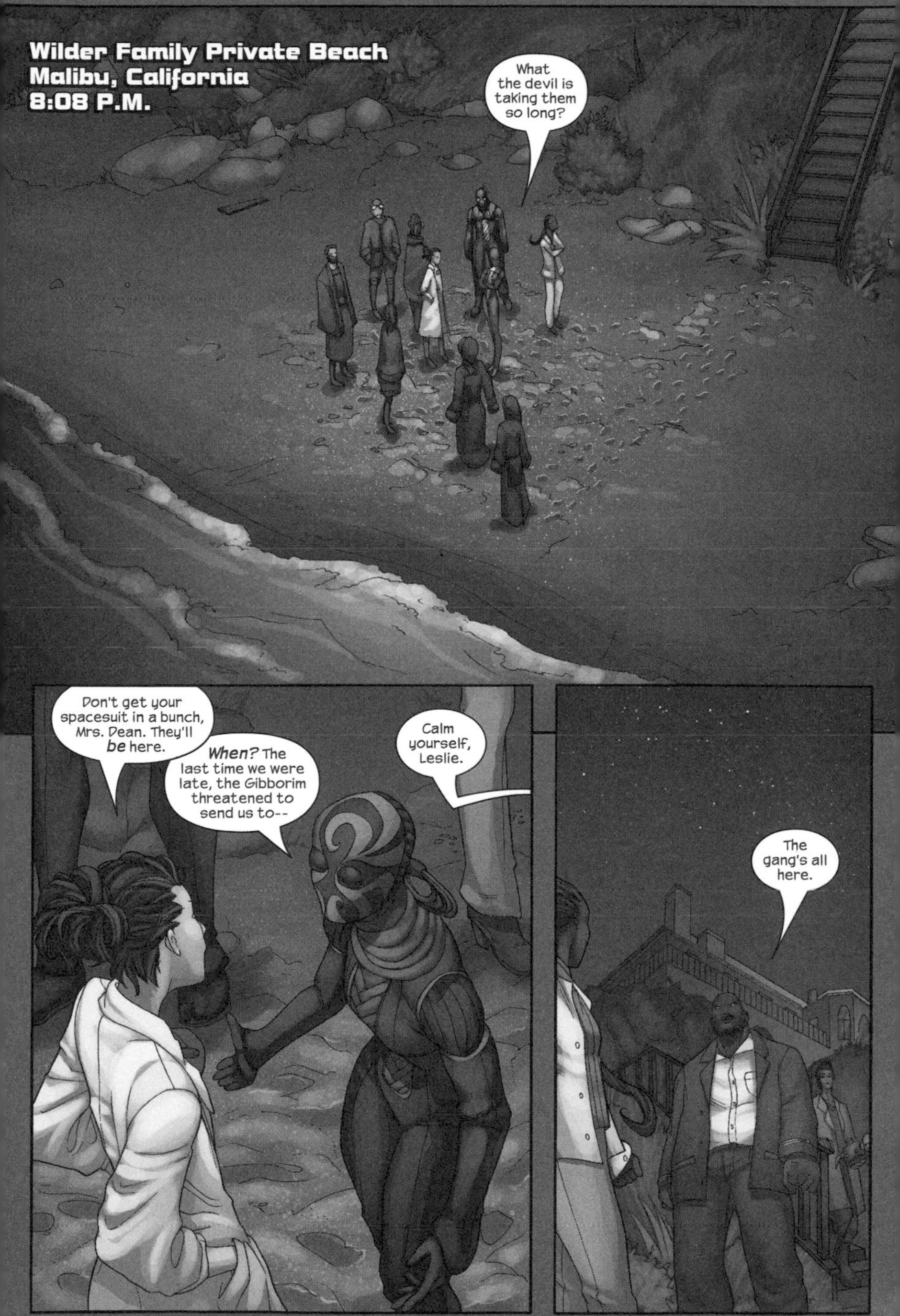
Wilder Family Private Beach
Malibu, California
8:08 P.M.
What the devil is taking them so long?
Don't get your spacesuit in a bunch, Mrs. Dean. They'll *be* here.
When? The last time we were late, the Gibborim threatened to send us to--
Calm yourself, Leslie.
The gang's all here.

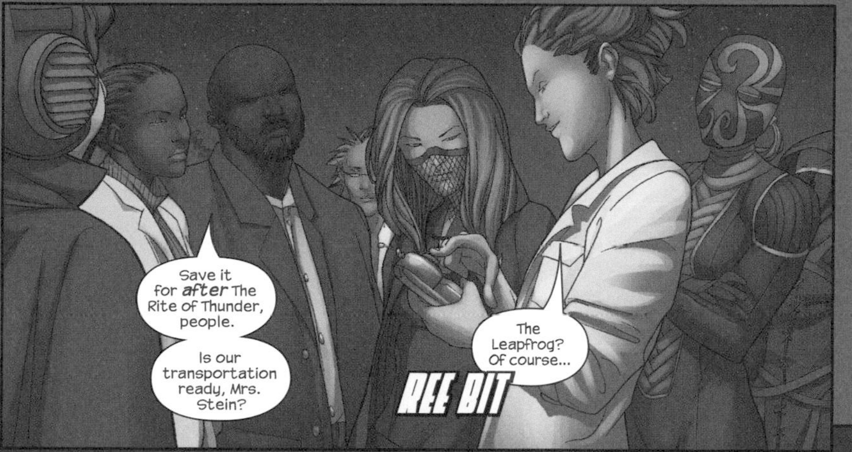
Save it for after The Rite of Thunder, people.
Is our transportation ready, Mrs. Stein?
The Leapfrog? Of course...
REE BIT

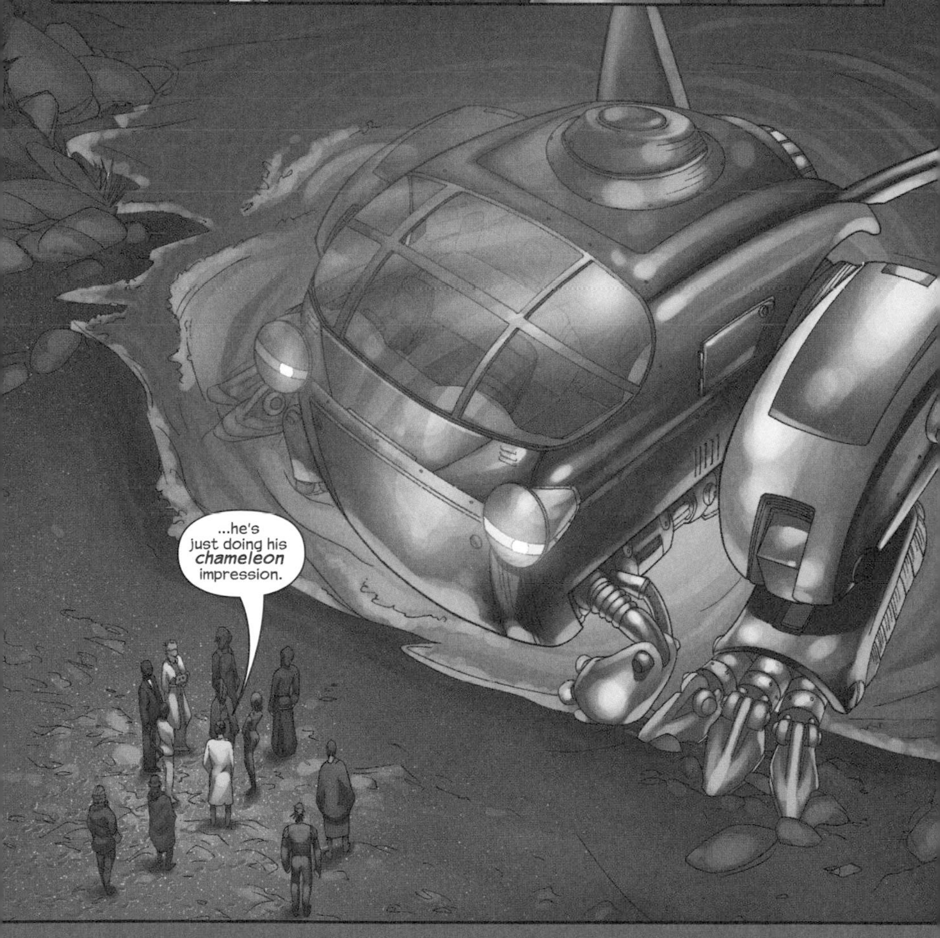
...he's just doing his chameleon impression.

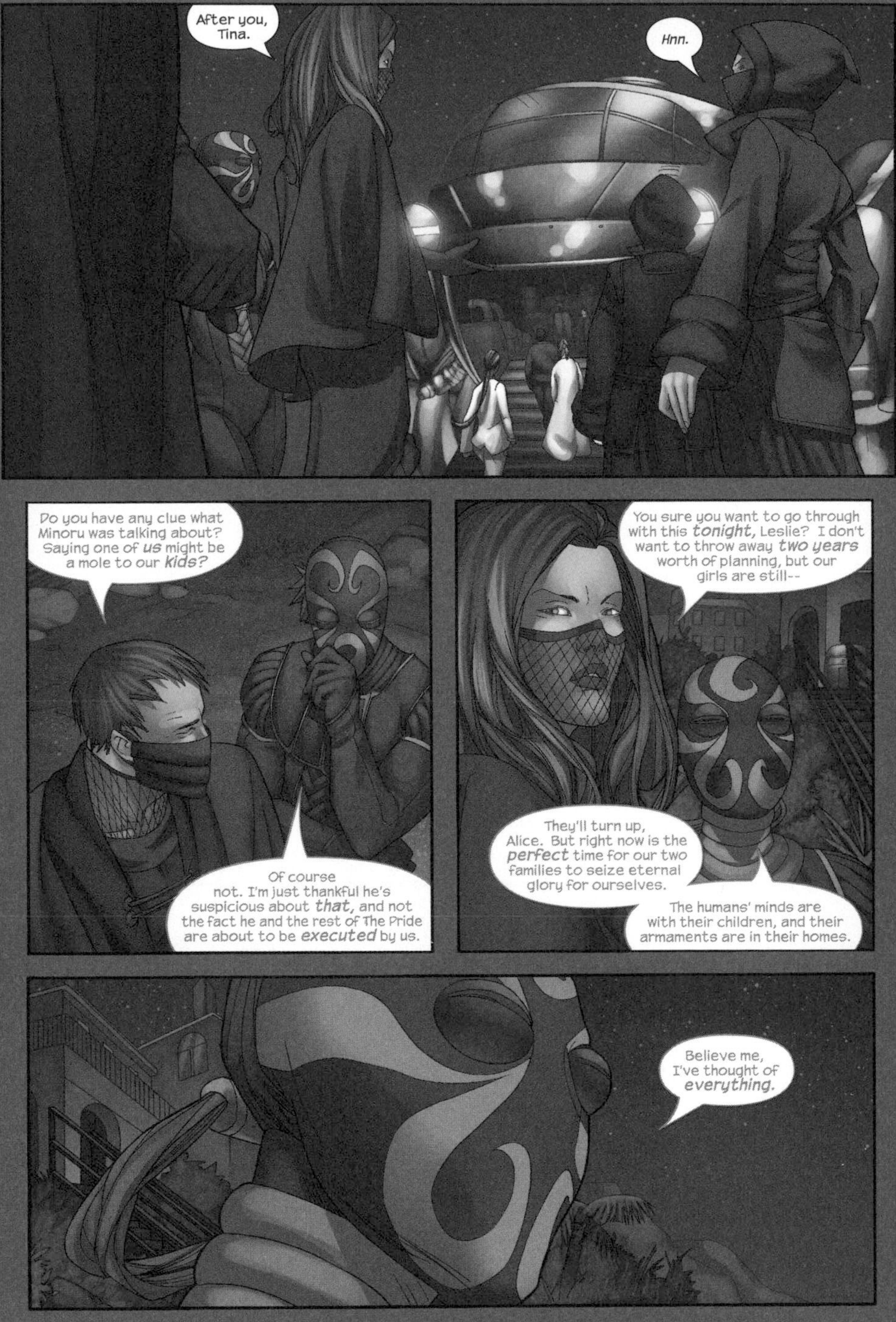
After you, Tina.
Hnn.
Do you have any clue what Minoru was talking about? Saying one of *us* might be a mole to our *kids?*
Of course not. I'm just thankful he's suspicious about *that,* and not the fact he and the rest of The Pride are about to be *executed* by us.
You sure you want to go through with this *tonight,* Leslie? I don't want to throw away *two years* worth of planning, but our girls are still--
They'll turn up, Alice. But right now is the *perfect* time for our two families to seize eternal glory for ourselves.
The humans' minds are with their children, and their armaments are in their homes.
Believe me, I've thought of *everything.*

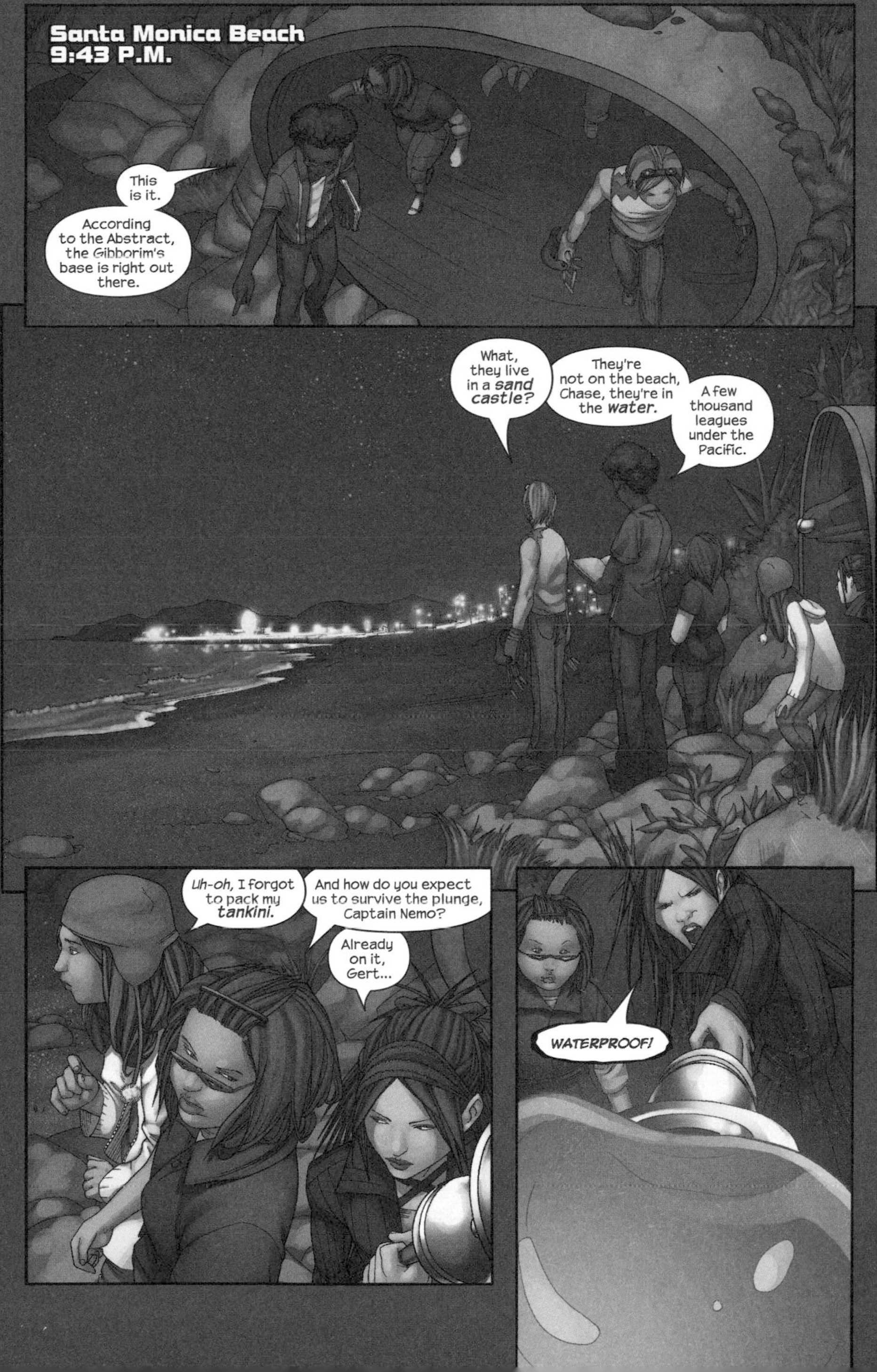
Santa Monica Beach
9:43 P.M.
This is it.
According to the Abstract, the Gibborim's base is right out there.
What, they live in a sand castle?
They're not on the beach, Chase, they're in the water.
A few thousand leagues under the Pacific.
Uh-oh, I forgot to pack my tankini.
And how do you expect us to survive the plunge, Captain Nemo?
Already on it, Gert...
WATERPROOF!

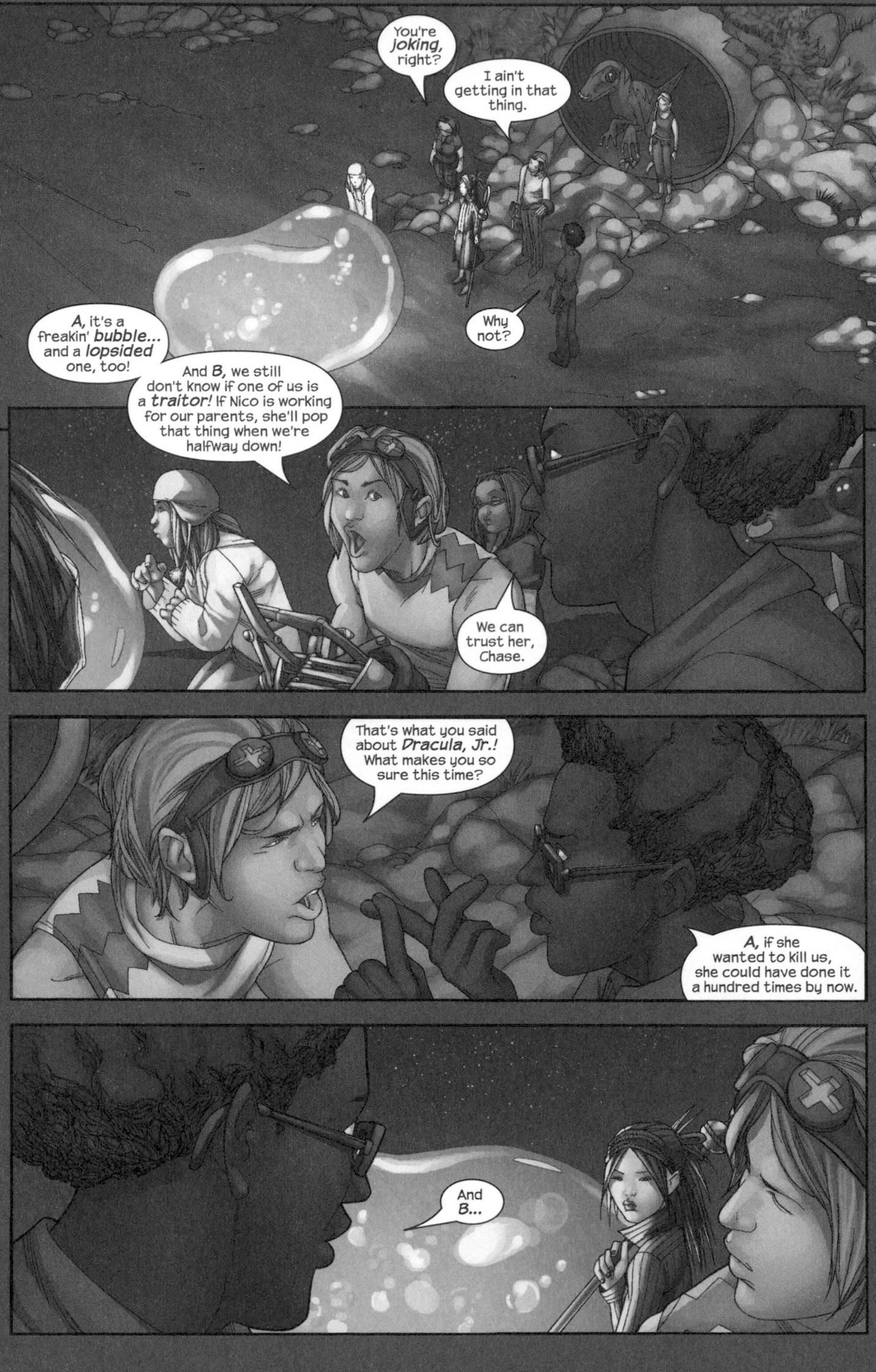
You're *joking,* right?
I ain't getting in that thing.
A, it's a freakin' ***bubble...*** and a ***lopsided*** one, too!
Why not?
And *B,* we still don't know if one of us is a ***traitor!*** If Nico is working for our parents, she'll pop that thing when we're halfway down!
We can trust her, Chase.
That's what you said about *Dracula, Jr.!* What makes you so sure this time?
A, if she wanted to kill us, she could have done it a hundred times by now.
And *B...*

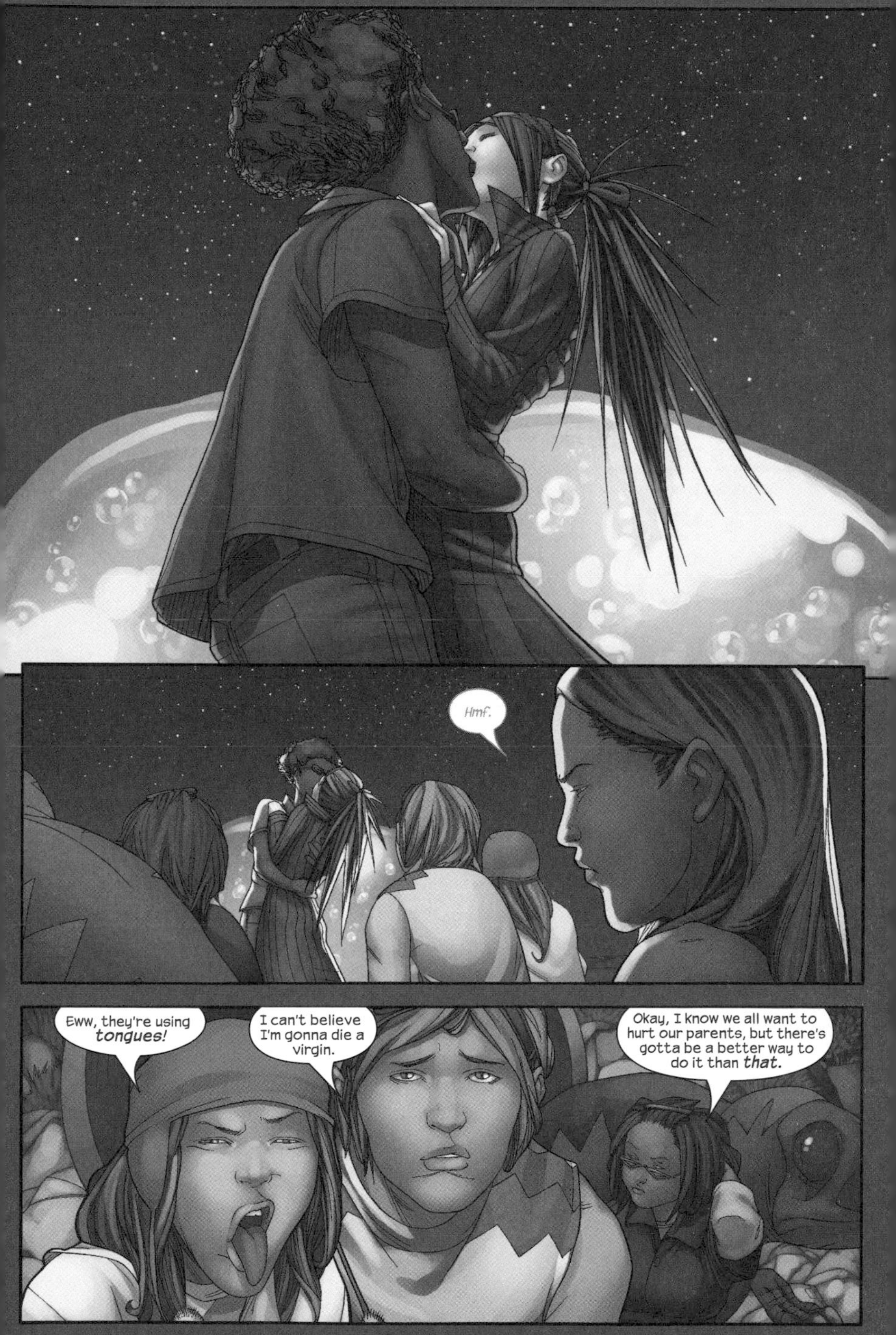
Hmf.
Eww, they're using *tongues!*
I can't believe I'm gonna die a virgin.
Okay, I know we all want to hurt our parents, but there's gotta be a better way to do it than *that.*

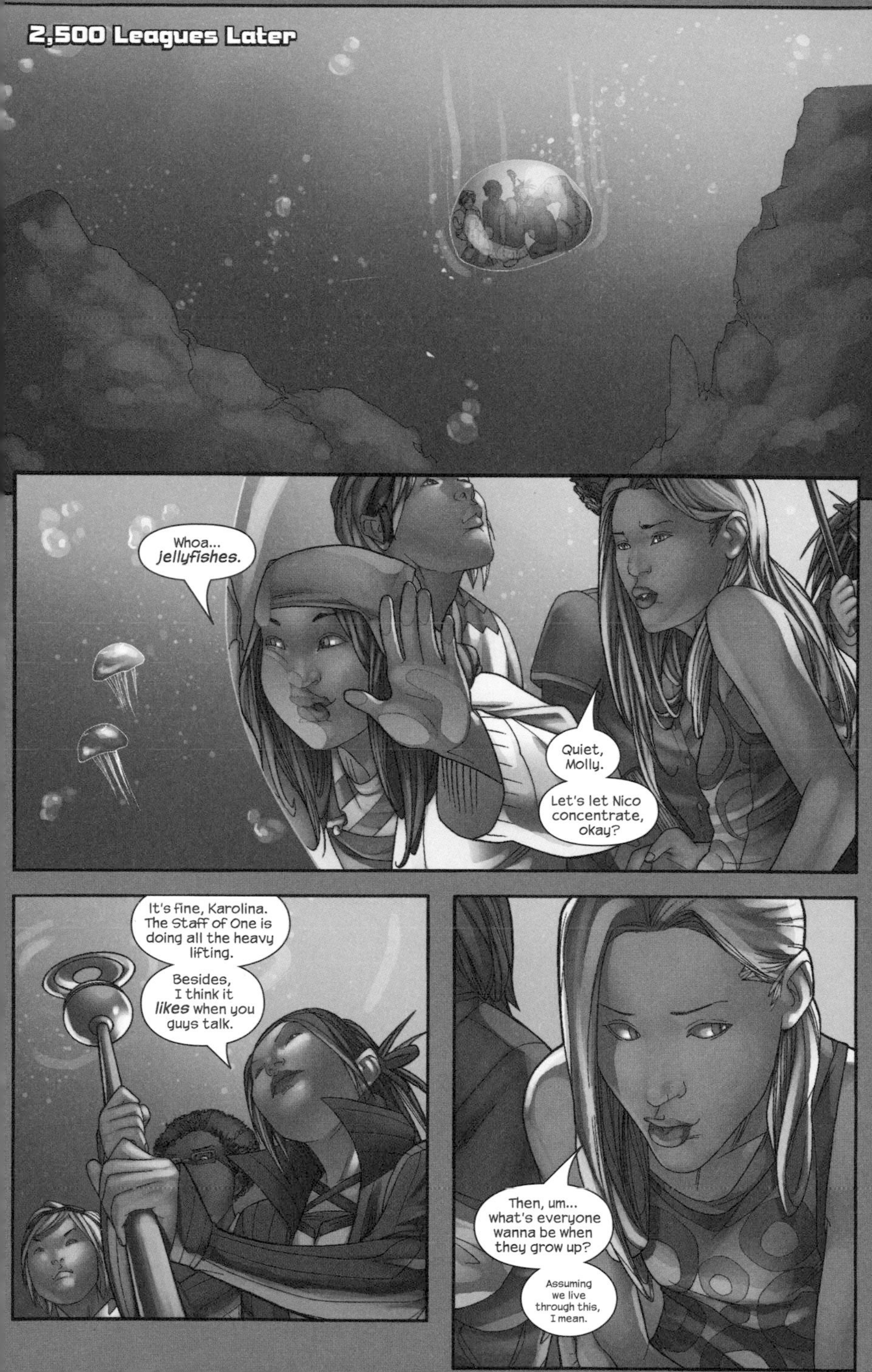
2,500 Leagues Later
Whoa... jellyfishes.
Quiet, Molly.
Let's let Nico concentrate, okay?
It's fine, Karolina. The Staff of One is doing all the heavy lifting.
Besides, I think it likes when you guys talk.
Then, um... what's everyone wanna be when they grow up?
Assuming we live through this, I mean.

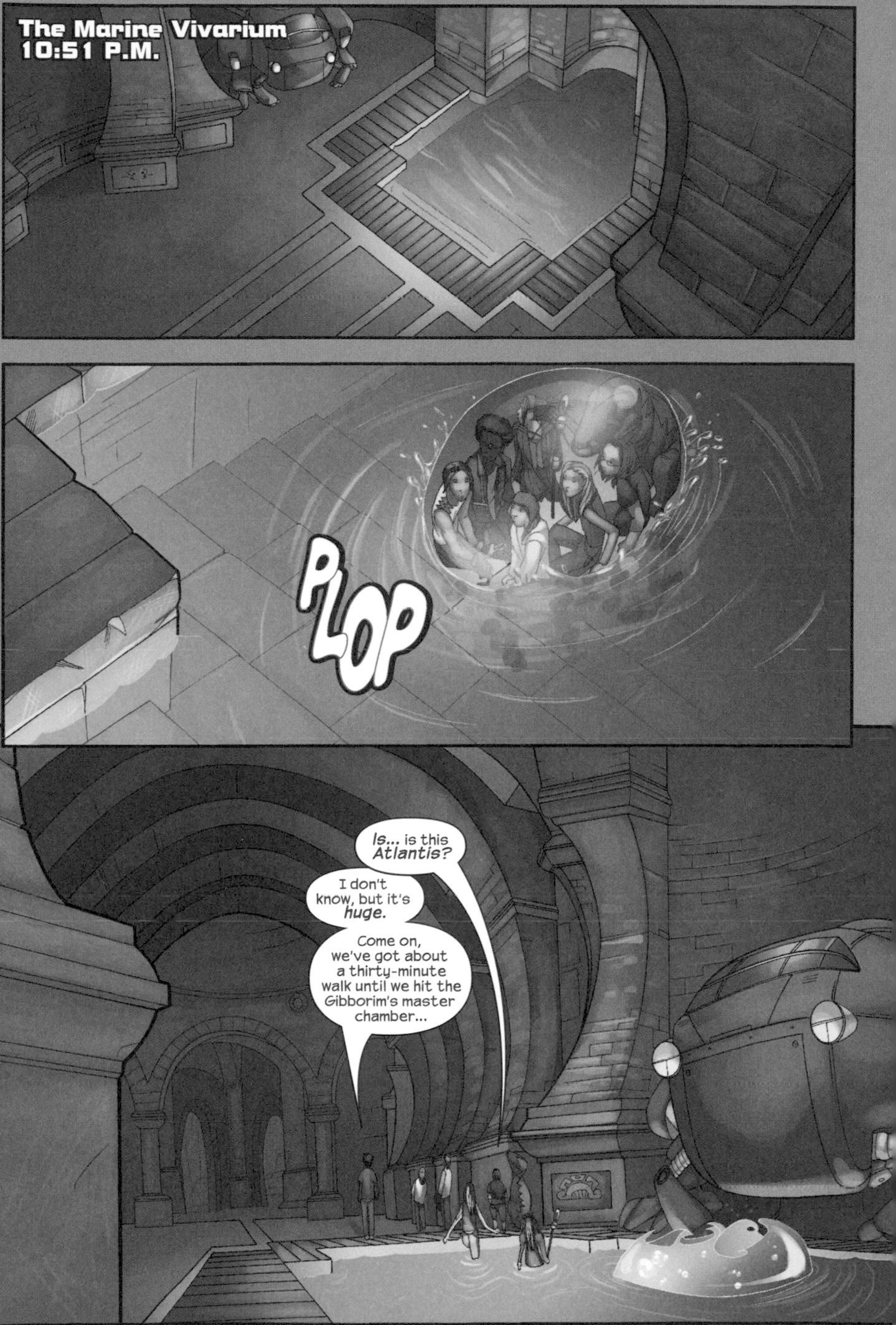
The Marine Vivarium
10:51 P.M.
PLOP
Is... is this Atlantis?
I don't know, but it's huge.
Come on, we've got about a thirty-minute walk until we hit the Gibborim's master chamber...

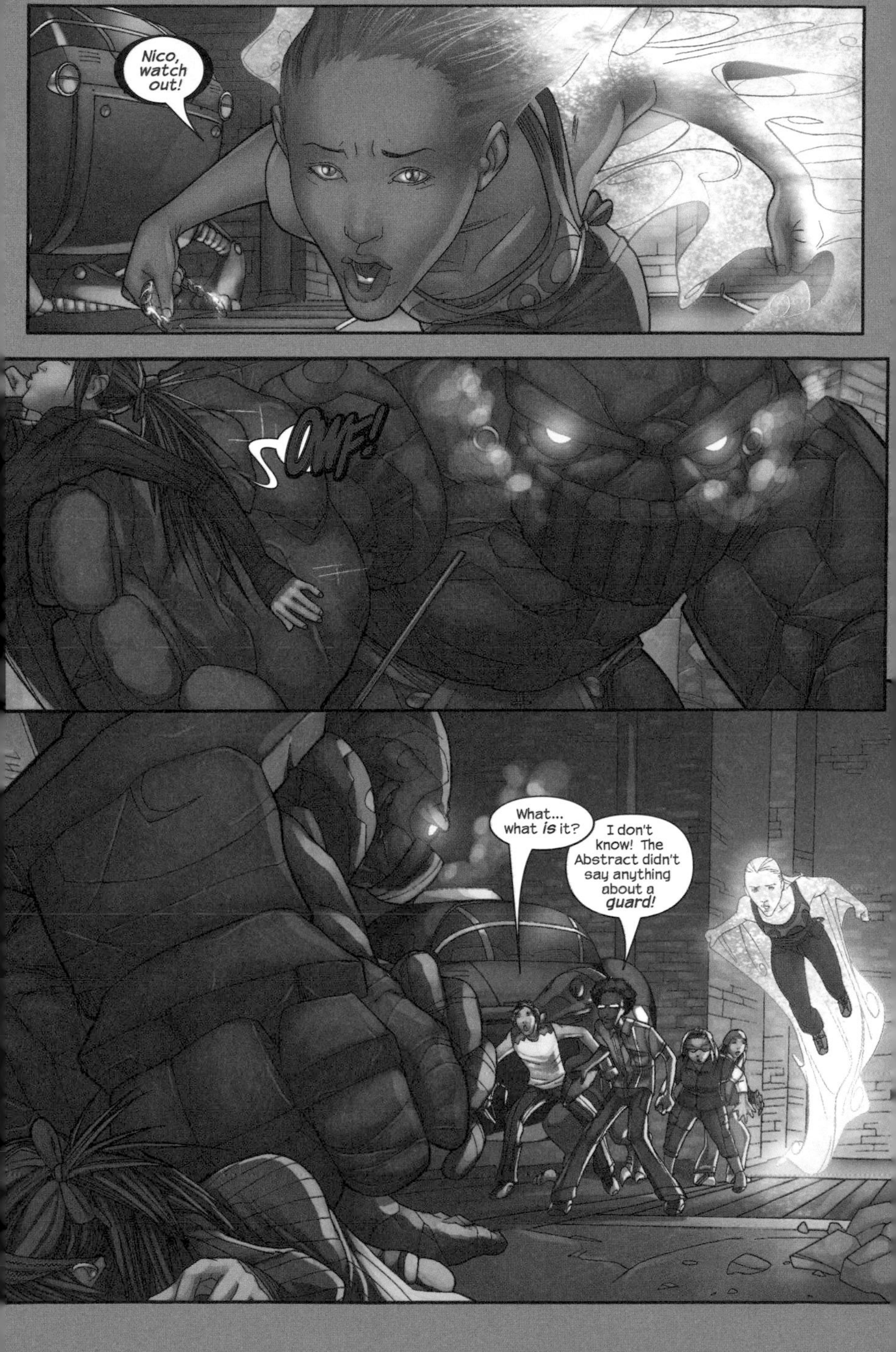
Nico, watch out!
SOWF!
What... what *is* it?
I don't know! The Abstract didn't say anything about a *guard*!

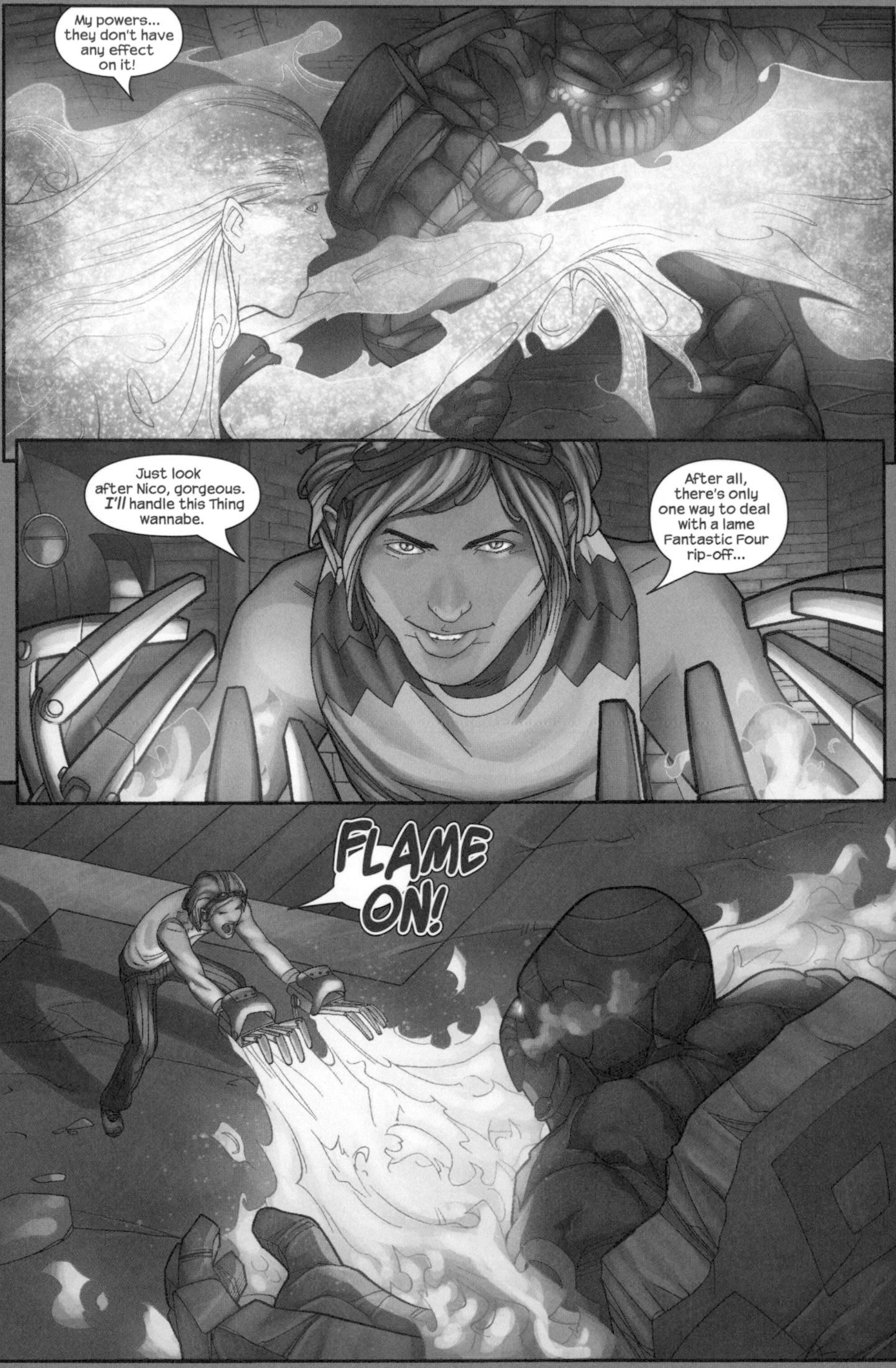
My powers... they don't have any effect on it!
Just look after Nico, gorgeous. *I'll* handle this Thing wannabe.
After all, there's only one way to deal with a lame Fantastic Four rip-off...
FLAME ON!

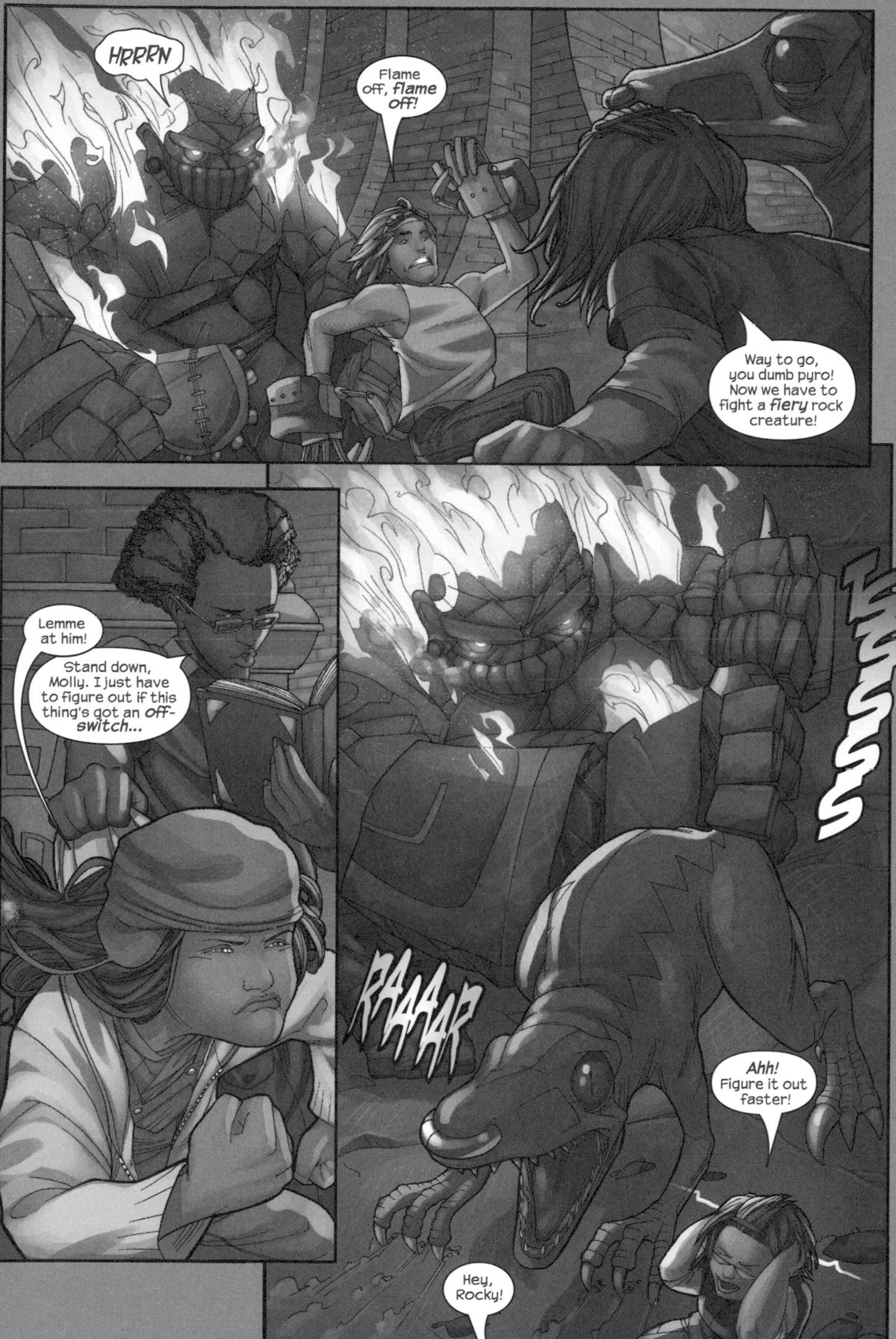
HRRRN
Flame off, flame off!
Way to go, you dumb pyro! Now we have to fight a fiery rock creature!
Lemme at him!
Stand down, Molly. I just have to figure out if this thing's got an off-switch...
TSSSSS
RAAAAR
Ahh! Figure it out faster!
Hey, Rocky!

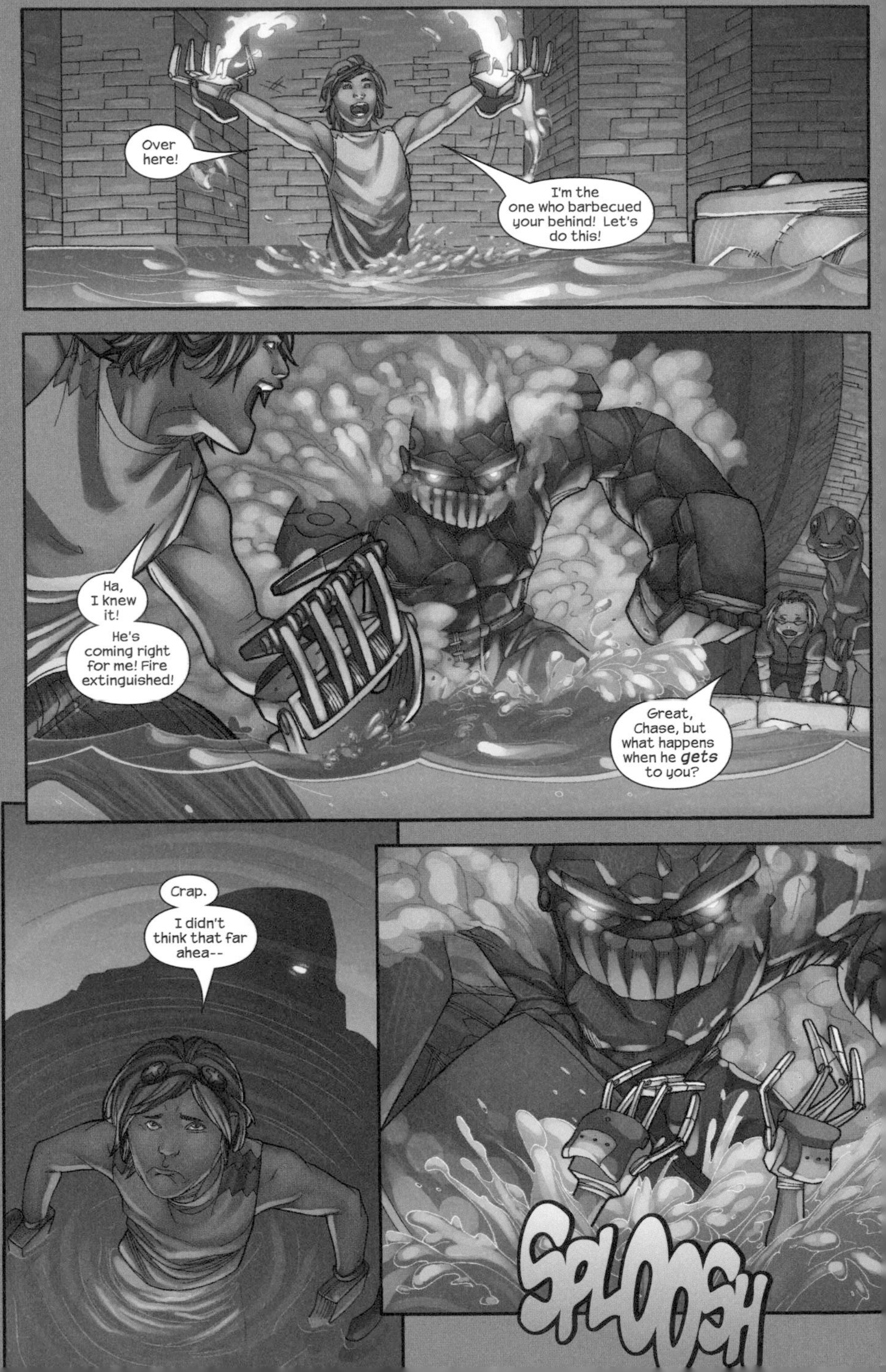
Over here!
I'm the one who barbecued your behind! Let's do this!
Ha, I knew it!
He's coming right for me! Fire extinguished!
Great, Chase, but what happens when he gets to you?
Crap.
I didn't think that far ahea--
SPLOOSH

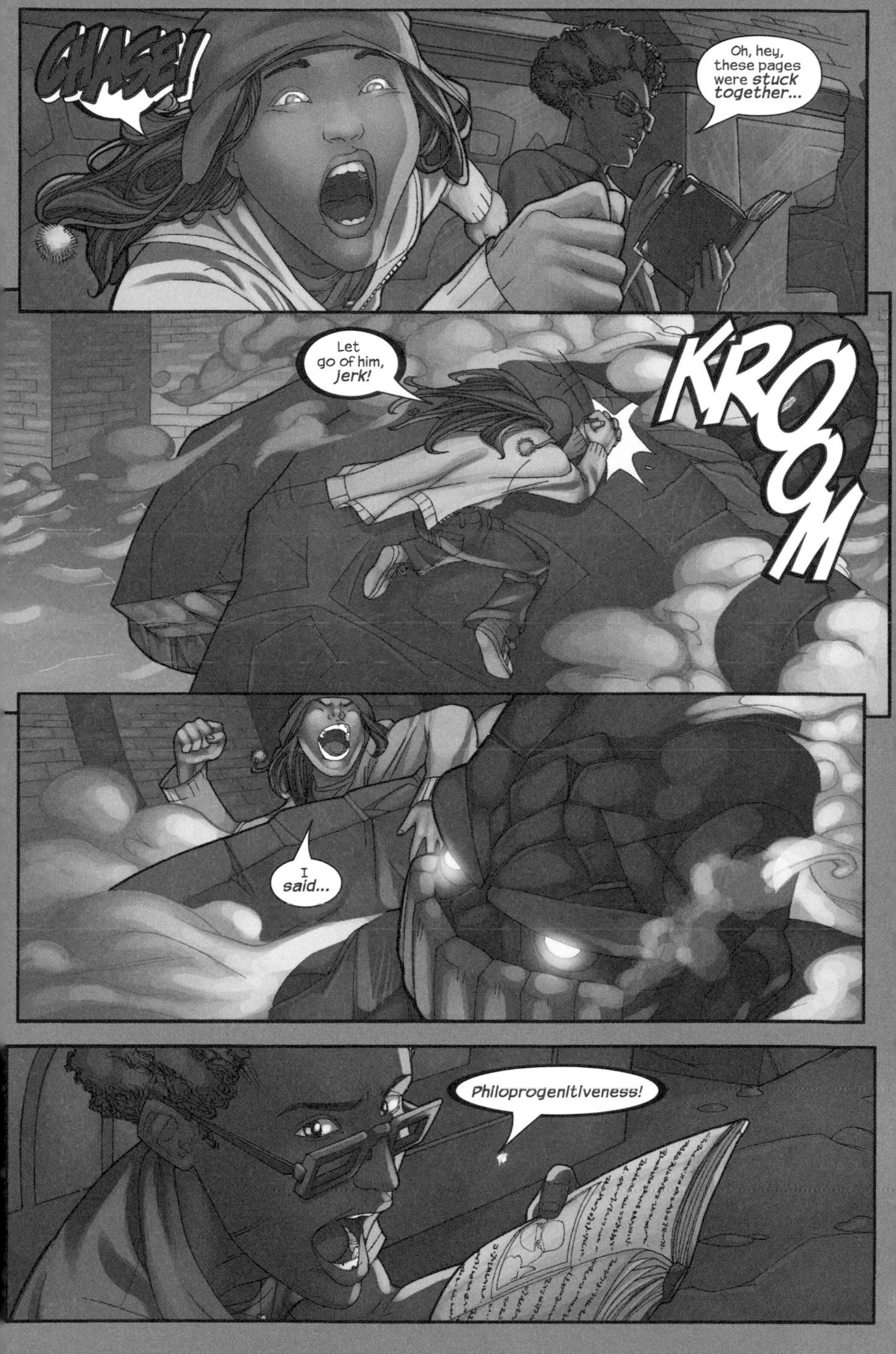
CHASE!
Oh, hey, these pages were *stuck together*...
Let go of him, *jerk!*
KROOM
I said...
Philoprogenitiveness!

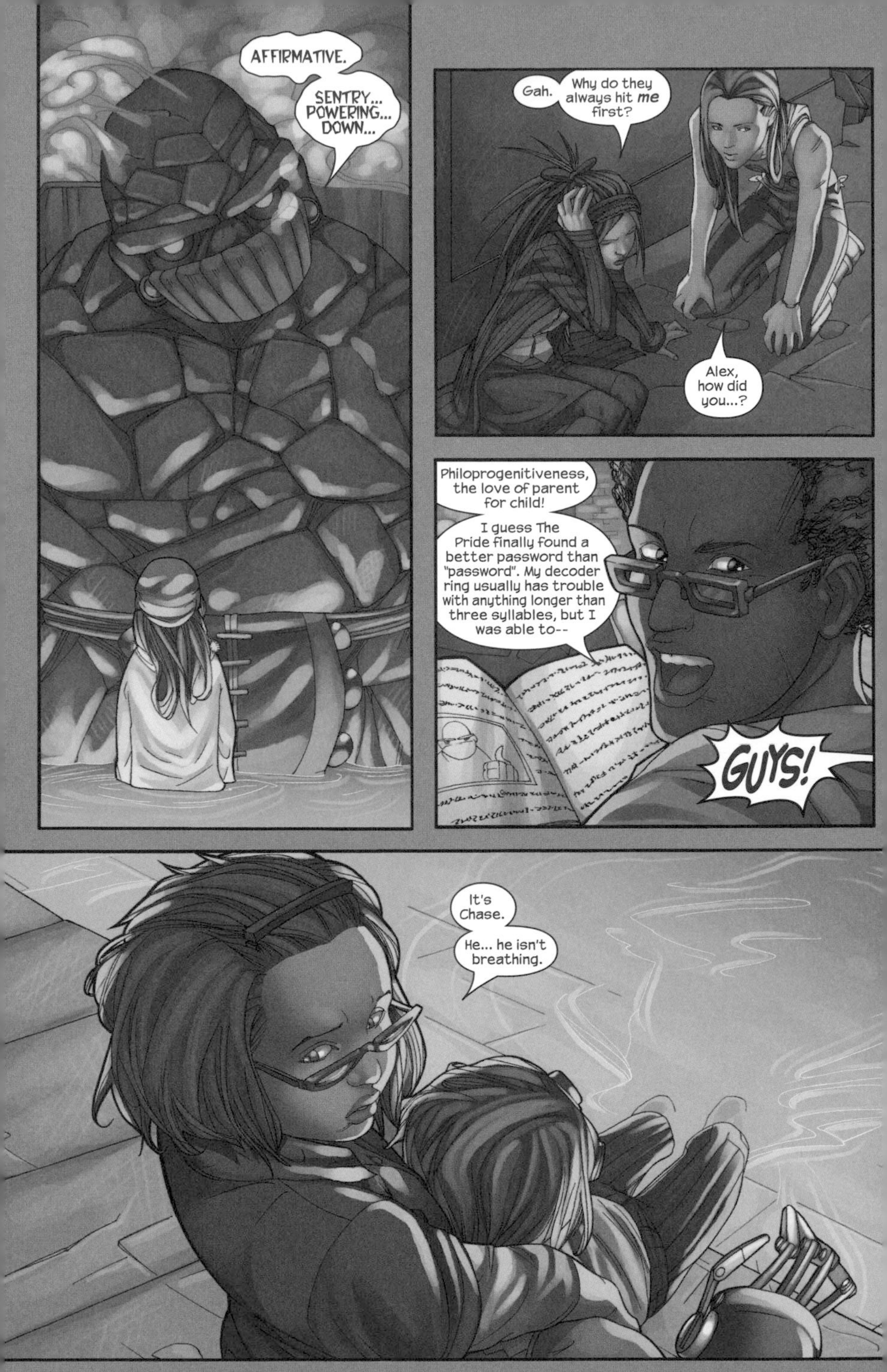
AFFIRMATIVE.
SENTRY... POWERING... DOWN...
Gah.
Why do they always hit *me* first?
Alex, how did you...?
Philoprogenitiveness, the love of parent for child!
I guess The Pride finally found a better password than "password". My decoder ring usually has trouble with anything longer than three syllables, but I was able to--
GUYS!
It's Chase.
He... he isn't breathing.

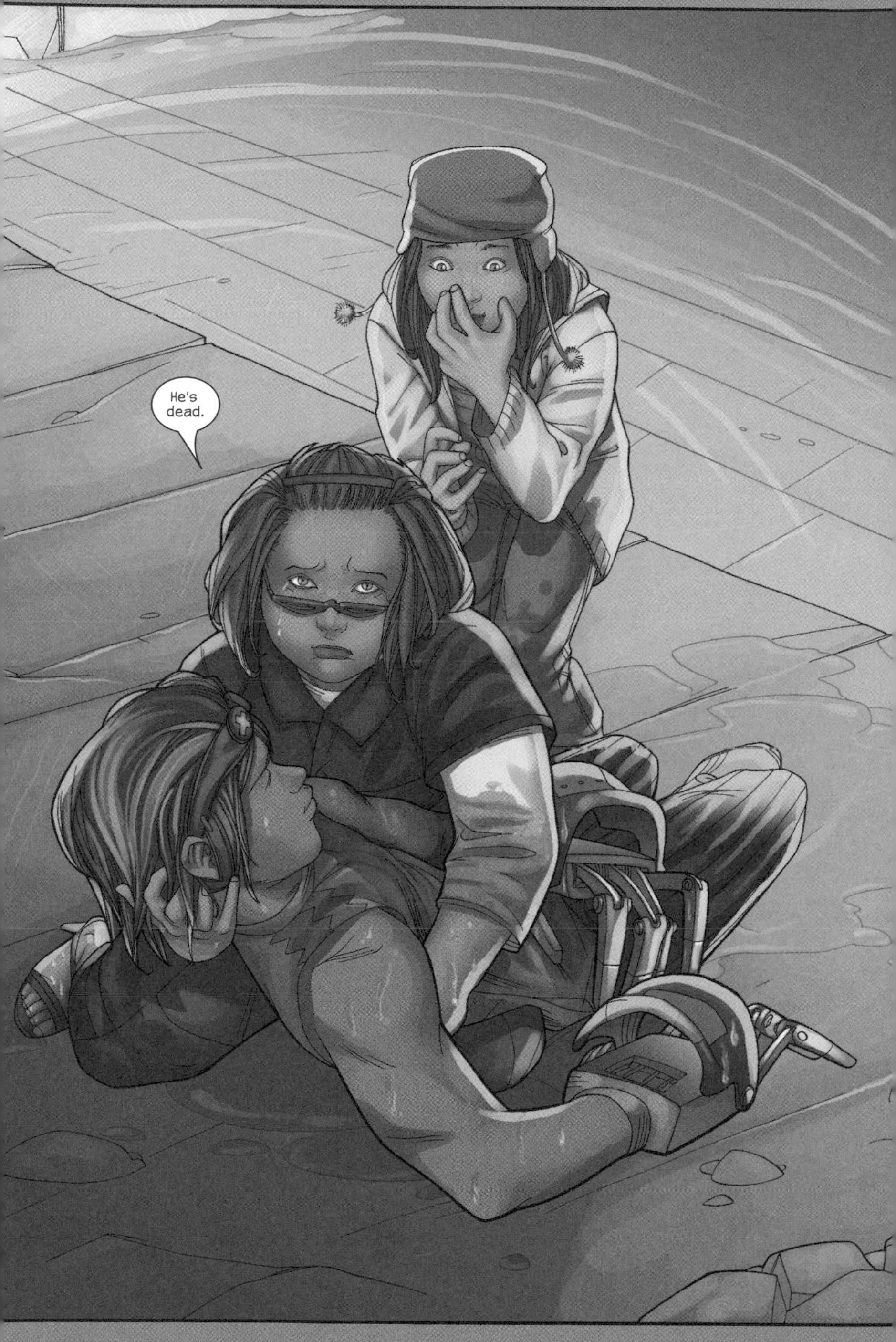
He's dead.

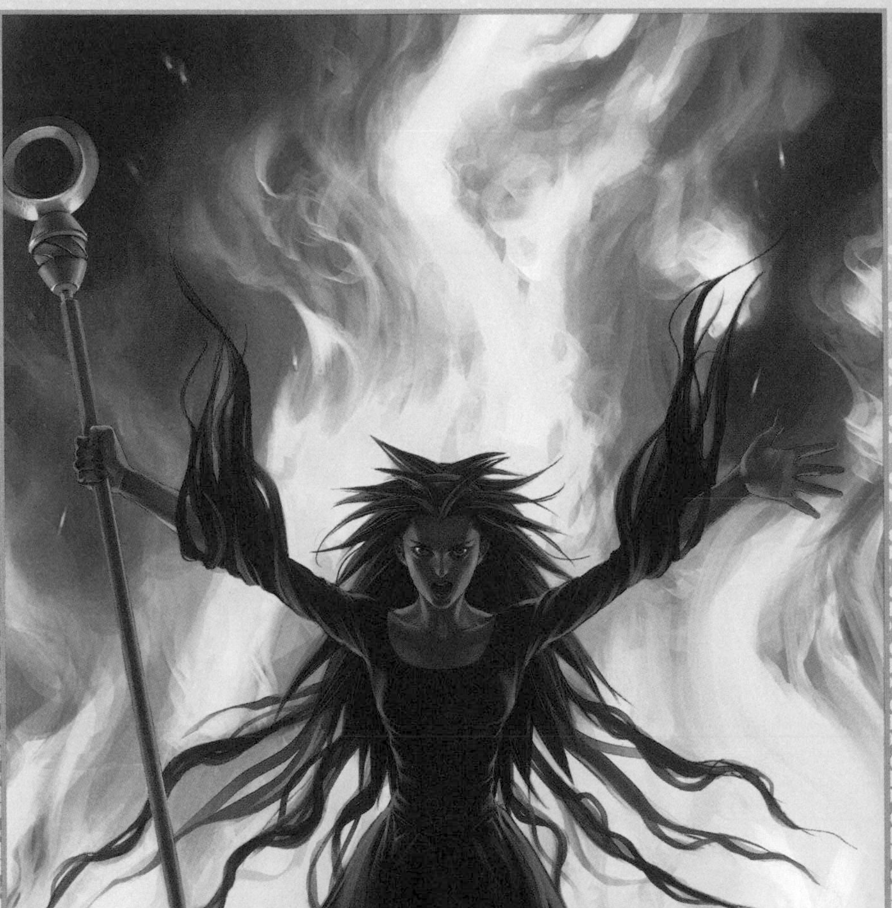

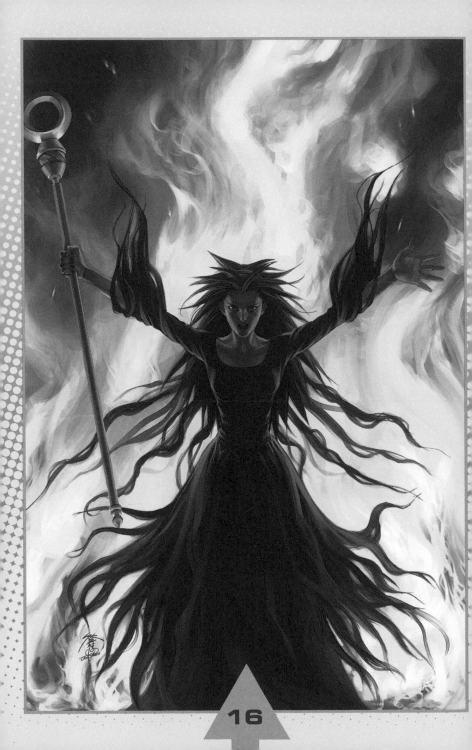

16

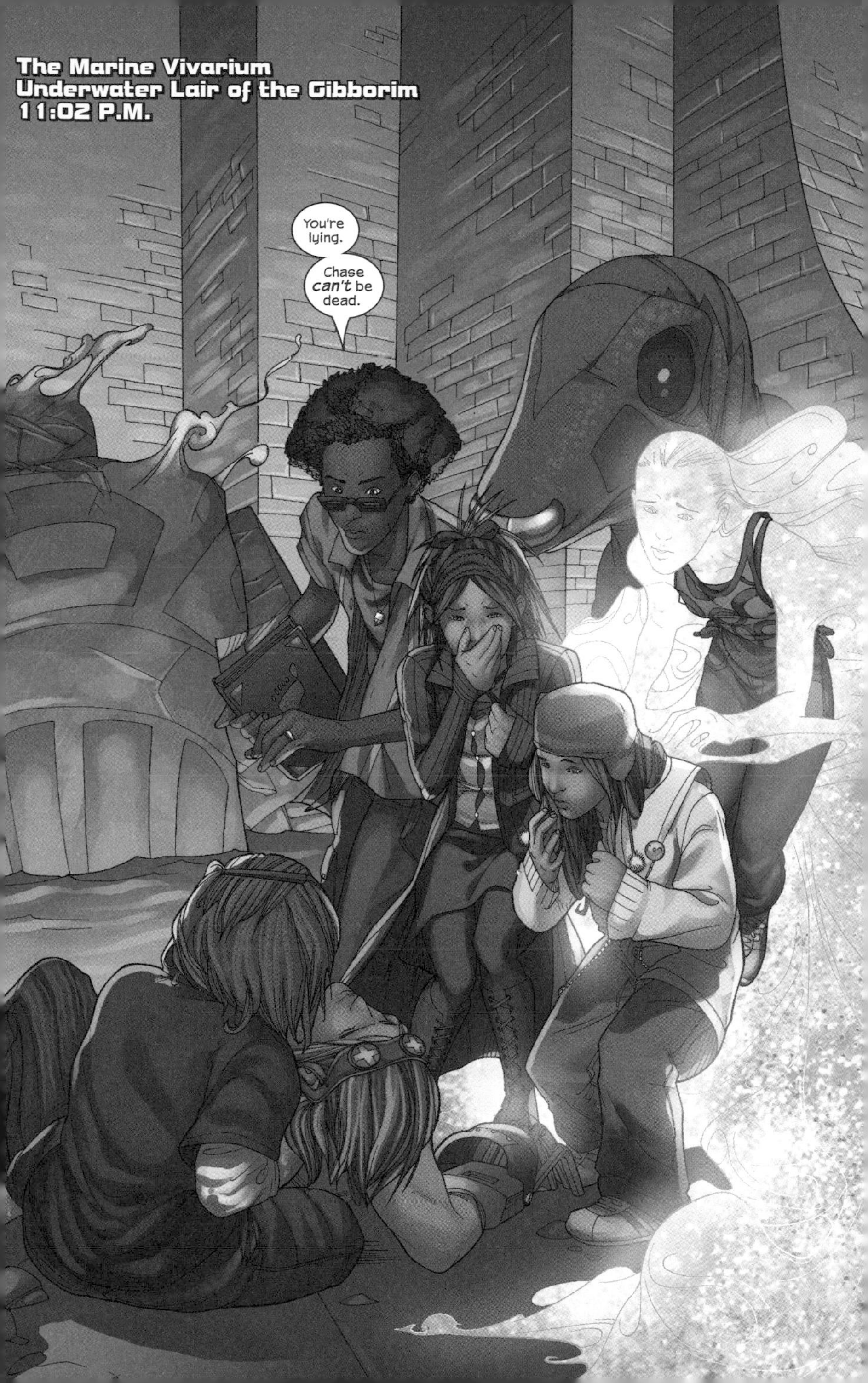
The Marine Vivarium
Underwater Lair of the Gibborim
11:02 P.M.
You're lying.
Chase can't be dead.

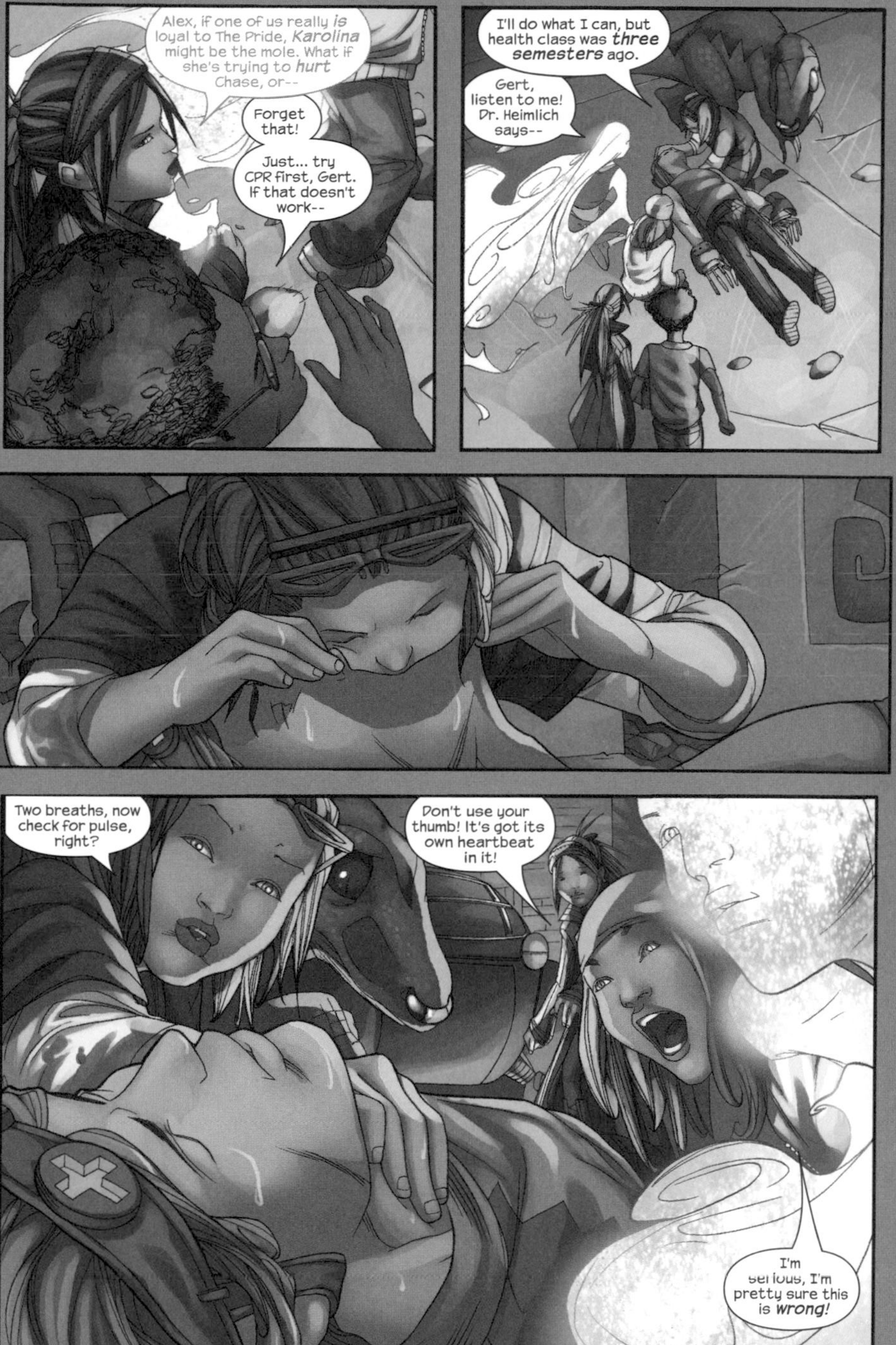

Alex, if one of us really *is* loyal to The Pride, *Karolina* might be the mole. What if she's trying to *hurt* Chase, or--
Forget that!
Just... try CPR first, Gert. If that doesn't work--
I'll do what I can, but health class was ***three semesters*** ago.
Gert, listen to me! Dr. Heimlich says--
Two breaths, now check for pulse, right?
Don't use your thumb! It's got its own heartbeat in it!
I'm serious, I'm pretty sure this is ***wrong!***

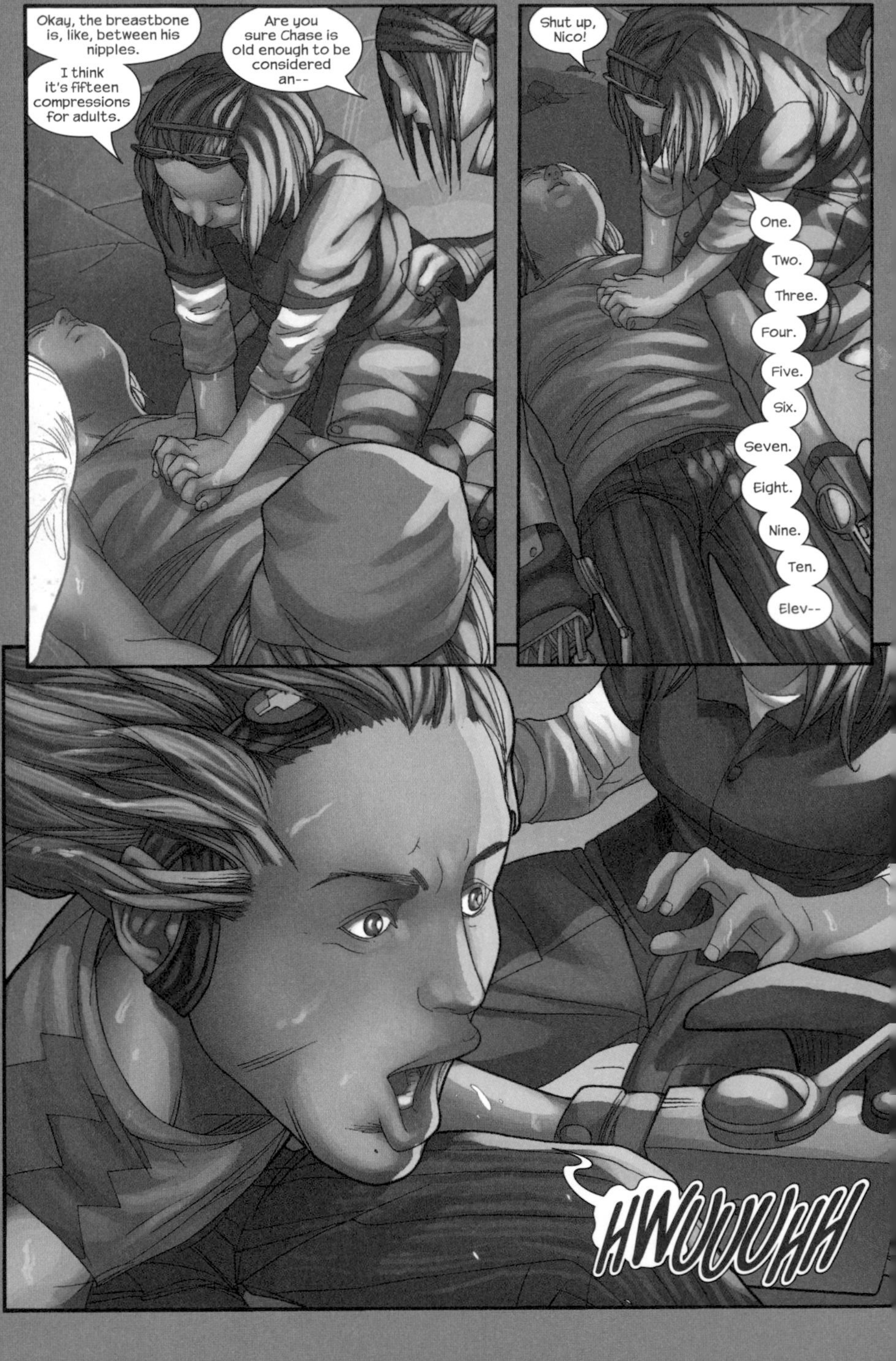
Okay, the breastbone is, like, between his nipples.
I think it's fifteen compressions for adults.
Are you sure Chase is old enough to be considered an--
Shut up, Nico!
One.
Two.
Three.
Four.
Five.
Six.
Seven.
Eight.
Nine.
Ten.
Elev--
HWUUUUHH

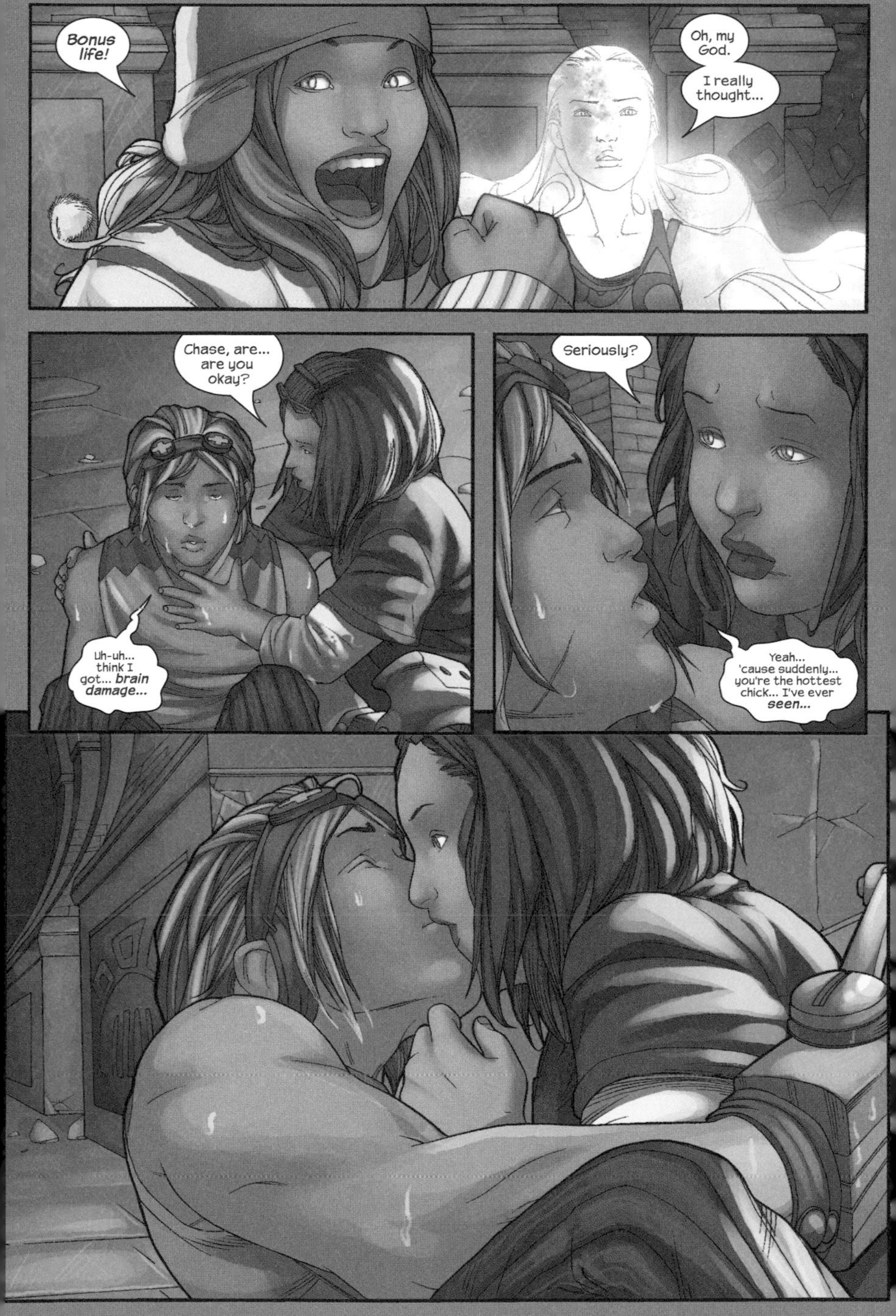
Bonus life!
Oh, my God.
I really thought...
Chase, are... are you okay?
Uh-uh... think I got... *brain damage*...
Seriously?
Yeah... 'cause suddenly... you're the hottest chick... I've ever *seen*...

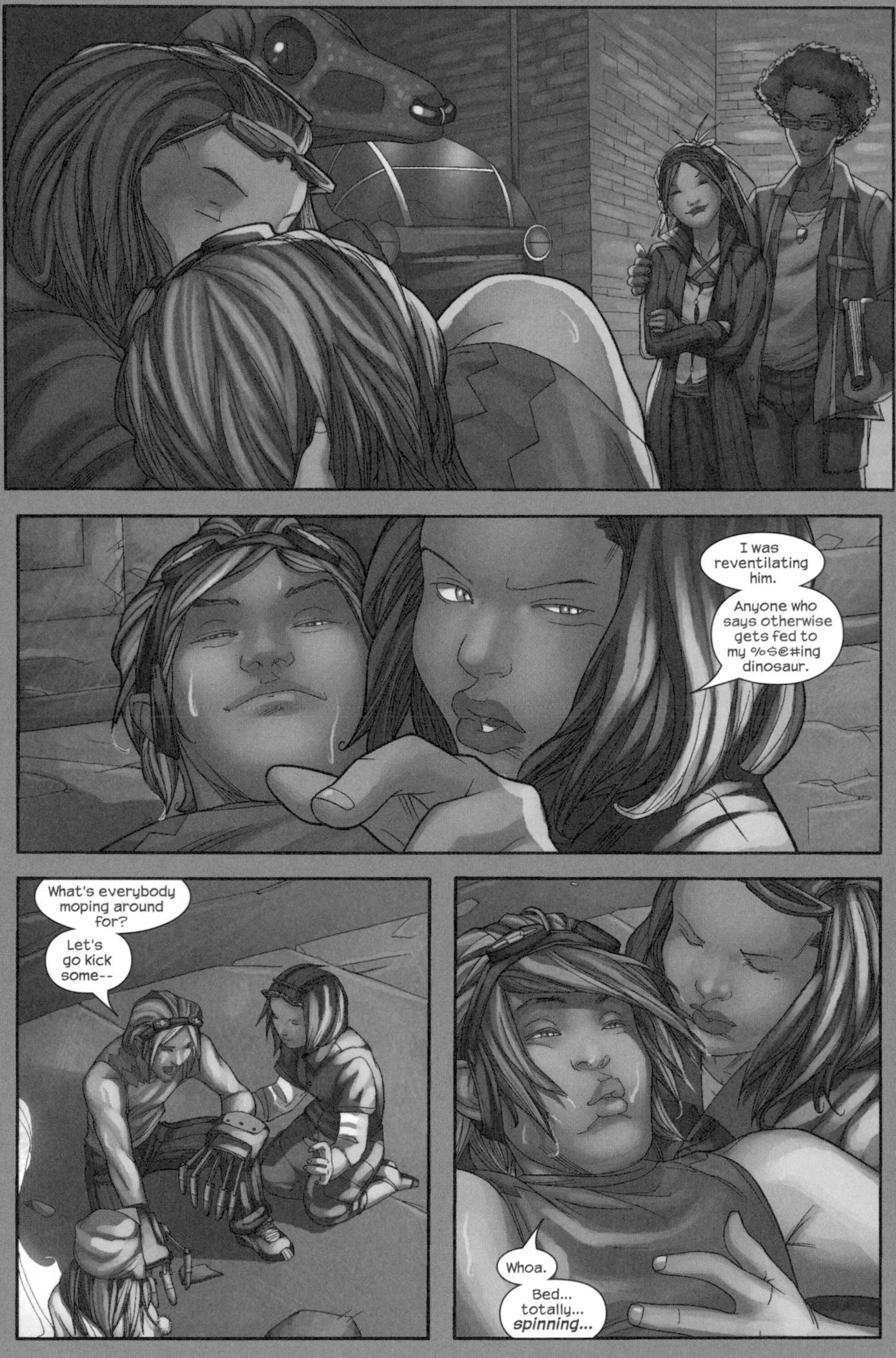

I was reventilating him.
Anyone who says otherwise gets fed to my %$@#ing dinosaur.
What's everybody moping around for?
Let's go kick some--
Whoa.
Bed... totally... *spinning*...

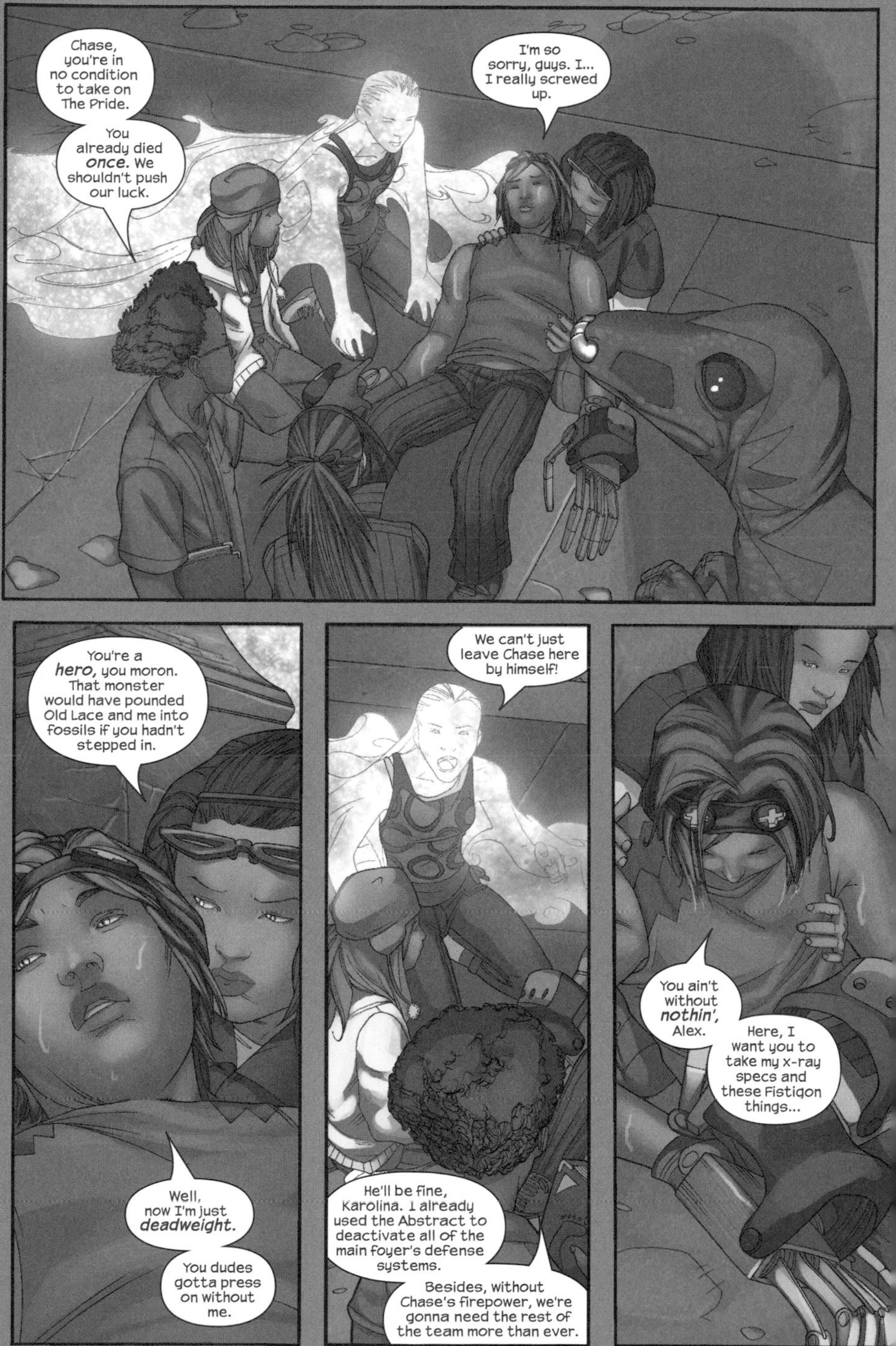
Chase, you're in no condition to take on The Pride.
You already died *once.* We shouldn't push our luck.
I'm so sorry, guys. I... I really screwed up.
You're a *hero,* you moron. That monster would have pounded Old Lace and me into fossils if you hadn't stepped in.
Well, now I'm just *deadweight.*
You dudes gotta press on without me.
We can't just leave Chase here by himself!
He'll be fine, Karolina. I already used the Abstract to deactivate all of the main foyer's defense systems.
Besides, without Chase's firepower, we're gonna need the rest of the team more than ever.
You ain't without *nothin',* Alex.
Here, I want you to take my x-ray specs and these Fistigon things...

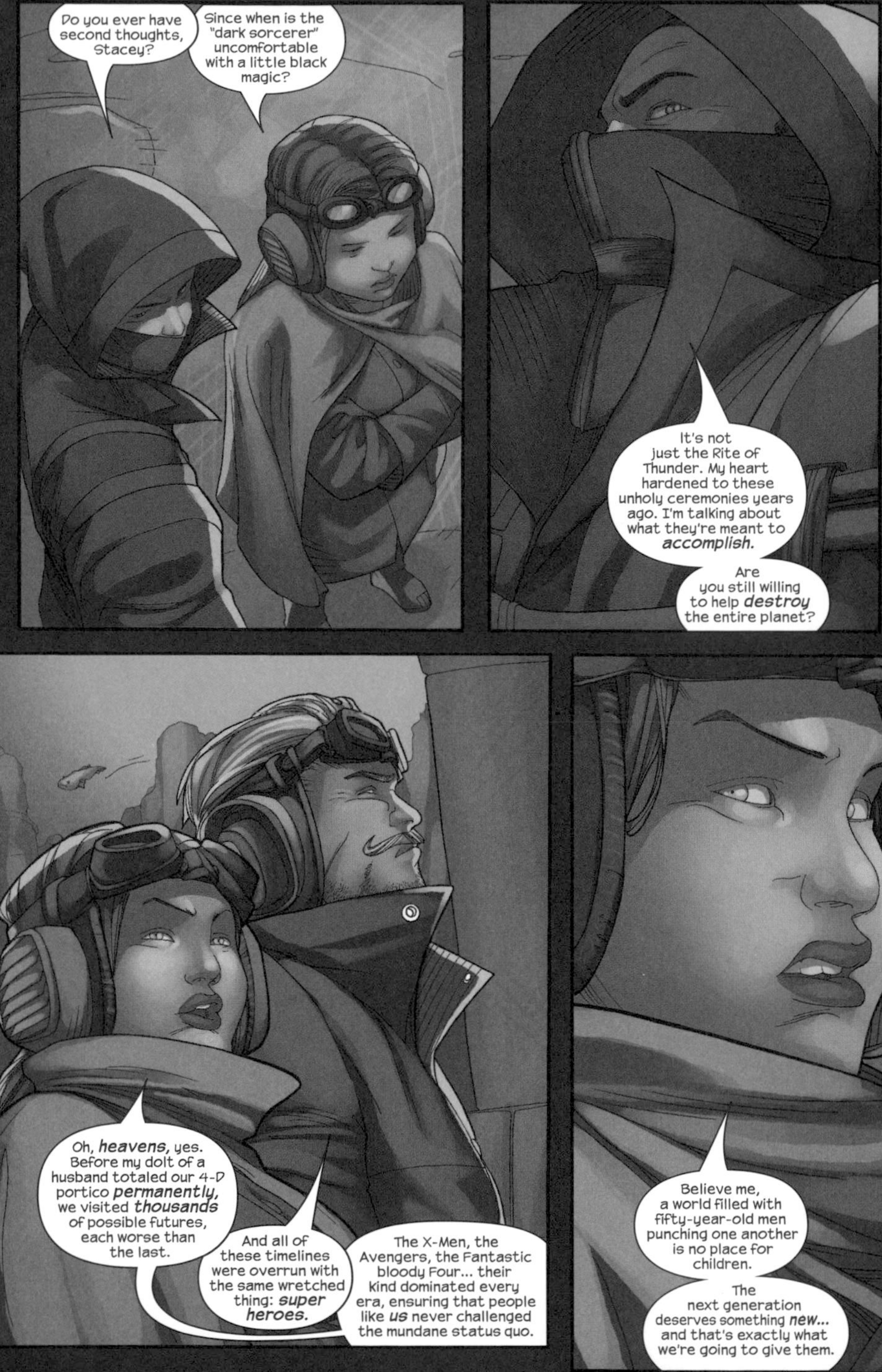
Do you ever have second thoughts, Stacey?
Since when is the "dark sorcerer" uncomfortable with a little black magic?
It's not just the Rite of Thunder. My heart hardened to these unholy ceremonies years ago. I'm talking about what they're meant to accomplish.
Are you still willing to help destroy the entire planet?
Oh, heavens, yes. Before my dolt of a husband totaled our 4-D portico permanently, we visited thousands of possible futures, each worse than the last.
And all of these timelines were overrun with the same wretched thing: super heroes.
The X-Men, the Avengers, the Fantastic bloody Four... their kind dominated every era, ensuring that people like us never challenged the mundane status quo.
Believe me, a world filled with fifty-year-old men punching one another is no place for children.
The next generation deserves something new... and that's exactly what we're going to give them.

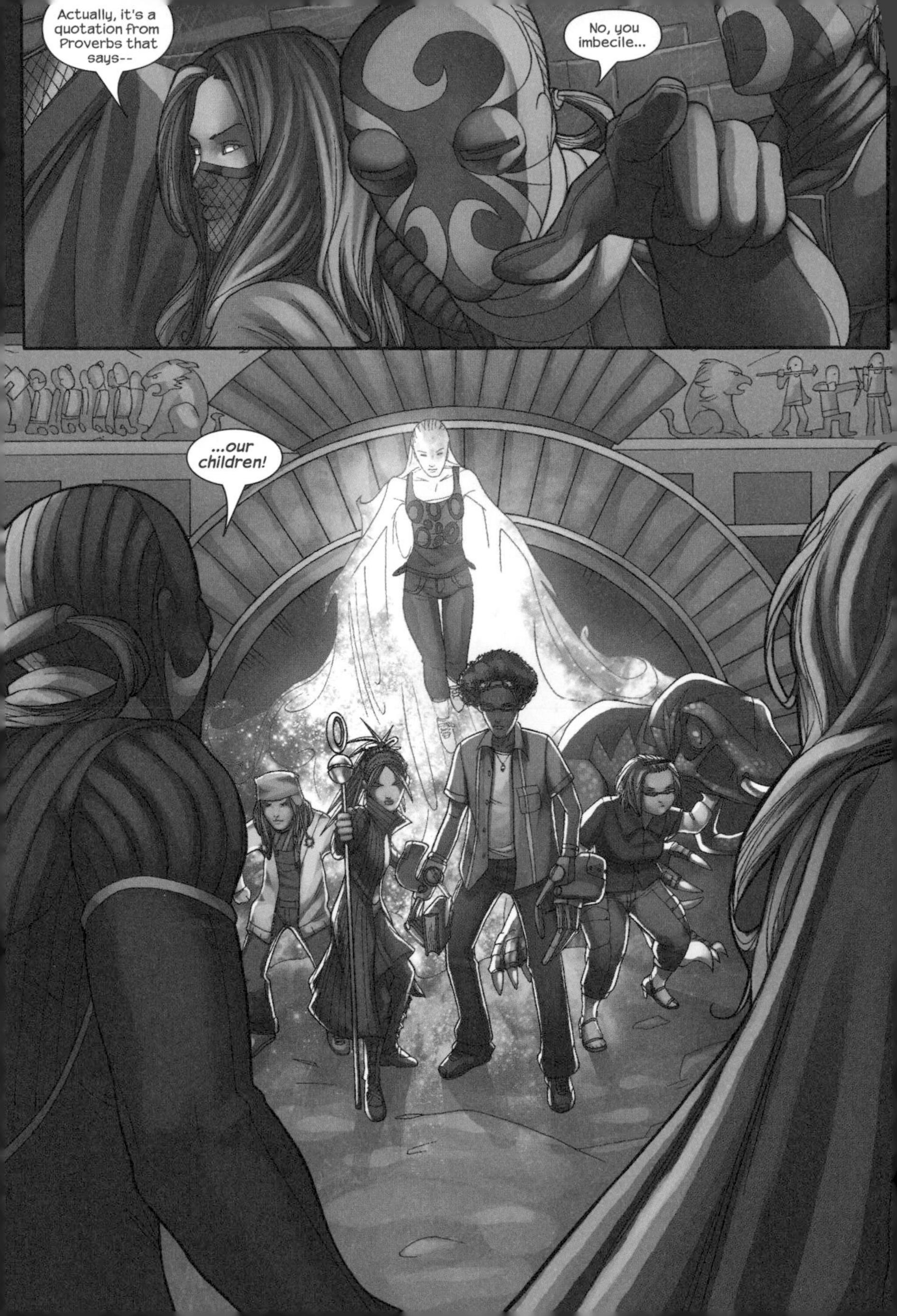
Actually, it's a quotation from Proverbs that says--
No, you imbecile...
...our children!

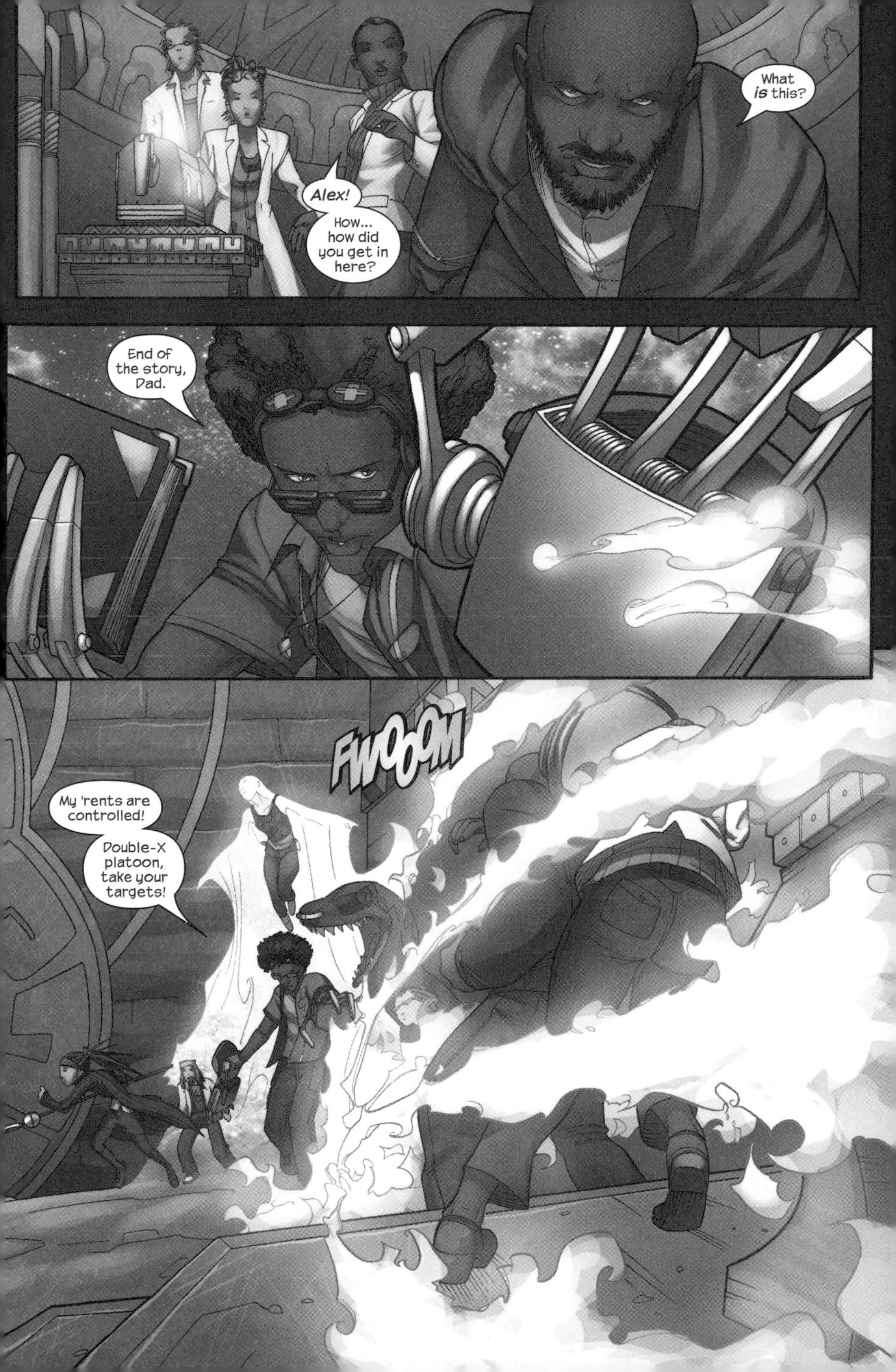
What is this?
Alex!
How... how did you get in here?
End of the story, Dad.
FWOOOM
My 'rents are controlled!
Double-X platoon, take your targets!

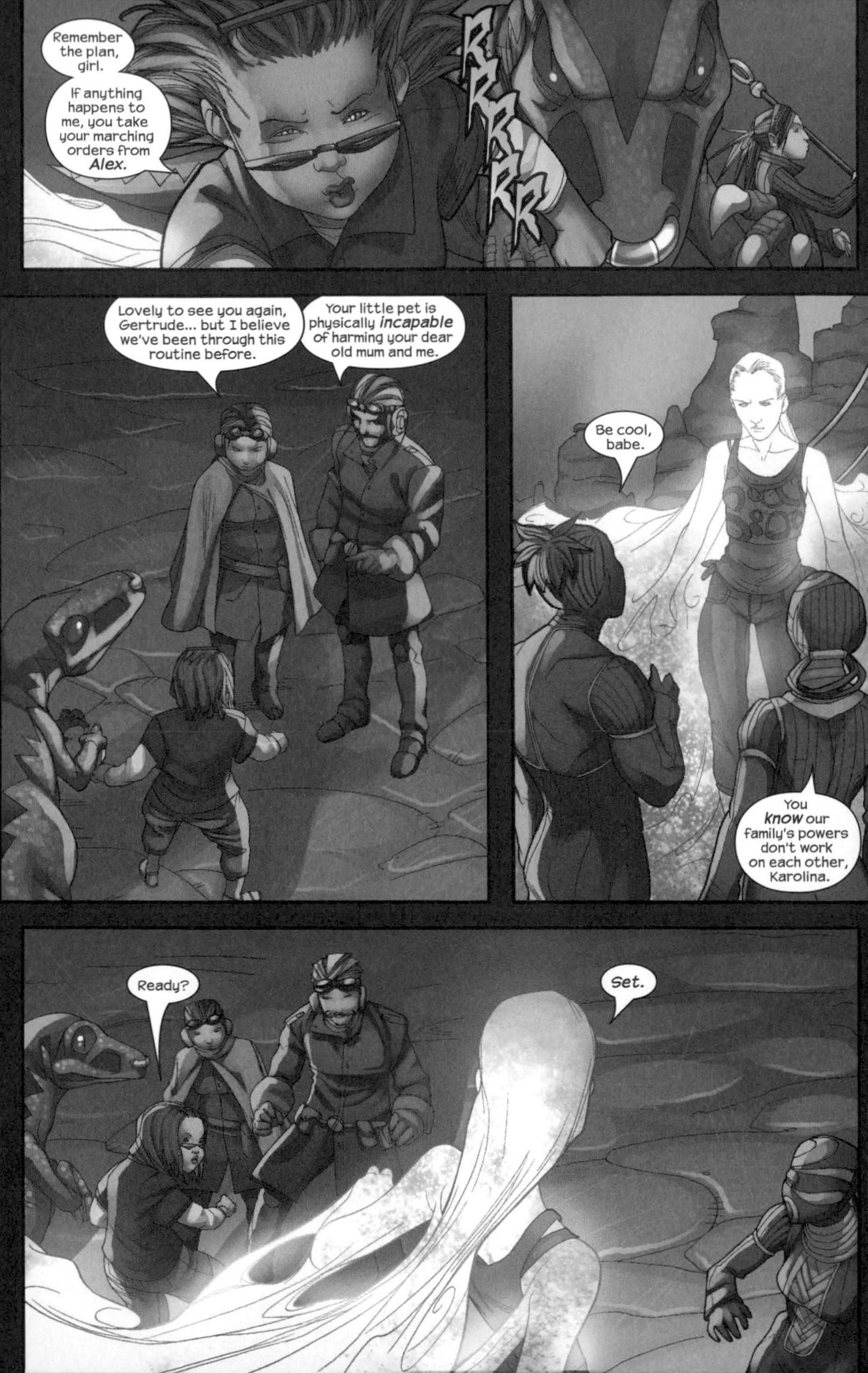

Remember the plan, girl.
If anything happens to me, you take your marching orders from *Alex.*
RRRRRR
Lovely to see you again, Gertrude... but I believe we've been through this routine before.
Your little pet is physically *incapable* of harming your dear old mum and me.
Be cool, babe.
You *KNOW* our family's powers don't work on each other, Karolina.
Ready?
Set.

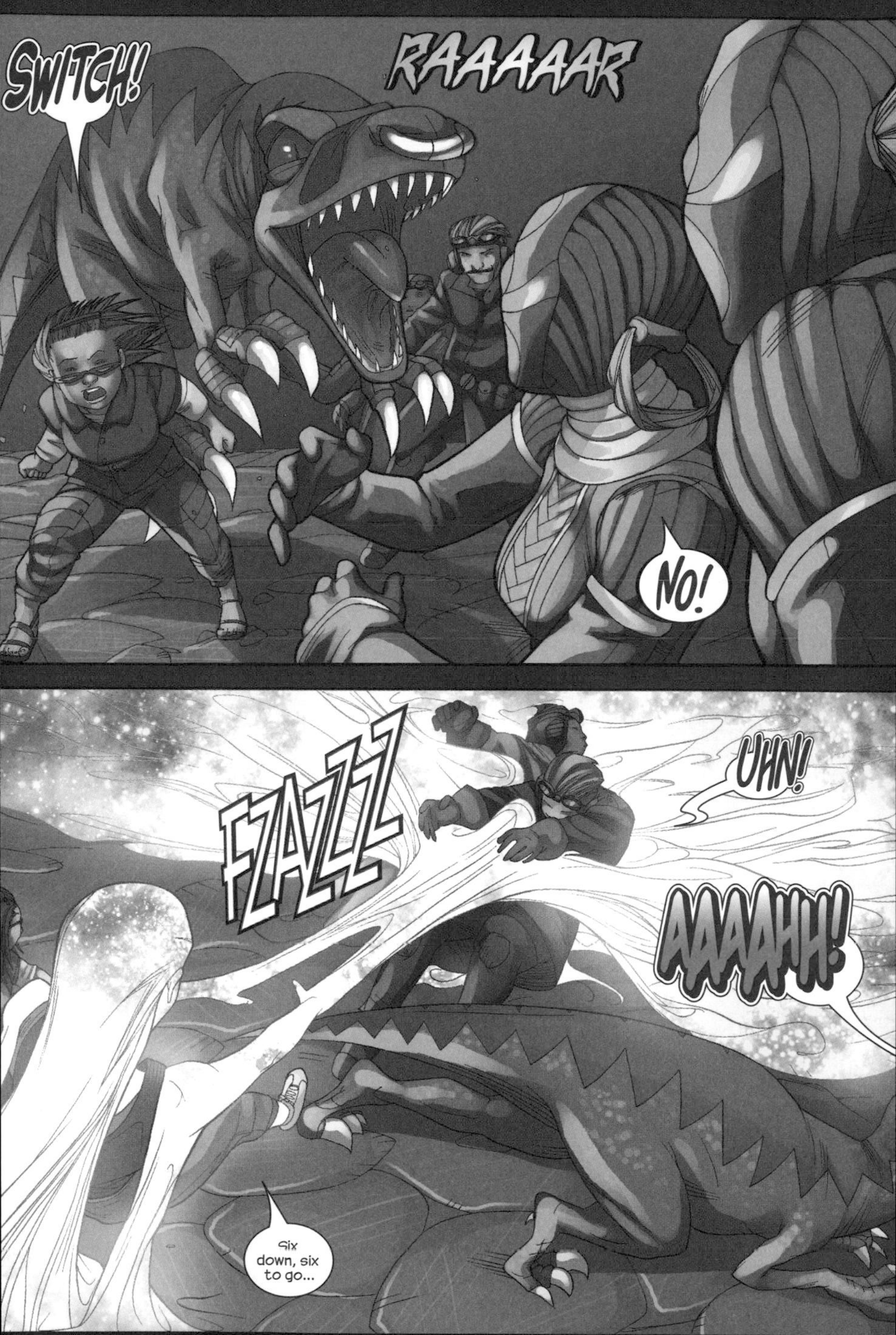
SWITCH!
RAAAAAR
NO!
FZAZZZ
UHN!
AAAAHH!
Six down, six to go...

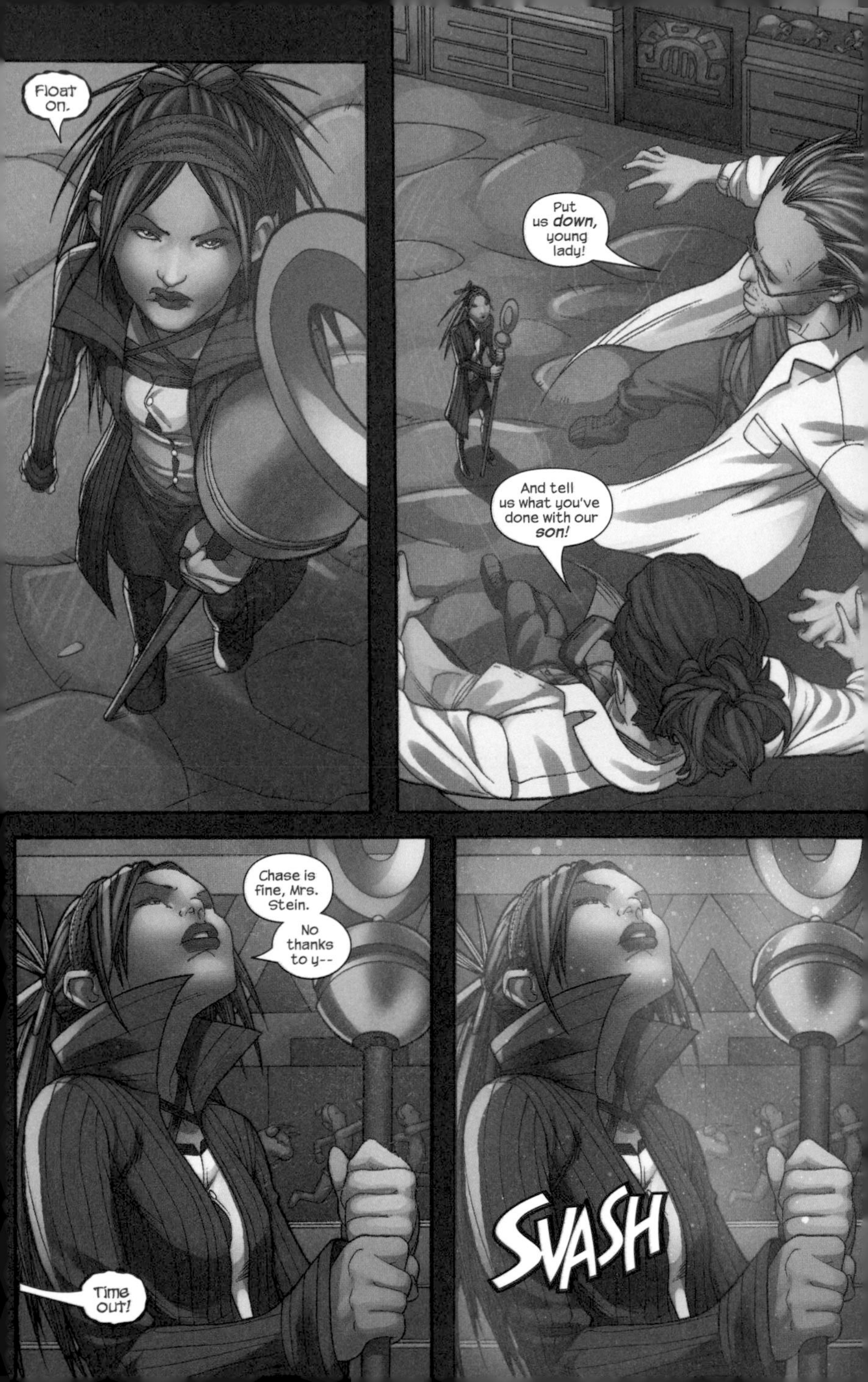
Float on.
Put us down, young lady!
And tell us what you've done with our son!
Chase is fine, Mrs. Stein.
No thanks to y--
Time out!
SVASH

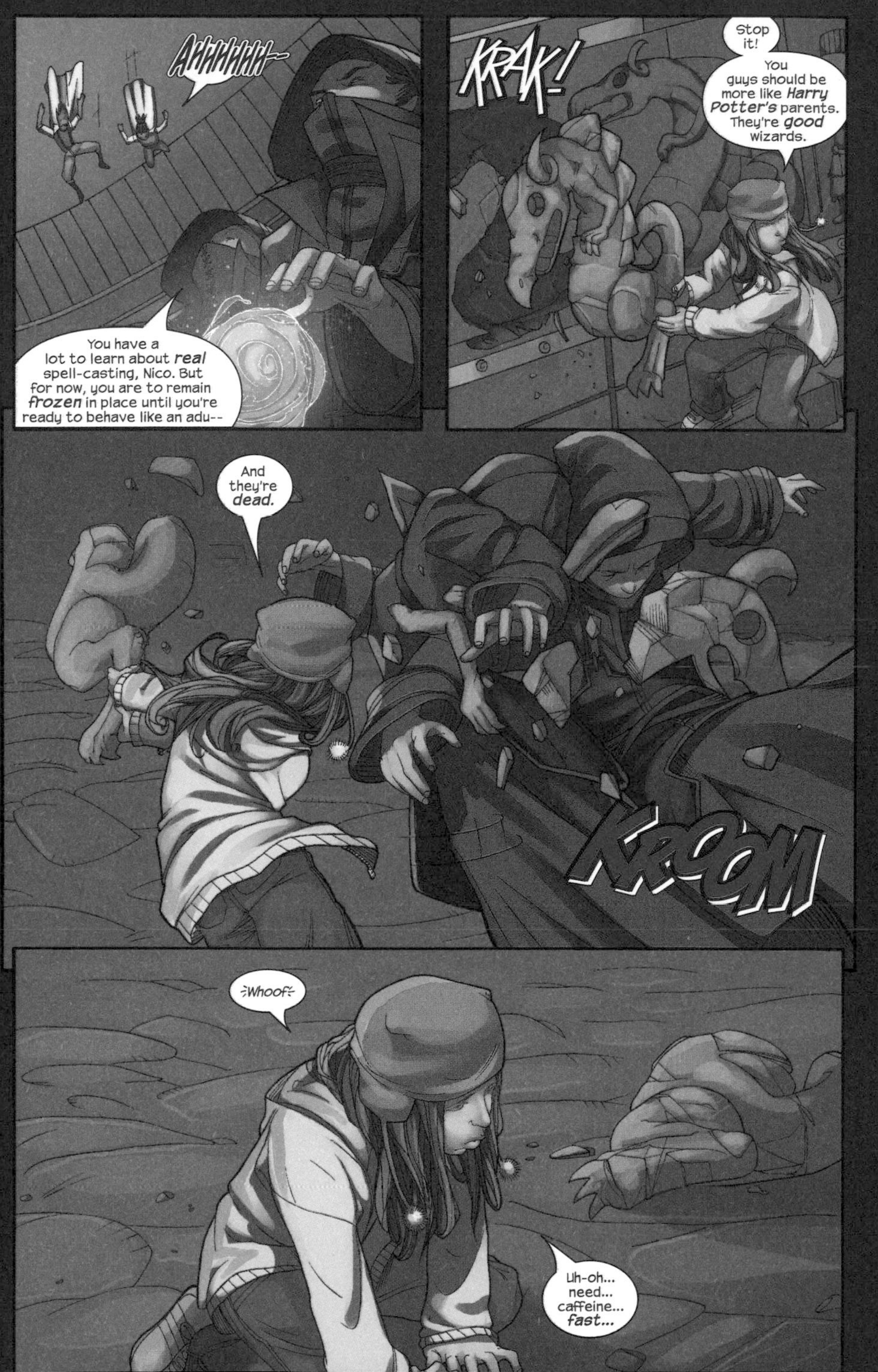
AHHHHHHH--
You have a lot to learn about real spell-casting, Nico. But for now, you are to remain frozen in place until you're ready to behave like an adu--
KRAK!
Stop it!
You guys should be more like Harry Potter's parents. They're good wizards.
And they're dead.
KROOM
Whoof
Uh-oh... need... caffeine... fast...

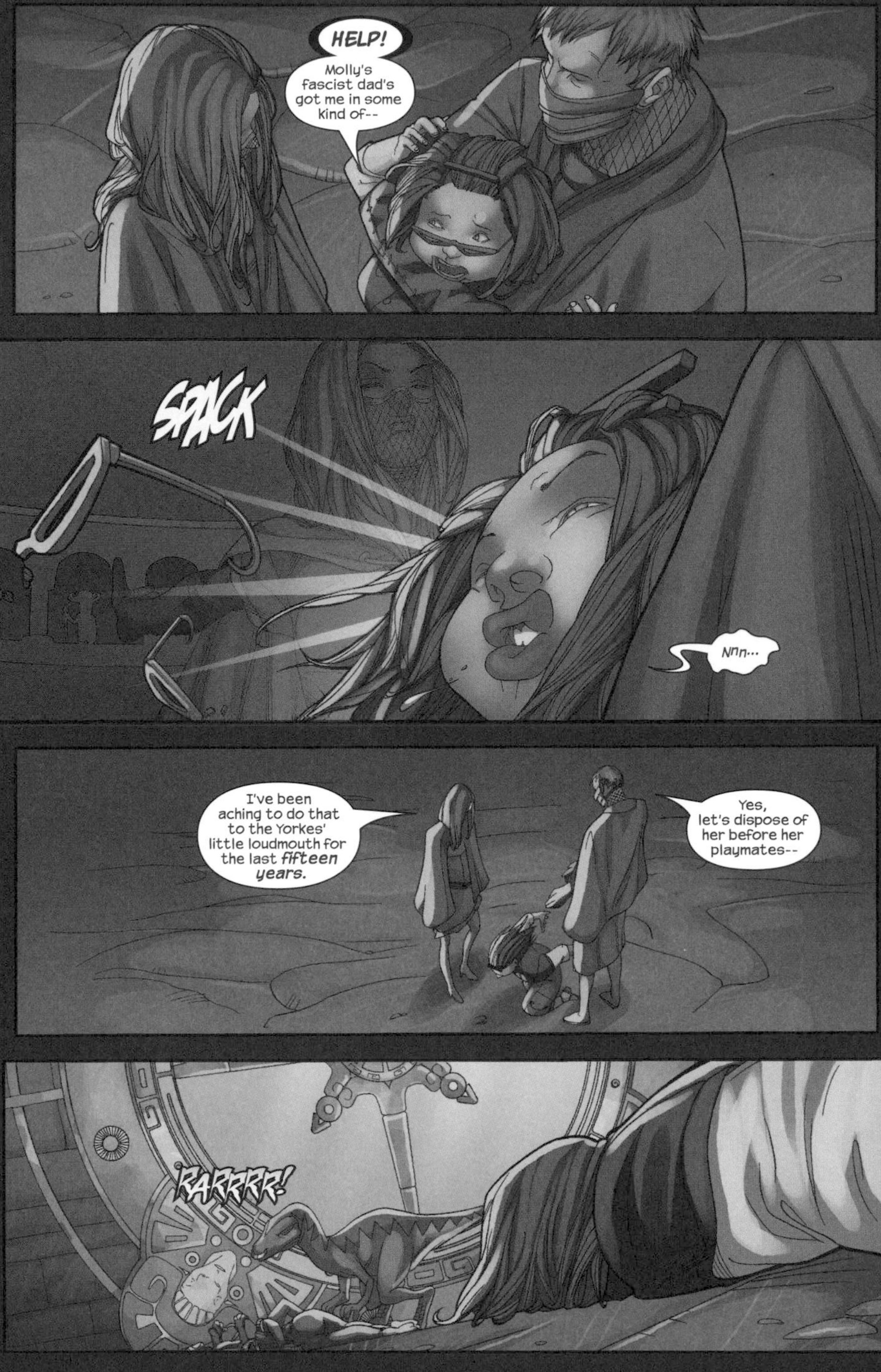
HELP!
Molly's fascist dad's got me in some kind of--
SPACK
Nnn...
I've been aching to do that to the Yorkes' little loudmouth for the last fifteen years.
Yes, let's dispose of her before her playmates--
RARRRR!

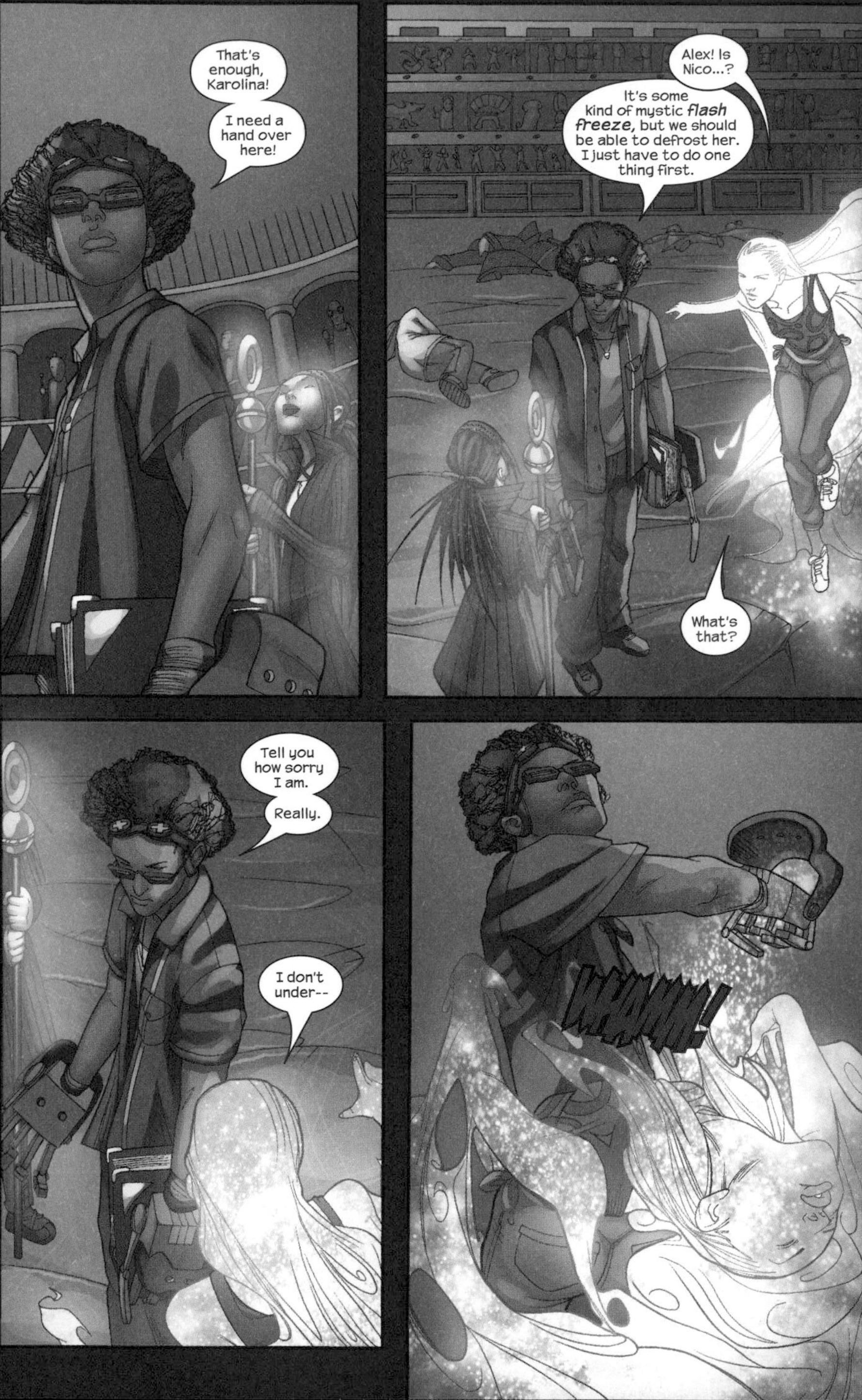

That's enough, Karolina!
I need a hand over here!
Alex! Is Nico...?
It's some kind of mystic flash freeze, but we should be able to defrost her. I just have to do one thing first.
What's that?
Tell you how sorry I am.
Really.
I don't under--
WHAMM!

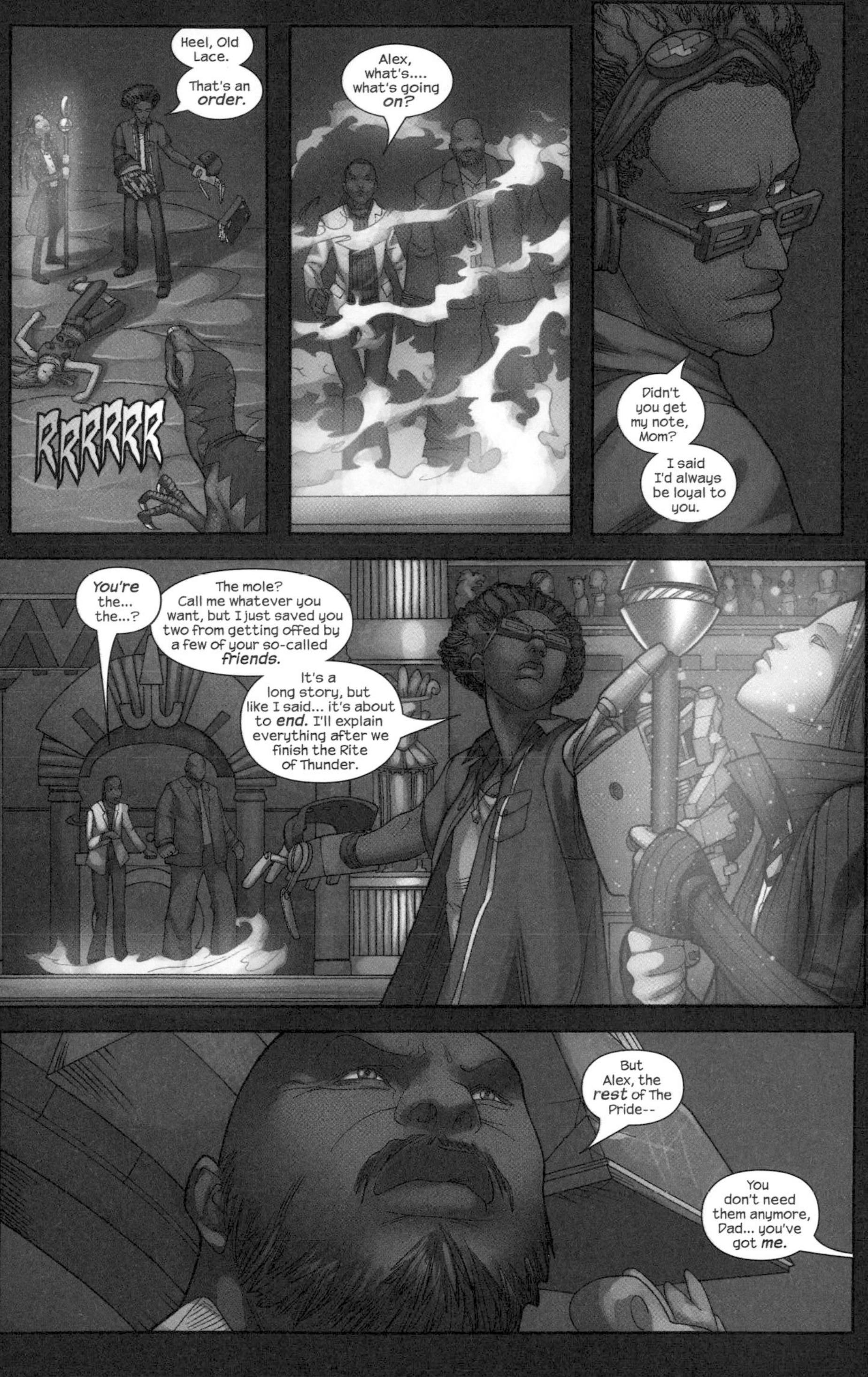

Heel, Old Lace.
That's an *order.*
RRRRRR
Alex, what's.... what's going *on?*
Didn't you get my note, Mom?
I said I'd always be loyal to you.
You're the... the...?
The mole? Call me whatever you want, but I just saved you two from getting offed by a few of your so-called *friends.*
It's a long story, but like I said... it's about to *end.* I'll explain everything after we finish the Rite of Thunder.
But Alex, the *rest* of The Pride--
You don't need them anymore, Dad... you've got *me.*

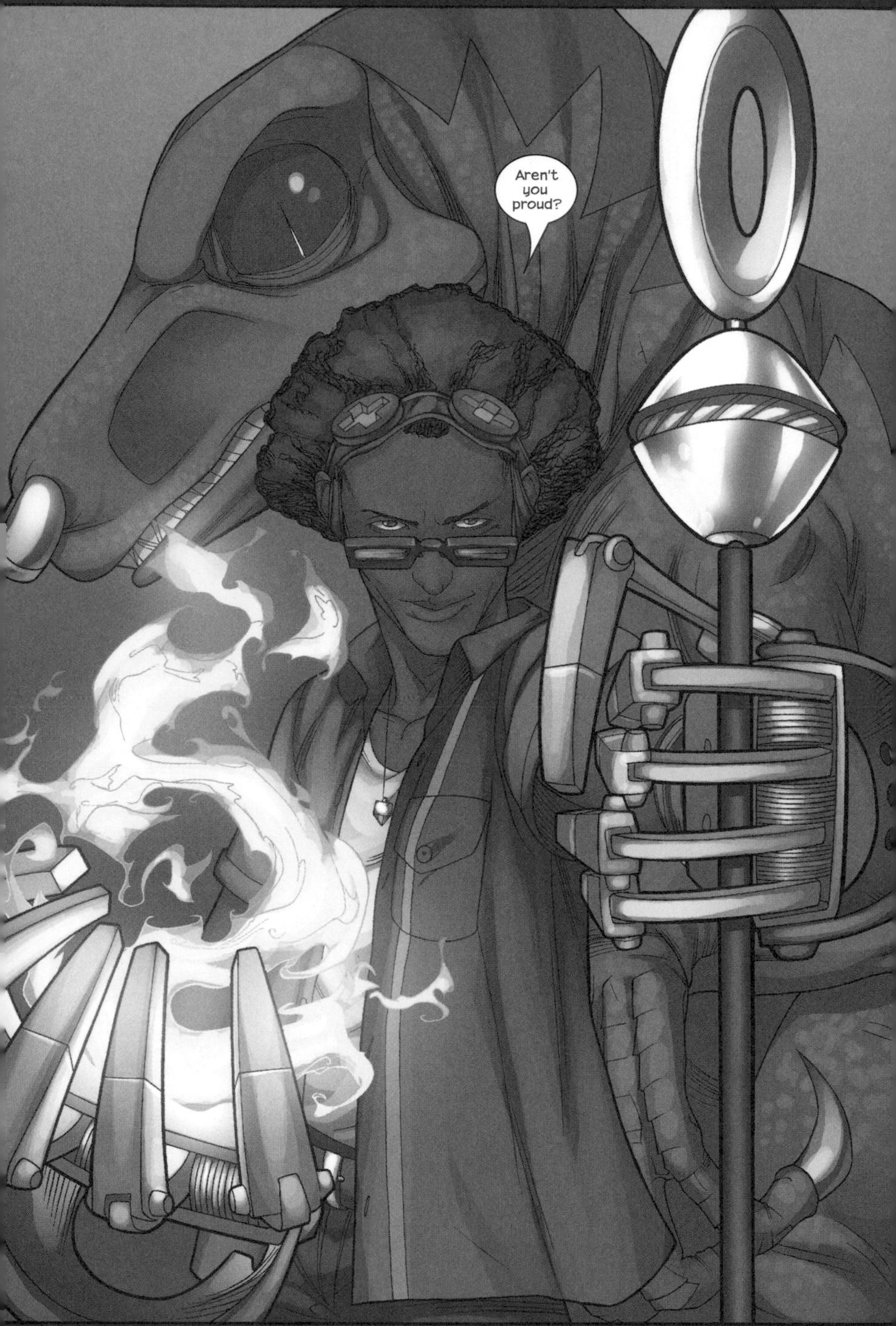
Aren't you proud?

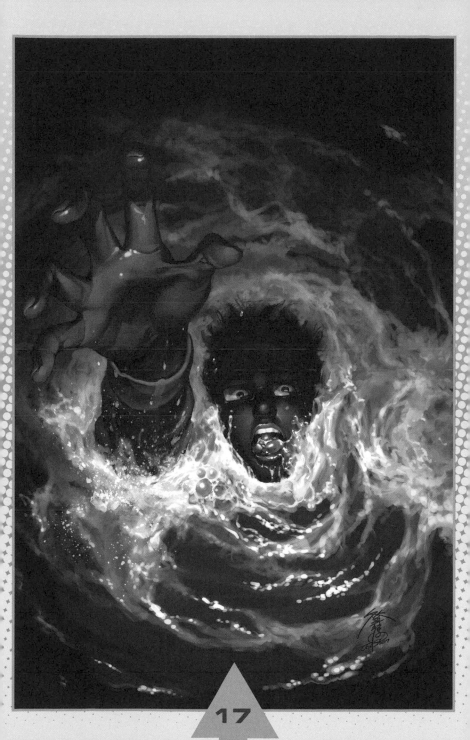

17

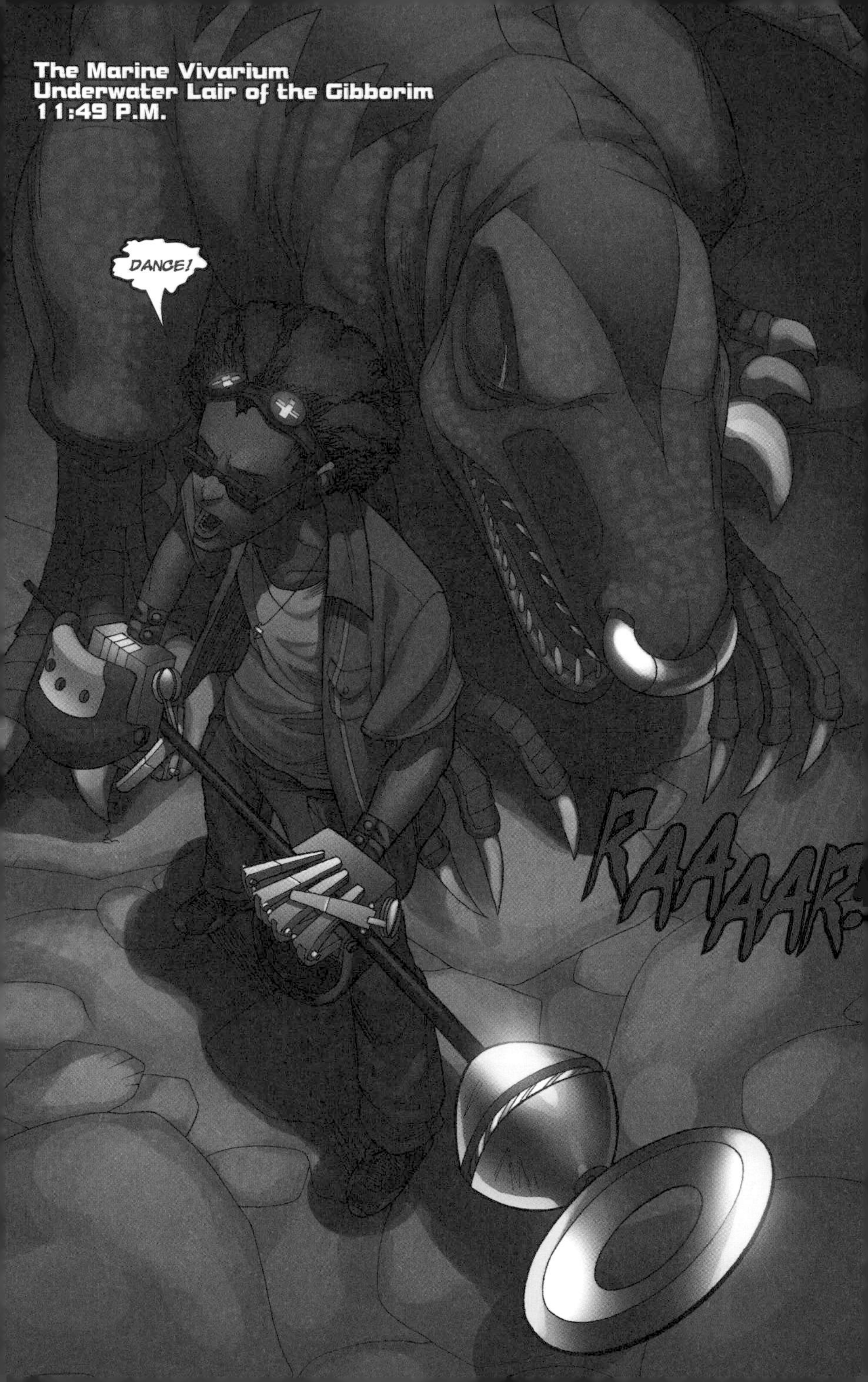
The Marine Vivarium
Underwater Lair of the Gibborim
11:49 P.M.
DANCE!
RAAAAR!

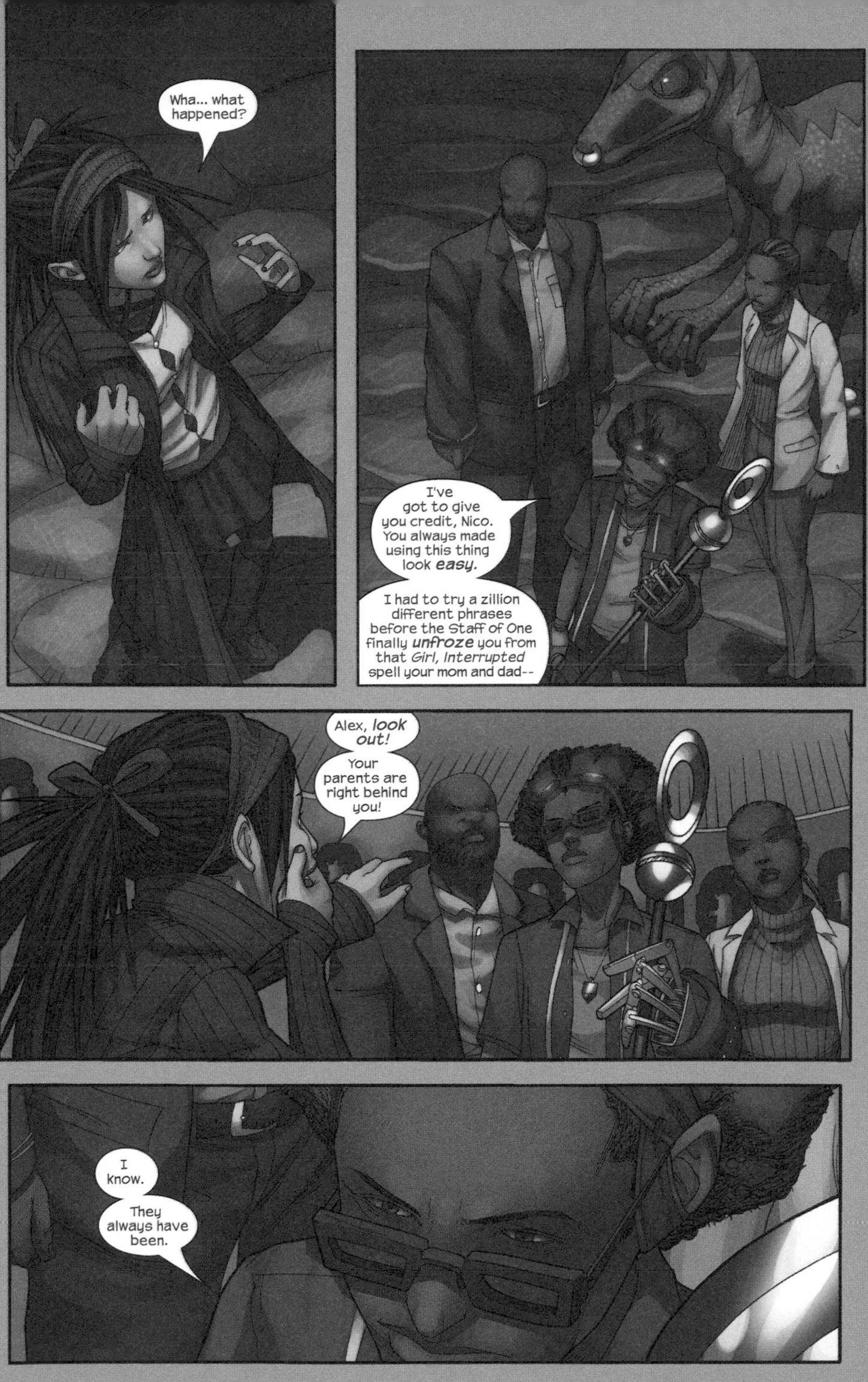

Wha... what happened?
I've got to give you credit, Nico. You always made using this thing look *easy.*
I had to try a zillion different phrases before the Staff of One finally *unfroze* you from that *Girl, Interrupted* spell your mom and dad--
Alex, *look out!*
Your parents are right behind you!
I know.
They always have been.

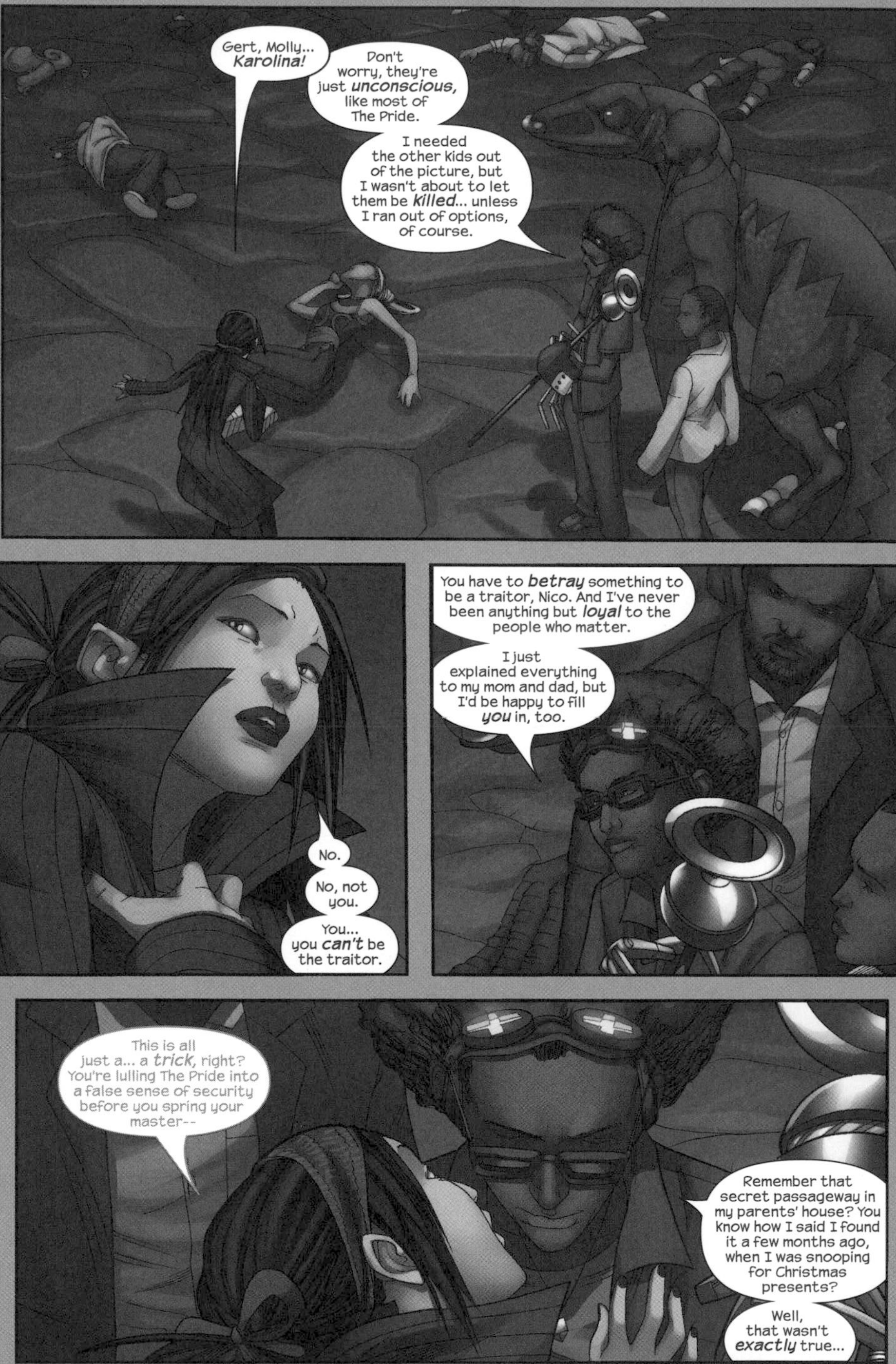

Gert, Molly... Karolina!
Don't worry, they're just unconscious, like most of The Pride.
I needed the other kids out of the picture, but I wasn't about to let them be killed... unless I ran out of options, of course.
No.
No, not you.
You... you can't be the traitor.
You have to betray something to be a traitor, Nico. And I've never been anything but loyal to the people who matter.
I just explained everything to my mom and dad, but I'd be happy to fill you in, too.
This is all just a... a trick, right? You're lulling The Pride into a false sense of security before you spring your master--
Remember that secret passageway in my parents' house? You know how I said I found it a few months ago, when I was snooping for Christmas presents?
Well, that wasn't exactly true...

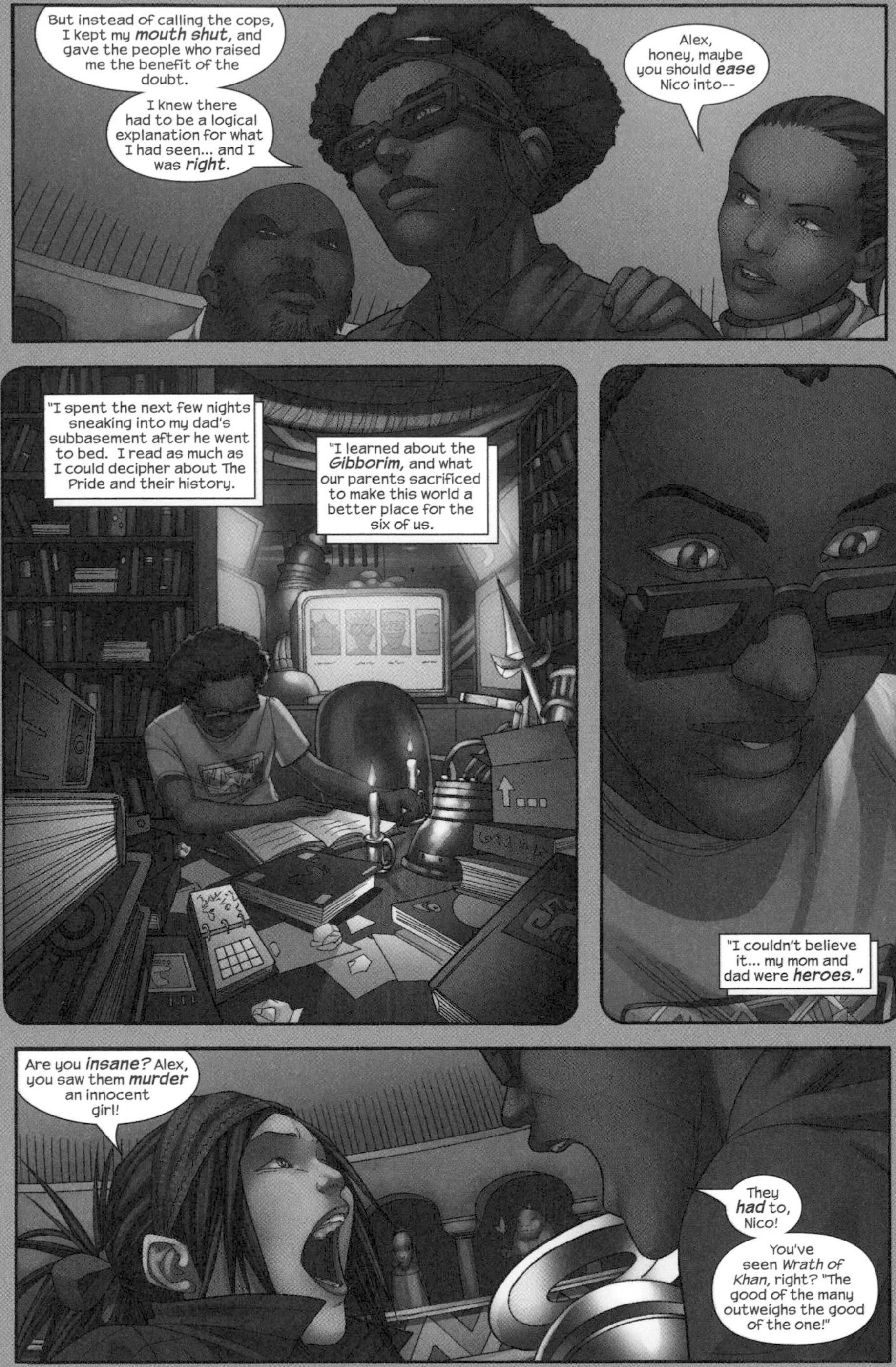
But instead of calling the cops, I kept my mouth shut, and gave the people who raised me the benefit of the doubt.
I knew there had to be a logical explanation for what I had seen... and I was right.
Alex, honey, maybe you should ease Nico into--
"I spent the next few nights sneaking into my dad's subbasement after he went to bed. I read as much as I could decipher about The Pride and their history.
"I learned about the Gibborim, and what our parents sacrificed to make this world a better place for the six of us.
"I couldn't believe it... my mom and dad were heroes."
Are you insane? Alex, you saw them murder an innocent girl!
They had to, Nico!
You've seen Wrath of Khan, right? "The good of the many outweighs the good of the one!"

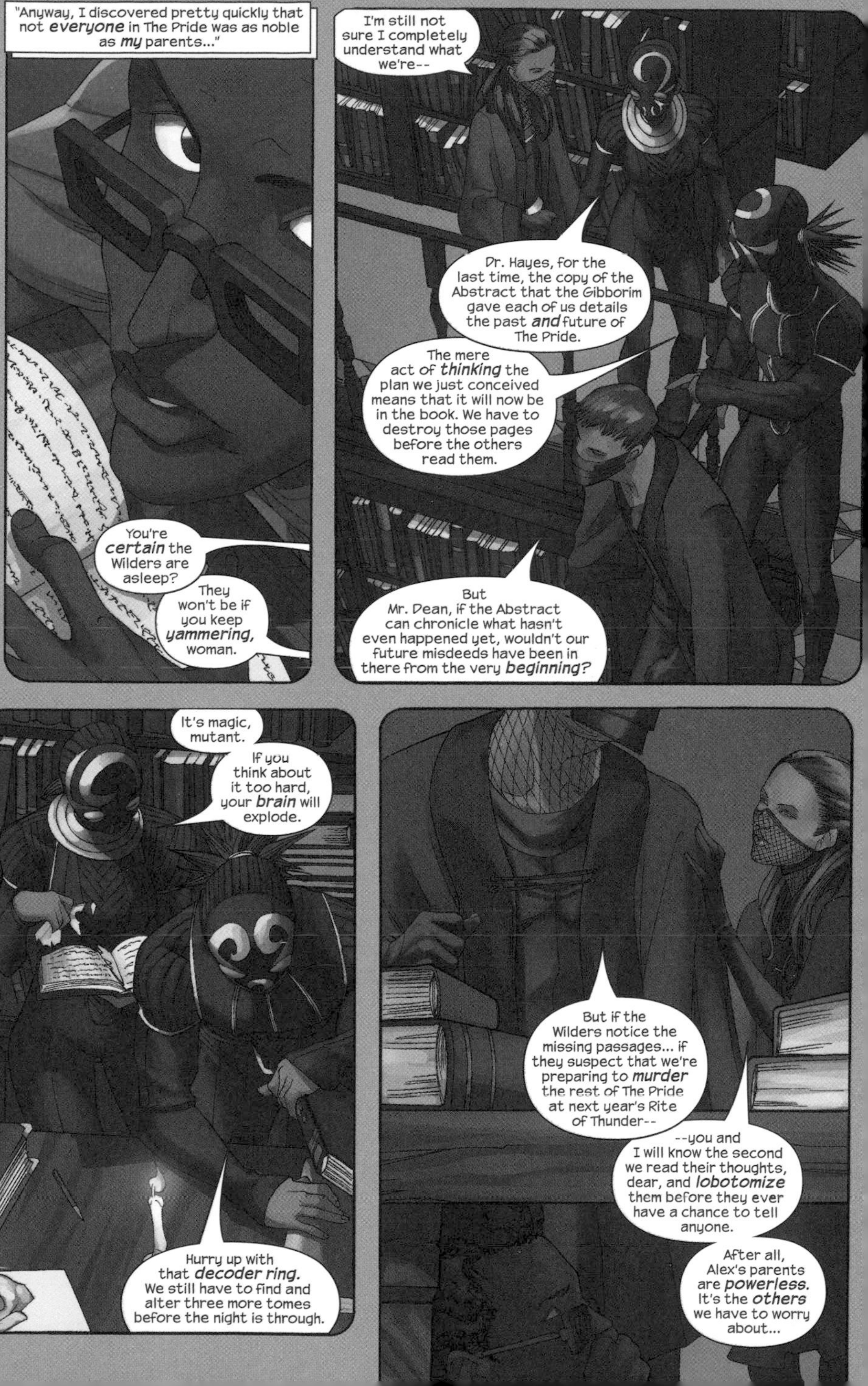
"Anyway, I discovered pretty quickly that not *everyone* in The Pride was as noble as *my* parents..."
You're *certain* the Wilders are asleep?
They won't be if you keep *yammering,* woman.
I'm still not sure I completely understand what we're--
Dr. Hayes, for the last time, the copy of the Abstract that the Gibborim gave each of us details the past *and* future of The Pride.
The mere act of *thinking* the plan we just conceived means that it will now be in the book. We have to destroy those pages before the others read them.
But Mr. Dean, if the Abstract can chronicle what hasn't even happened yet, wouldn't our future misdeeds have been in there from the very *beginning?*
It's magic, mutant.
If you think about it too hard, your *brain* will explode.
Hurry up with that *decoder ring.* We still have to find and alter three more tomes before the night is through.
But if the Wilders notice the missing passages... if they suspect that we're preparing to *murder* the rest of The Pride at next year's Rite of Thunder--
--you and I will know the second we read their thoughts, dear, and *lobotomize* them before they ever have a chance to tell anyone.
After all, Alex's parents are *powerless.* It's the *others* we have to worry about...

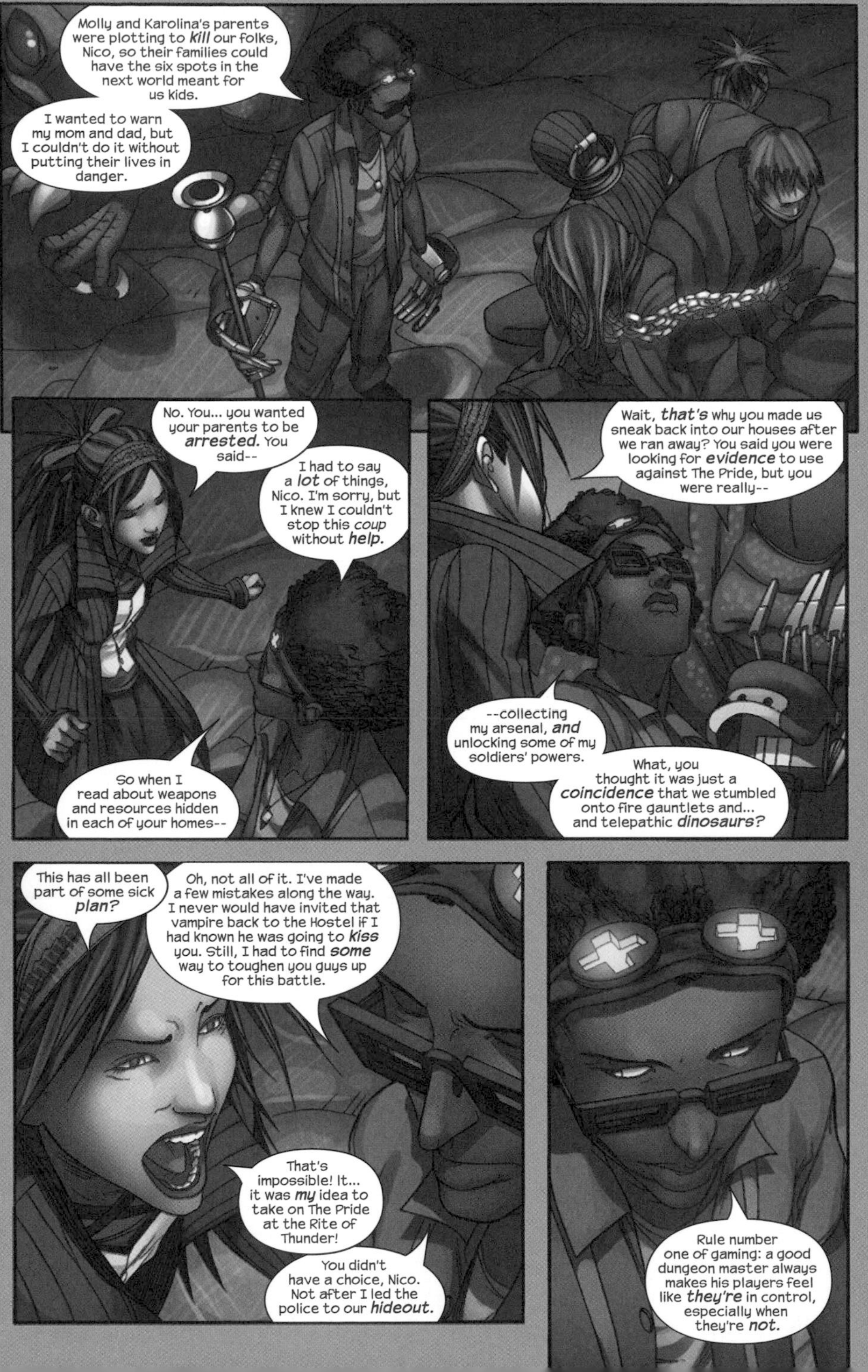
Molly and Karolina's parents were plotting to kill our folks, Nico, so their families could have the six spots in the next world meant for us kids.
I wanted to warn my mom and dad, but I couldn't do it without putting their lives in danger.
No. You... you wanted your parents to be arrested. You said--
I had to say a lot of things, Nico. I'm sorry, but I knew I couldn't stop this coup without help.
So when I read about weapons and resources hidden in each of your homes--
Wait, that's why you made us sneak back into our houses after we ran away? You said you were looking for evidence to use against The Pride, but you were really--
--collecting my arsenal, and unlocking some of my soldiers' powers.
What, you thought it was just a coincidence that we stumbled onto fire gauntlets and... and telepathic dinosaurs?
This has all been part of some sick plan?
Oh, not all of it. I've made a few mistakes along the way. I never would have invited that vampire back to the Hostel if I had known he was going to kiss you. Still, I had to find some way to toughen you guys up for this battle.
That's impossible! It... it was my idea to take on The Pride at the Rite of Thunder!
You didn't have a choice, Nico. Not after I led the police to our hideout.
Rule number one of gaming: a good dungeon master always makes his players feel like they're in control, especially when they're not.

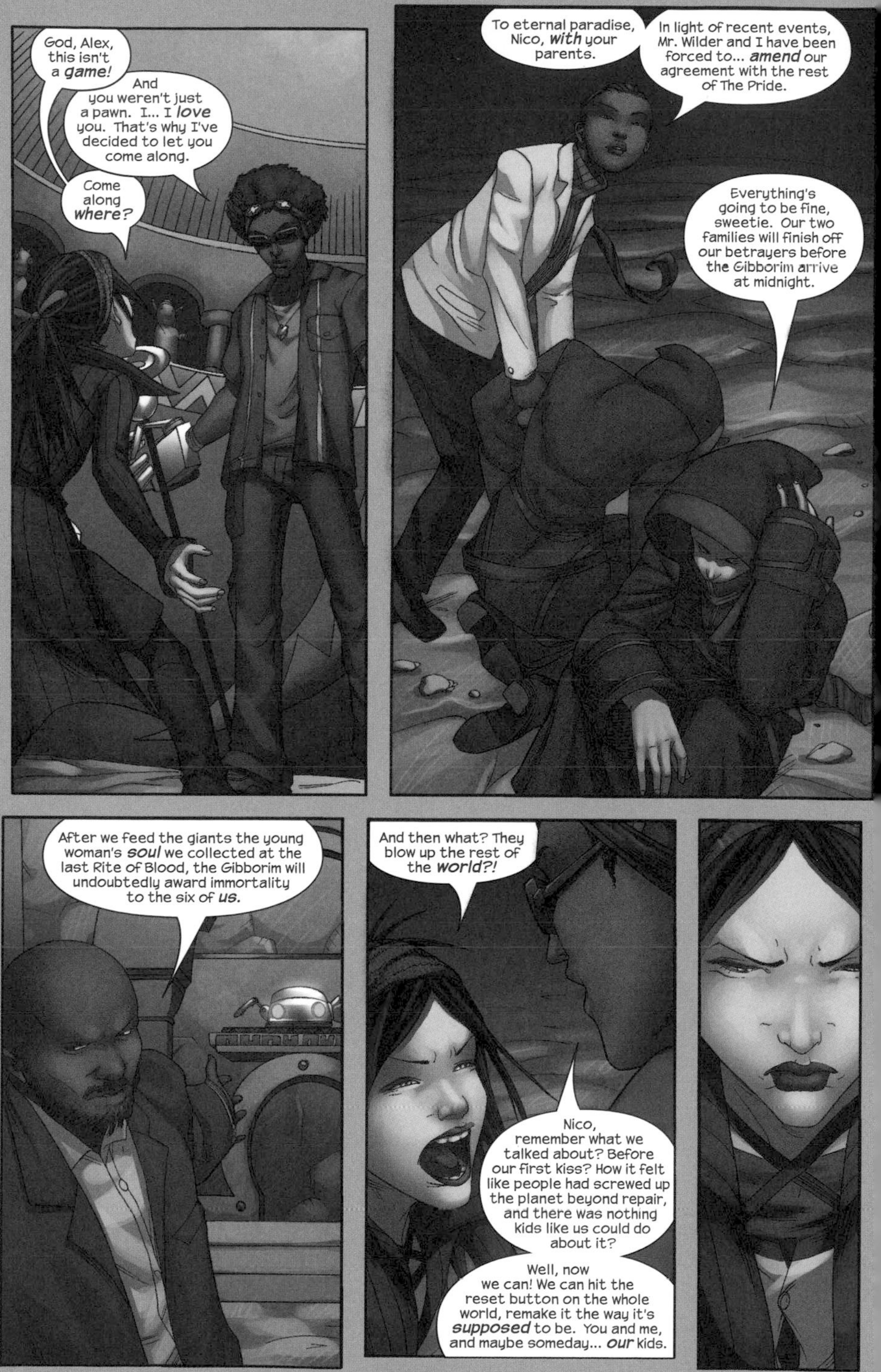
God, Alex, this isn't a game!
And you weren't just a pawn. I... I love you. That's why I've decided to let you come along.
Come along where?
To eternal paradise, Nico, with your parents.
In light of recent events, Mr. Wilder and I have been forced to... amend our agreement with the rest of The Pride.
Everything's going to be fine, sweetie. Our two families will finish off our betrayers before the Gibborim arrive at midnight.
After we feed the giants the young woman's soul we collected at the last Rite of Blood, the Gibborim will undoubtedly award immortality to the six of us.
And then what? They blow up the rest of the world?!
Nico, remember what we talked about? Before our first kiss? How it felt like people had screwed up the planet beyond repair, and there was nothing kids like us could do about it?
Well, now we can! We can hit the reset button on the whole world, remake it the way it's supposed to be. You and me, and maybe someday... our kids.

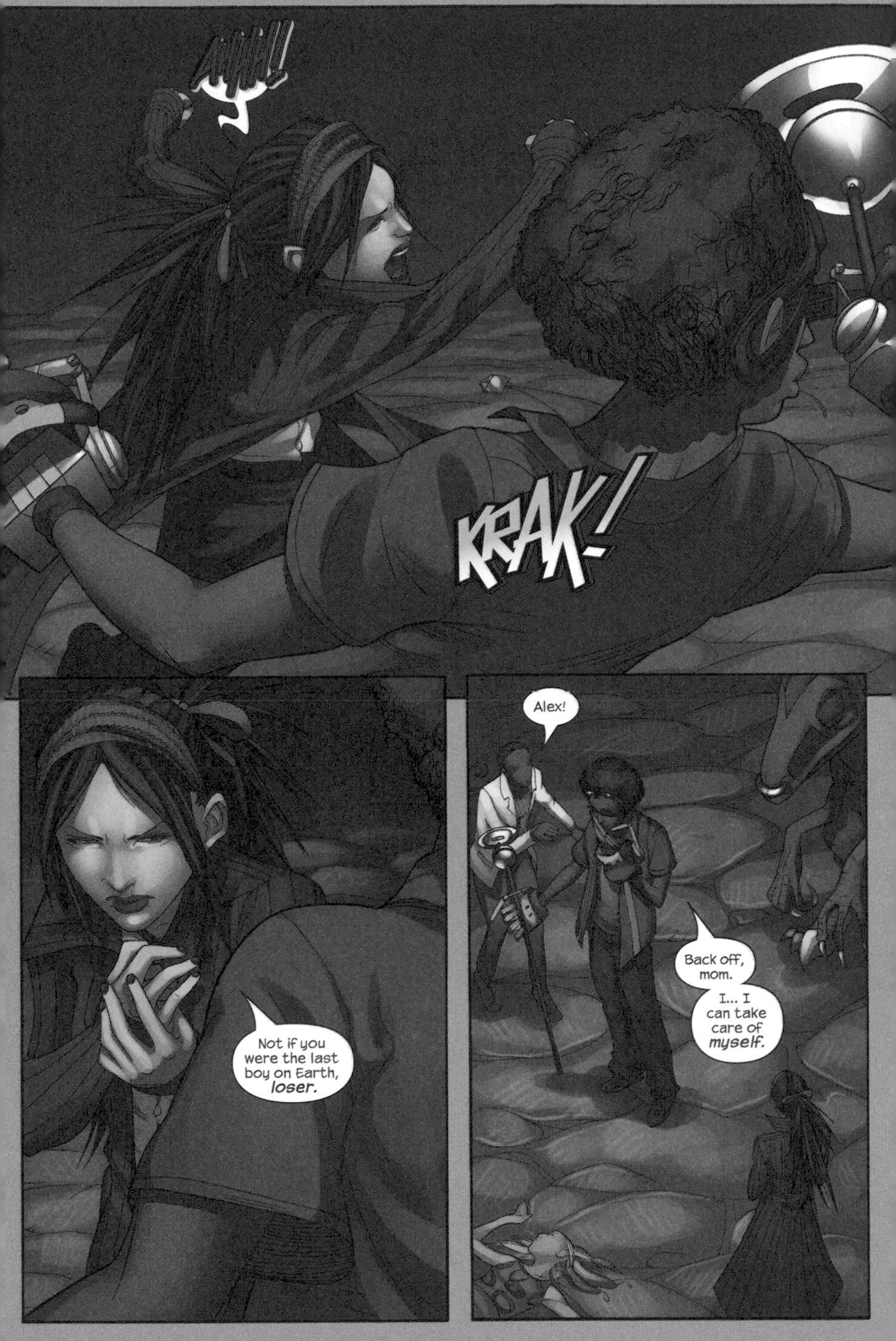
AHHH!!
KRAK!
Not if you were the last boy on Earth, *loser.*
Alex!
Back off, mom.
I... I can take care of *myself.*

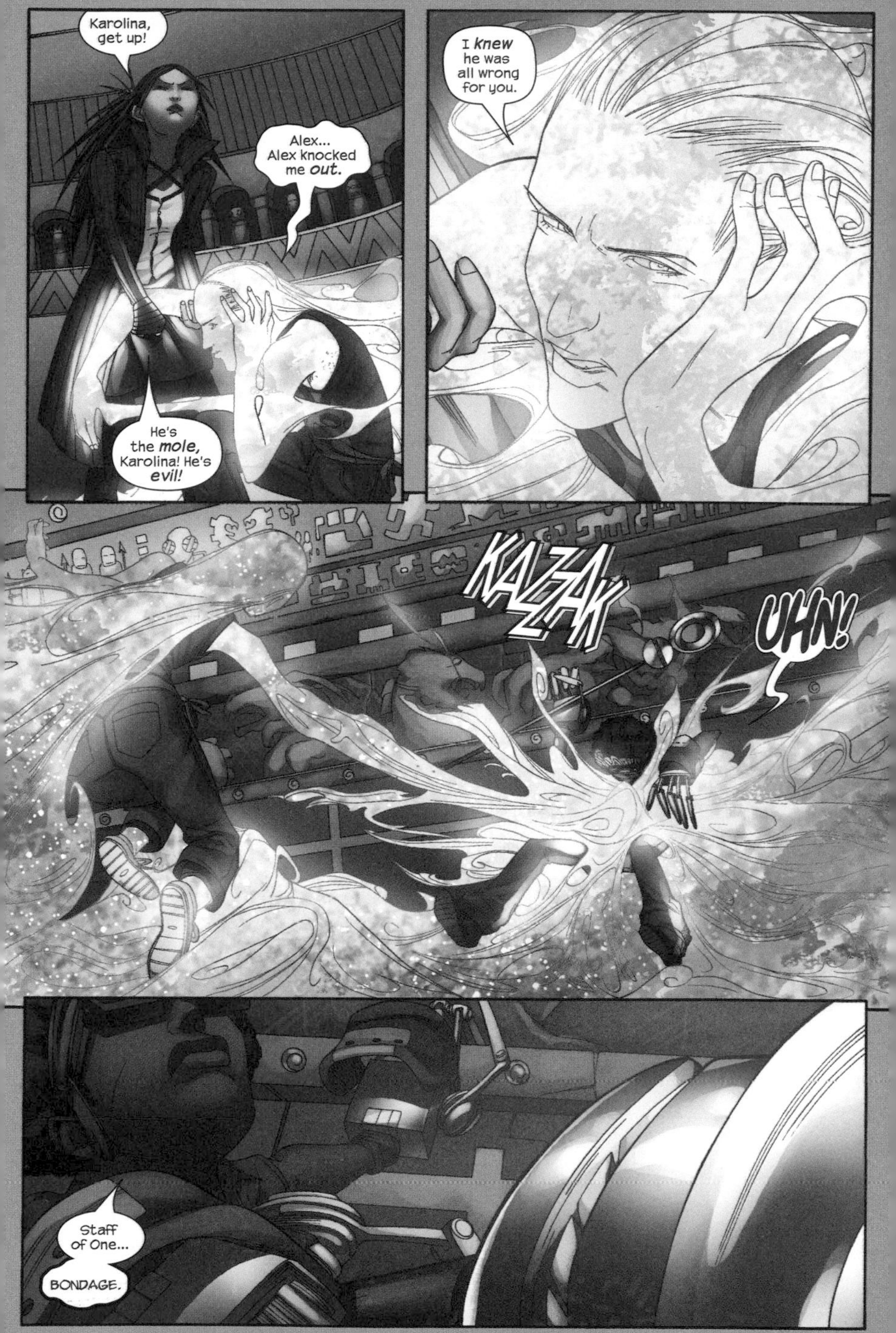
Karolina, get up!
Alex... Alex knocked me *out.*
He's the *mole,* Karolina! He's *evil!*
I *knew* he was all wrong for you.
KAZZAK
UHN!
Staff of One...
BONDAGE.

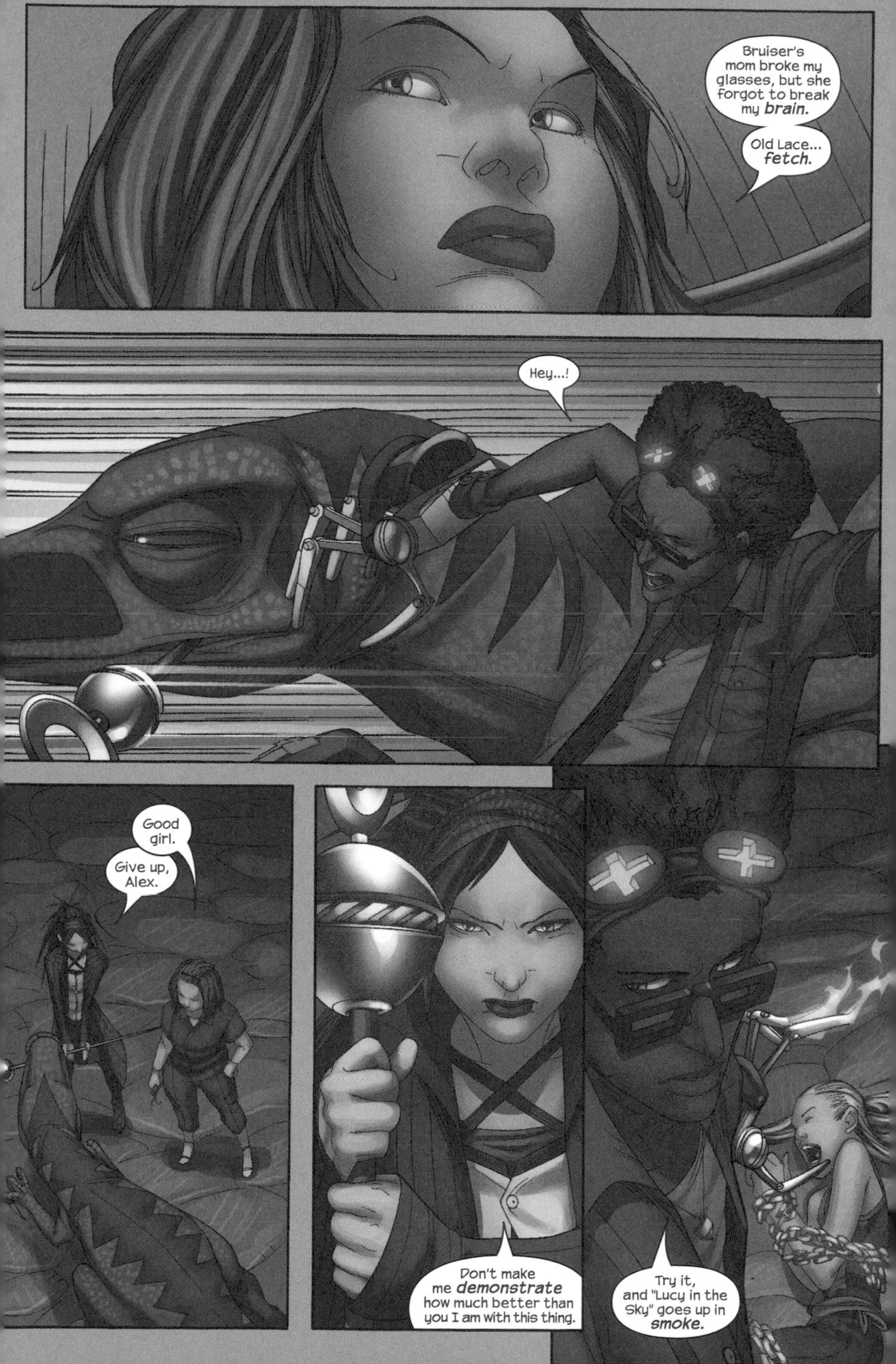
Bruiser's mom broke my glasses, but she forgot to break my brain.
Old Lace... fetch.
Hey...!
Good girl.
Give up, Alex.
Don't make me demonstrate how much better than you I am with this thing.
Try it, and "Lucy in the Sky" goes up in smoke.

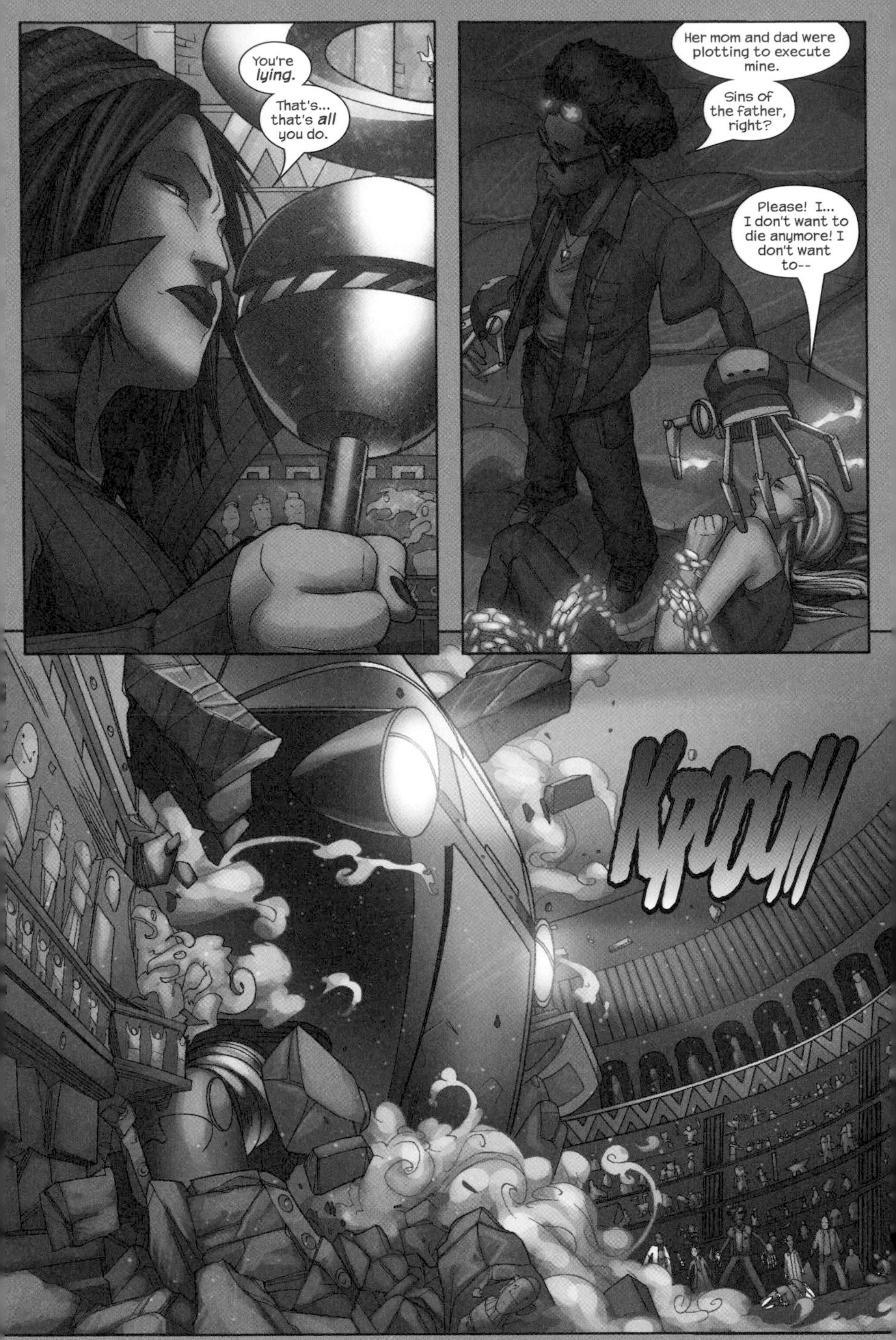
You're *lying.*
That's... that's *all* you do.
Her mom and dad were plotting to execute mine.
Sins of the father, right?
Please! I... I don't want to die anymore! I don't want to--
KROOOM

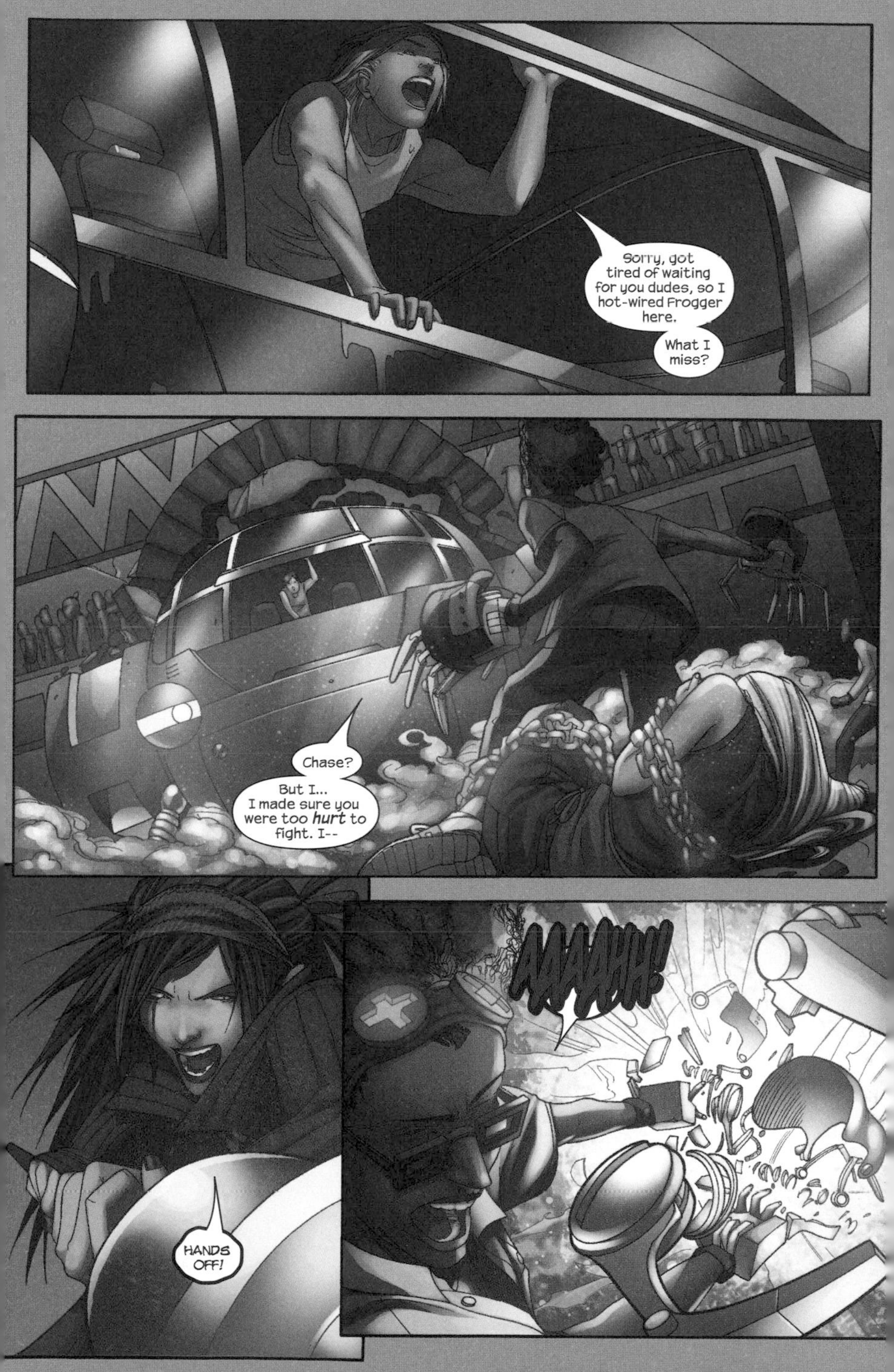
Sorry, got tired of waiting for you dudes, so I hot-wired Frogger here.
What I miss?
Chase?
But I... I made sure you were too *hurt* to fight. I--
HANDS OFF!
AAAAHH!

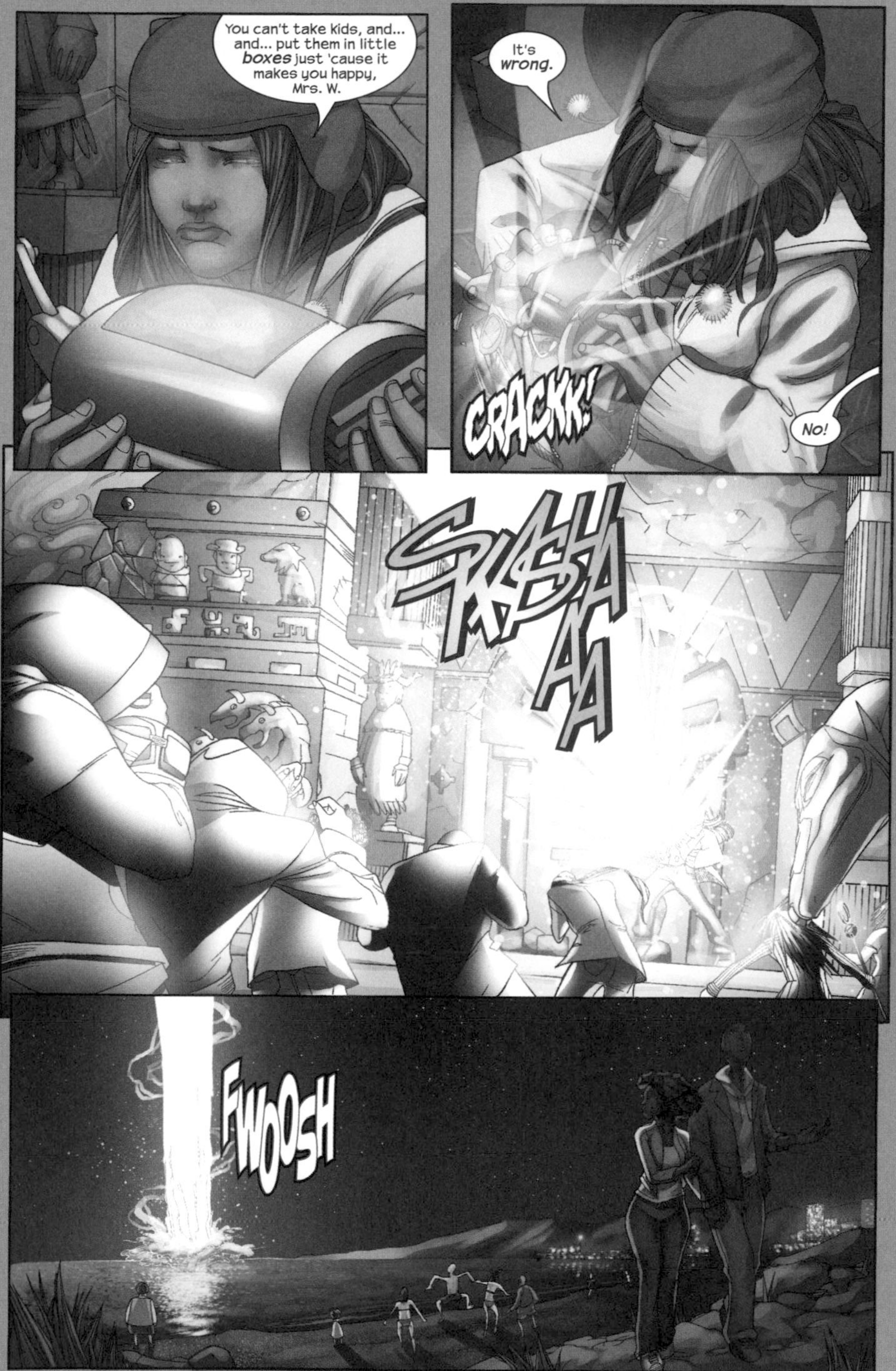

You can't take kids, and... and... put them in little *boxes* just 'cause it makes you happy, Mrs. W.
It's *wrong*.
CRACKK!
No!
SKASHAAA
FWOOSH

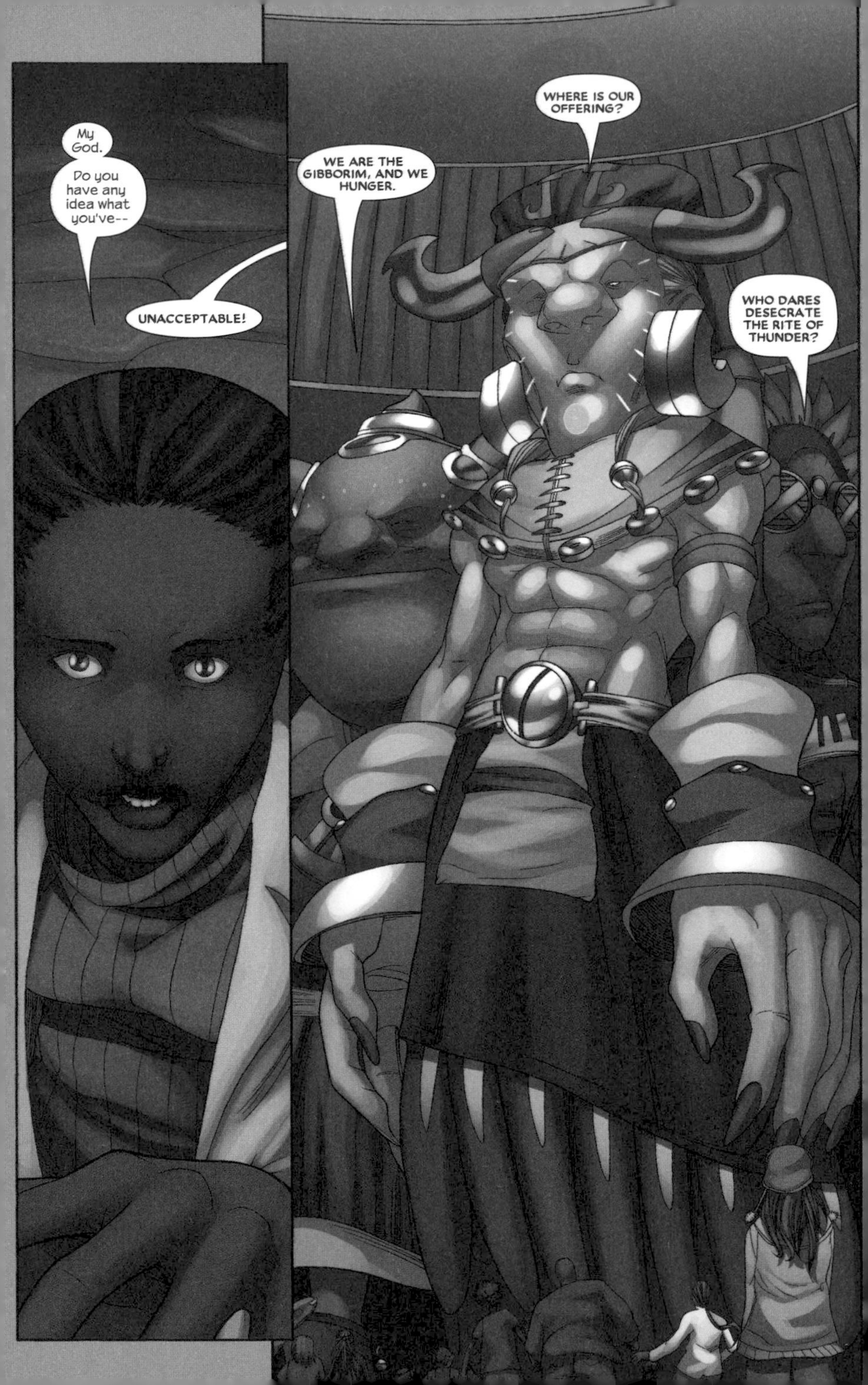
My God.
Do you have any idea what you've--
UNACCEPTABLE!
WE ARE THE GIBBORIM, AND WE HUNGER.
WHERE IS OUR OFFERING?
WHO DARES DESECRATE THE RITE OF THUNDER?

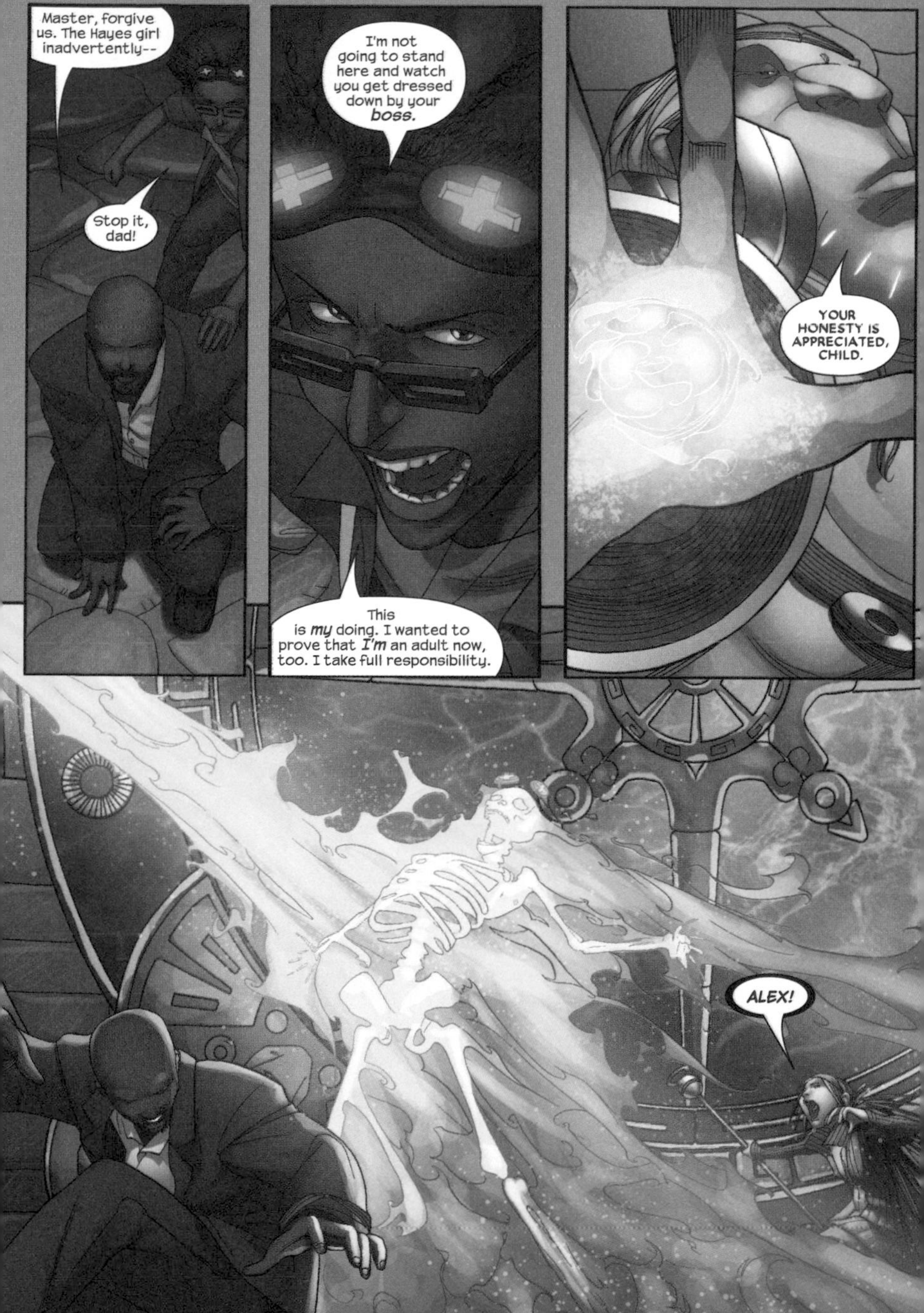
Master, forgive us. The Hayes girl inadvertently--
Stop it, dad!
I'm not going to stand here and watch you get dressed down by your boss.
This is my doing. I wanted to prove that I'm an adult now, too. I take full responsibility.
YOUR HONESTY IS APPRECIATED, CHILD.
ALEX!

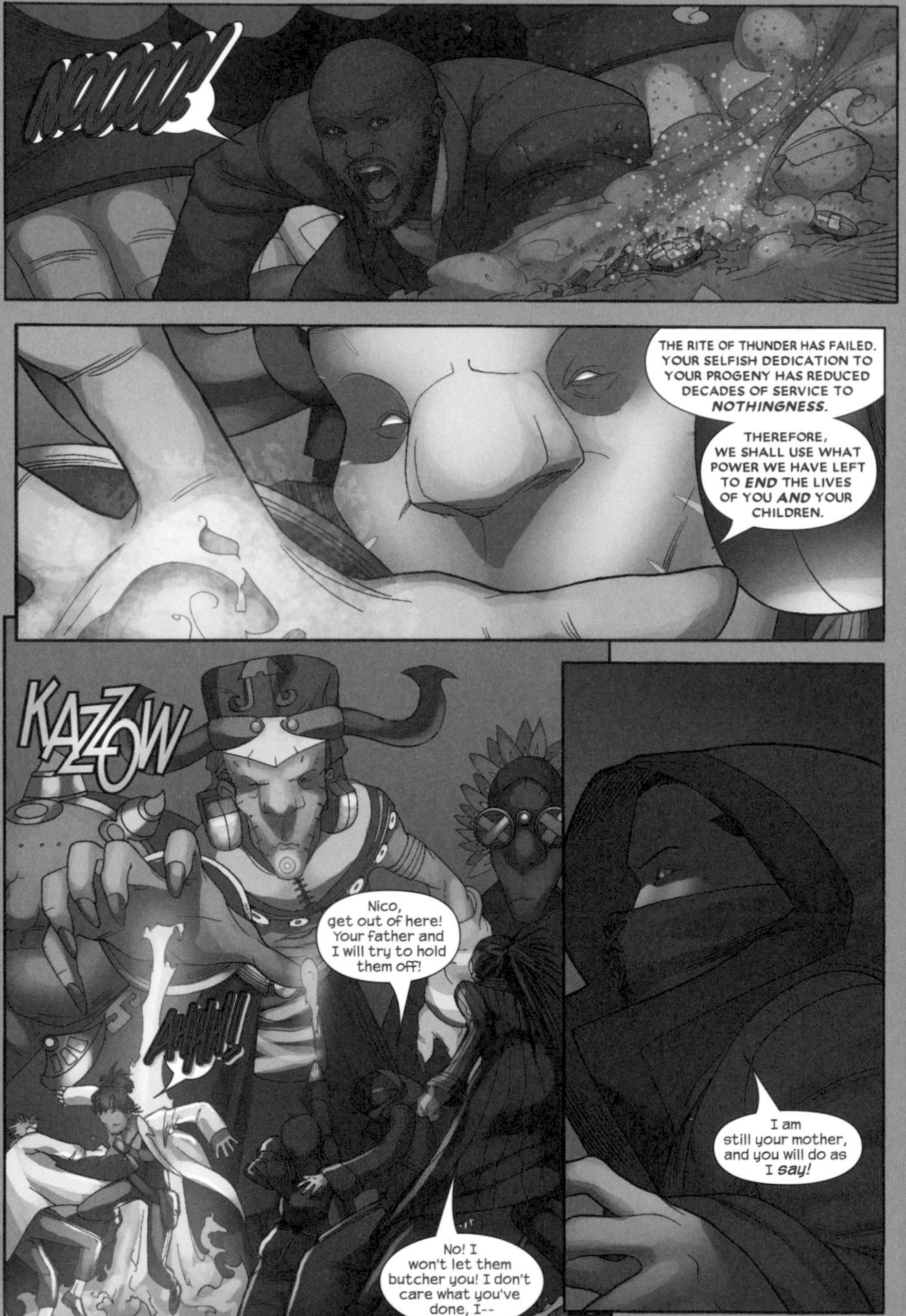
NOOOO!
THE RITE OF THUNDER HAS FAILED. YOUR SELFISH DEDICATION TO YOUR PROGENY HAS REDUCED DECADES OF SERVICE TO *NOTHINGNESS.*
THEREFORE, WE SHALL USE WHAT POWER WE HAVE LEFT TO *END* THE LIVES OF YOU *AND* YOUR CHILDREN.
KAZZOW
Nico, get out of here! Your father and I will try to hold them off!
AHHH!!
No! I won't let them butcher you! I don't care what you've done, I--
I am still your mother, and you will do as I *say!*

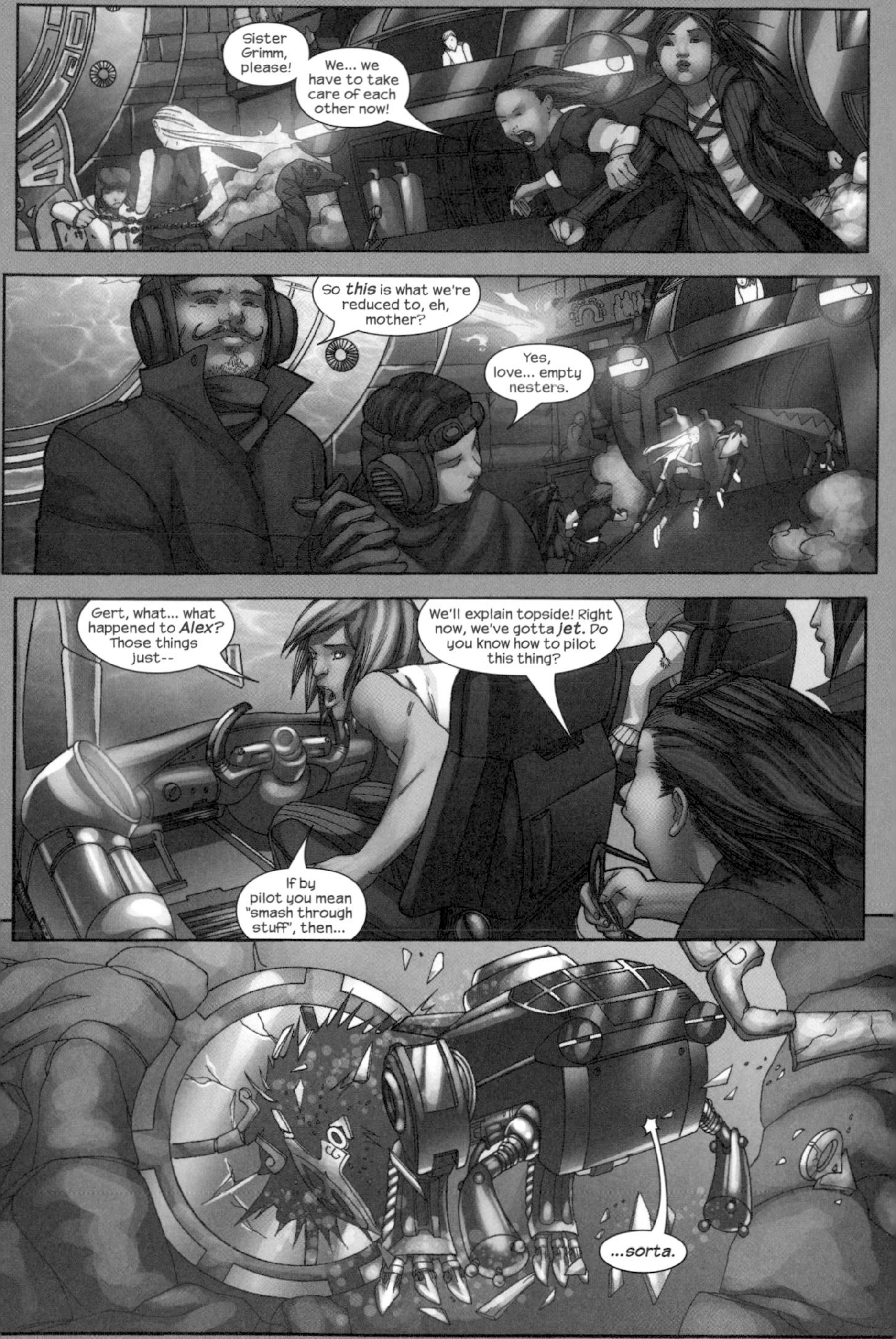
Sister Grimm, please!
We... we have to take care of each other now!
So *this* is what we're reduced to, eh, mother?
Yes, love... empty nesters.
Gert, what... what happened to *Alex?* Those things just--
We'll explain topside! Right now, we've gotta *jet.* Do you know how to pilot this thing?
If by pilot you mean "smash through stuff", then...
...sorta.

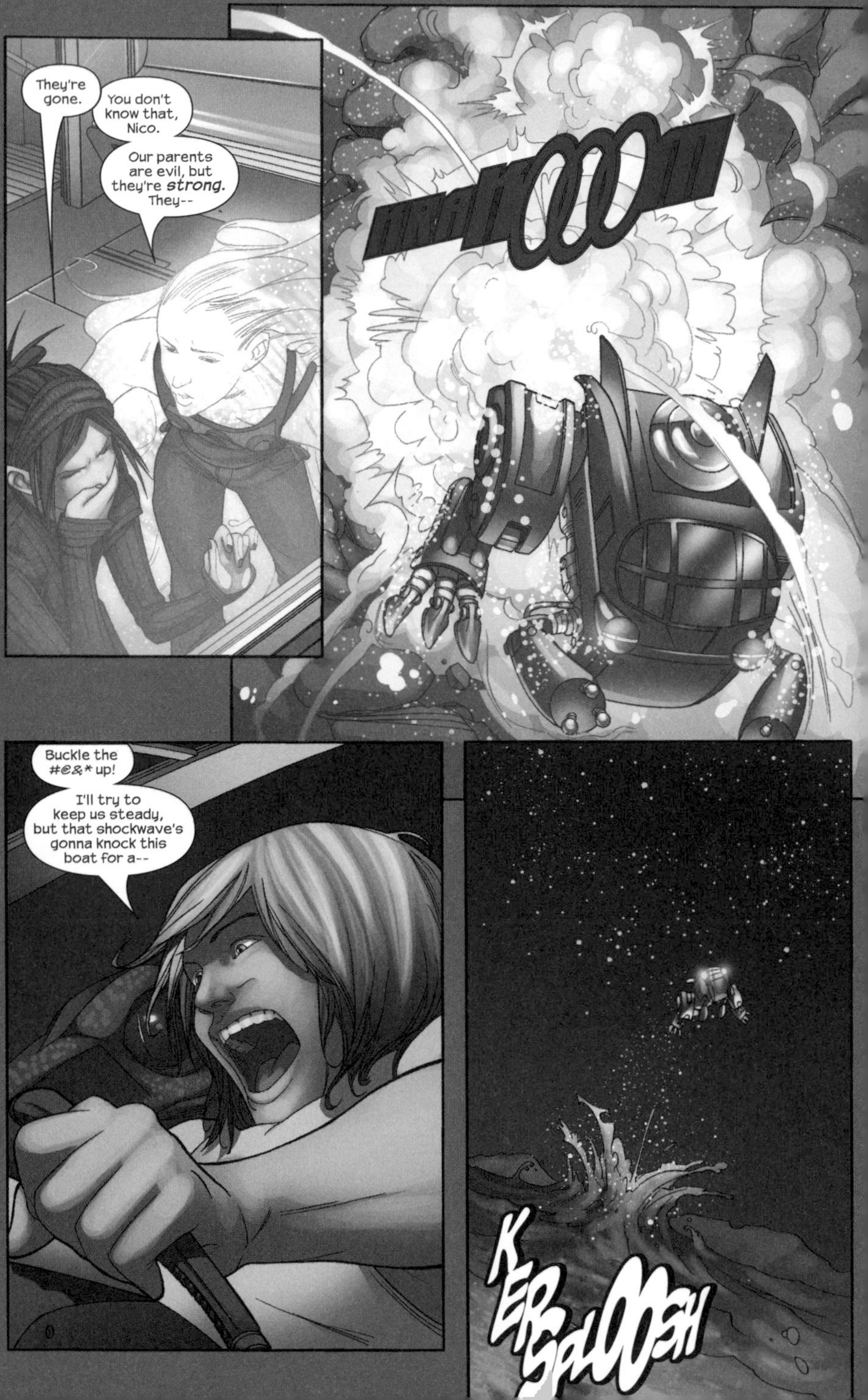
They're gone.
You don't know that, Nico.
Our parents are evil, but they're *strong.* They--
KRAKOOOM
Buckle the #@&* up!
I'll try to keep us steady, but that shockwave's gonna knock this boat for a--
KERSPLOOSH

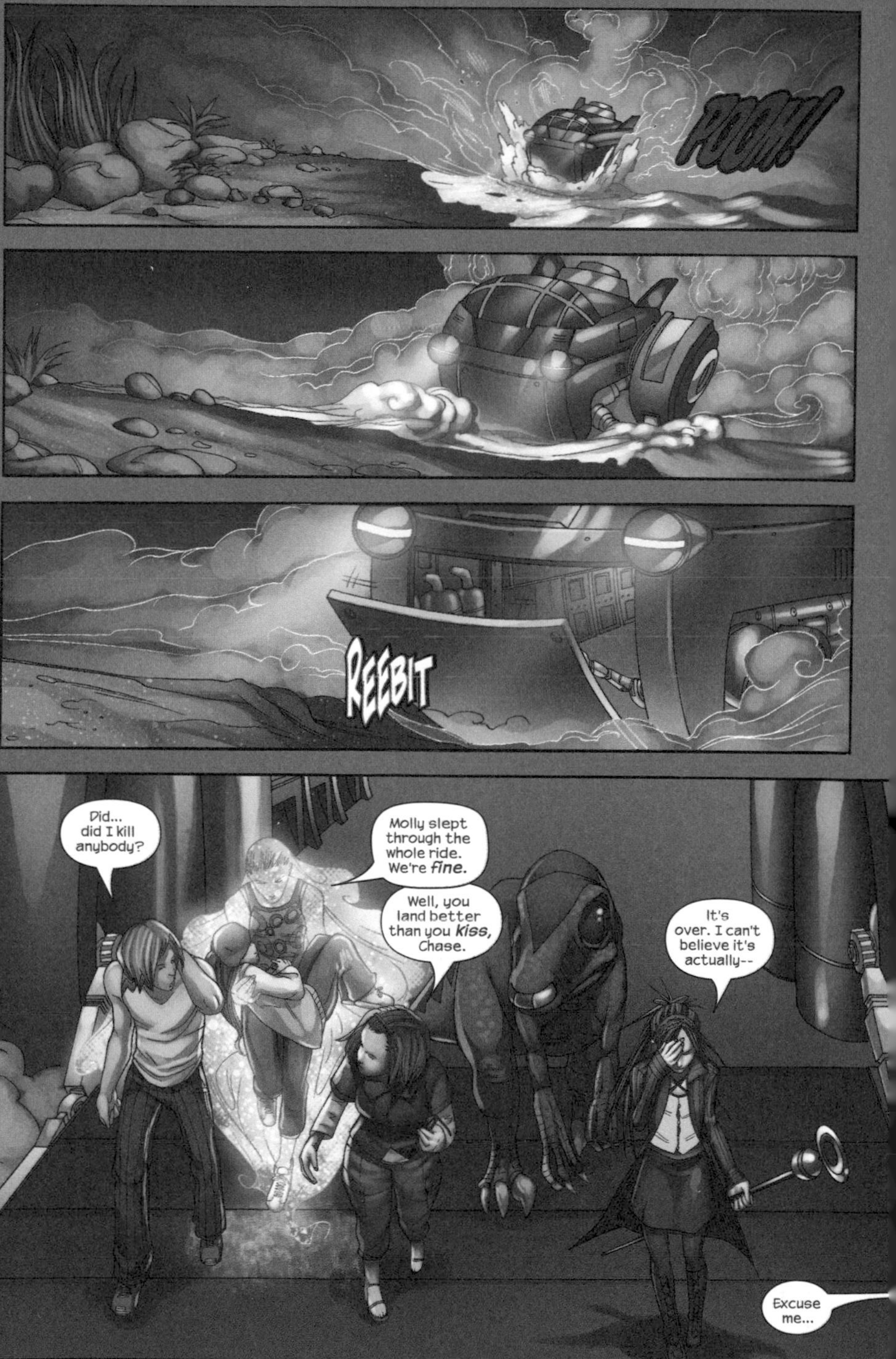
POOM!
REEBIT
Did... did I kill anybody?
Molly slept through the whole ride. We're *fine.*
Well, you land better than you *kiss,* Chase.
It's over. I can't believe it's actually--
Excuse me...

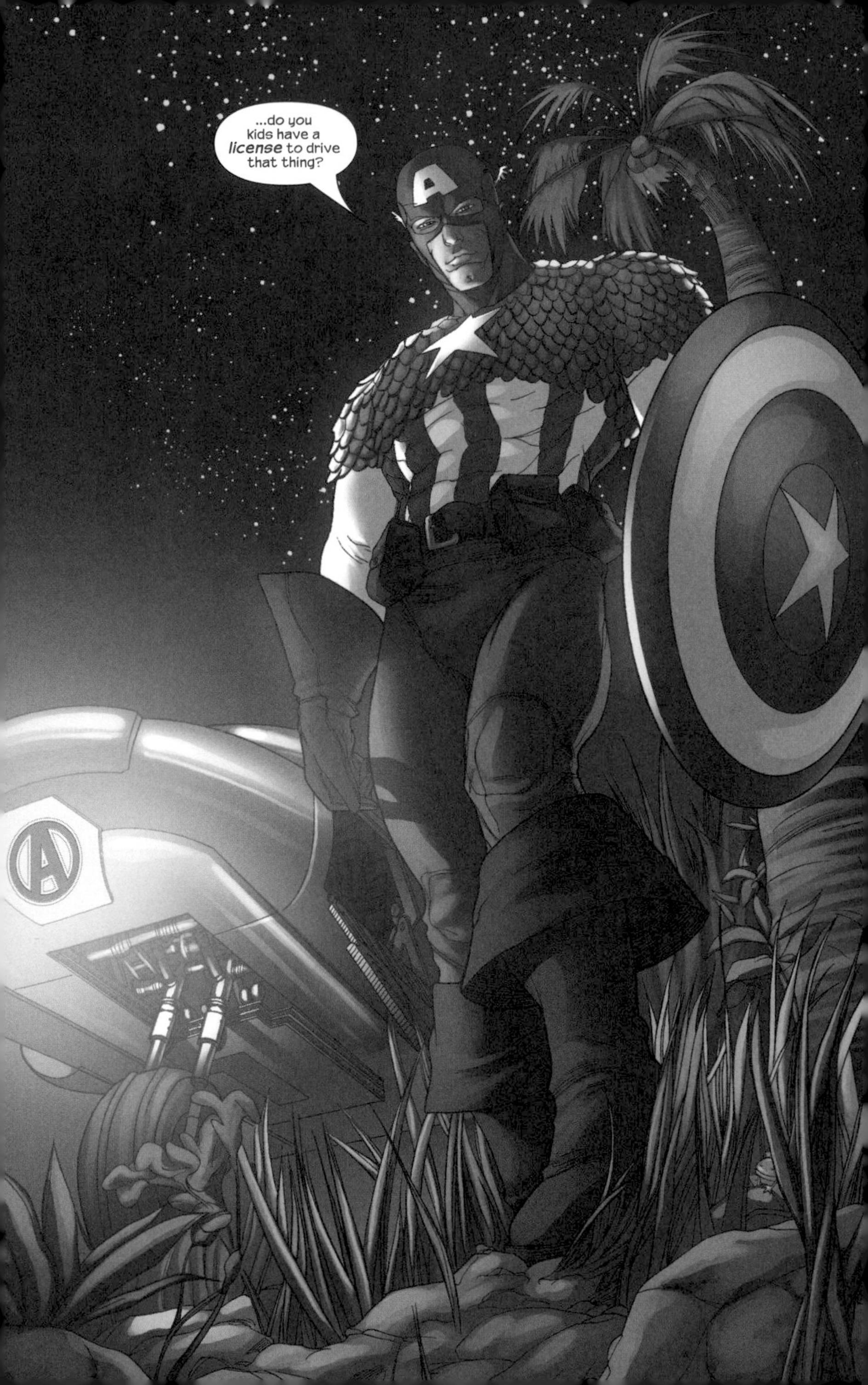
...do you kids have a *license* to drive that thing?

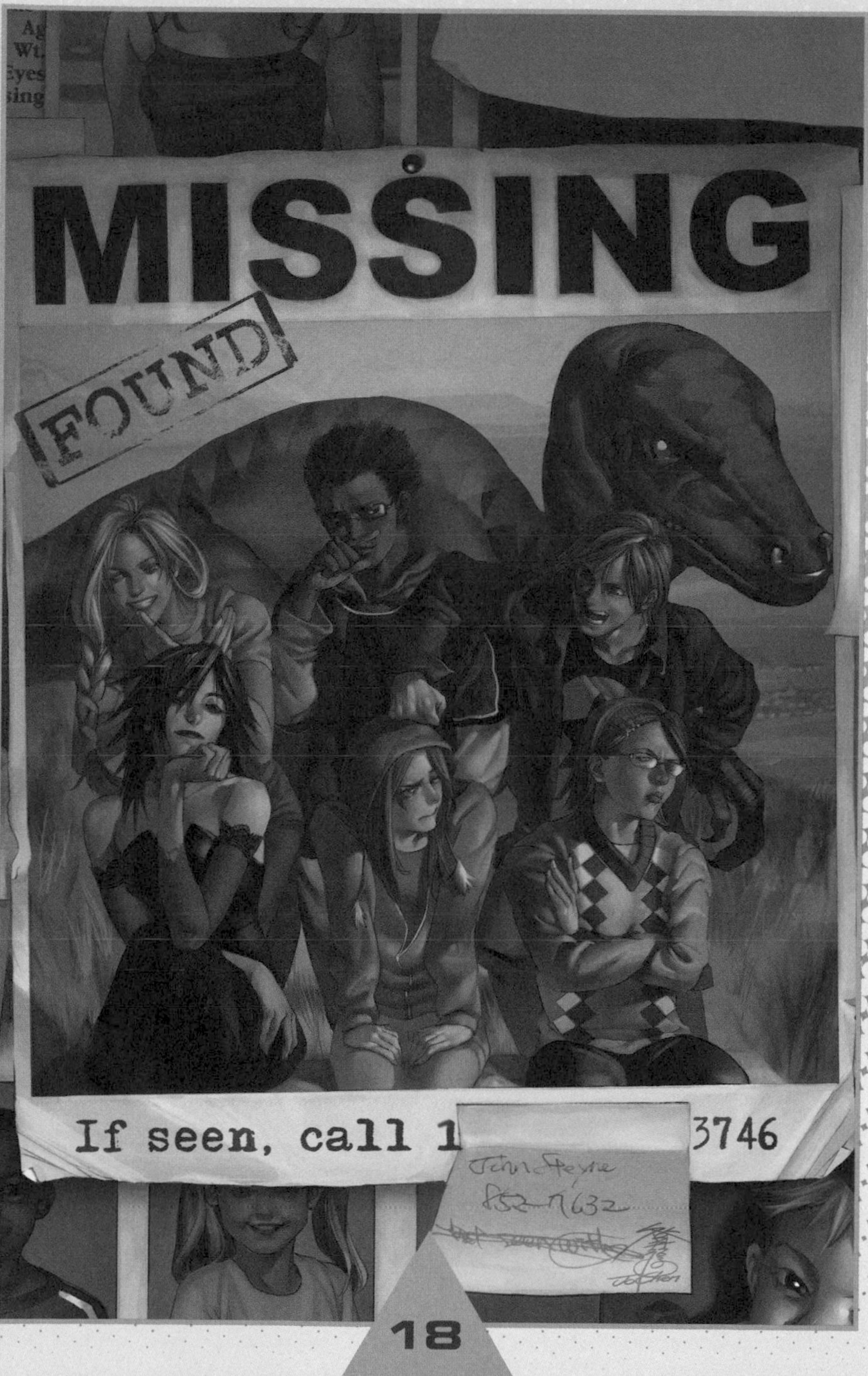
MISSING
FOUND
If seen, call 1
3746

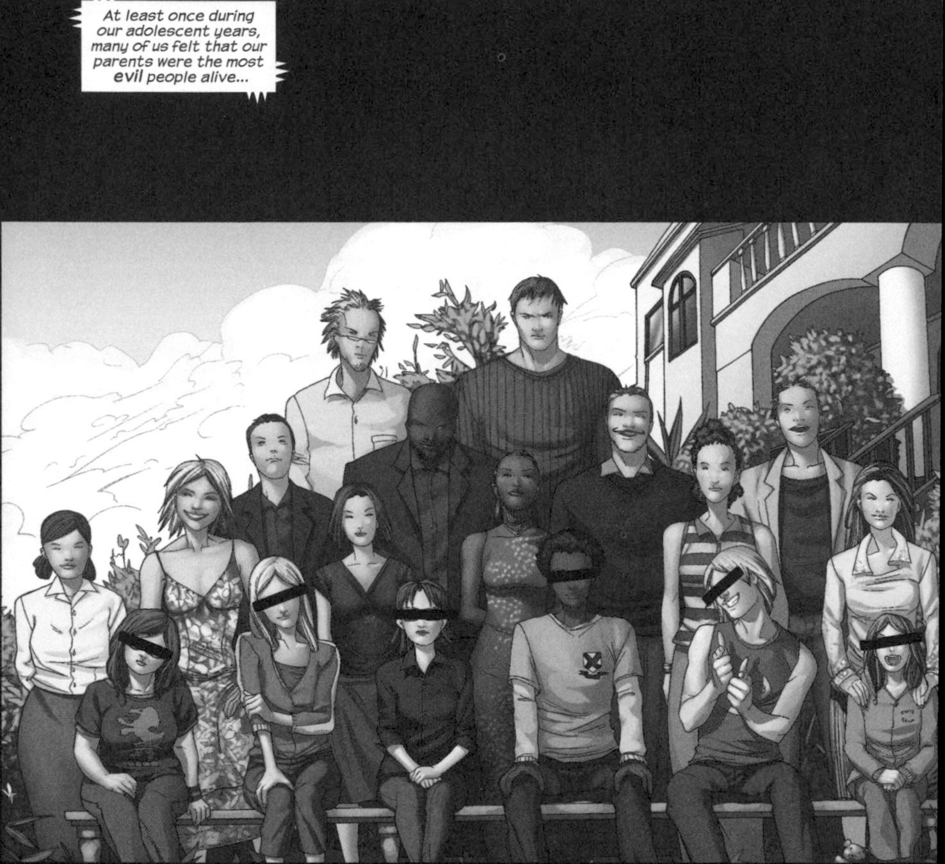
At least once during our adolescent years, many of us felt that our parents were the most **evil** people alive...

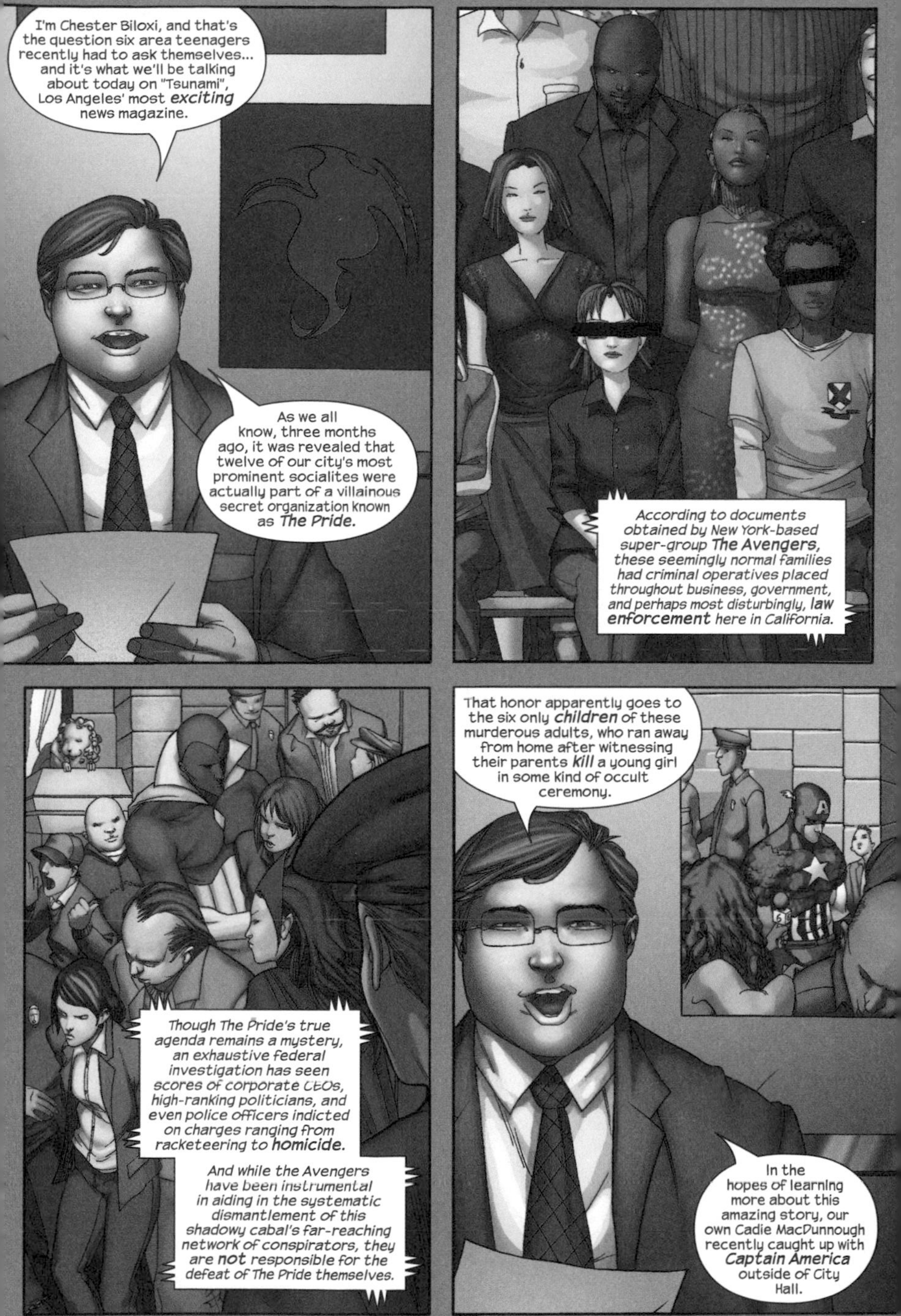
I'm Chester Biloxi, and that's the question six area teenagers recently had to ask themselves... and it's what we'll be talking about today on "Tsunami", Los Angeles' most exciting news magazine.
As we all know, three months ago, it was revealed that twelve of our city's most prominent socialites were actually part of a villainous secret organization known as The Pride.
According to documents obtained by New York-based super-group The Avengers, these seemingly normal families had criminal operatives placed throughout business, government, and perhaps most disturbingly, law enforcement here in California.
Though The Pride's true agenda remains a mystery, an exhaustive federal investigation has seen scores of corporate CEOs, high-ranking politicians, and even police officers indicted on charges ranging from racketeering to homicide.
And while the Avengers have been instrumental in aiding in the systematic dismantlement of this shadowy cabal's far-reaching network of conspirators, they are not responsible for the defeat of The Pride themselves.
That honor apparently goes to the six only children of these murderous adults, who ran away from home after witnessing their parents kill a young girl in some kind of occult ceremony.
In the hopes of learning more about this amazing story, our own Cadie MacDunnough recently caught up with Captain America outside of City Hall.

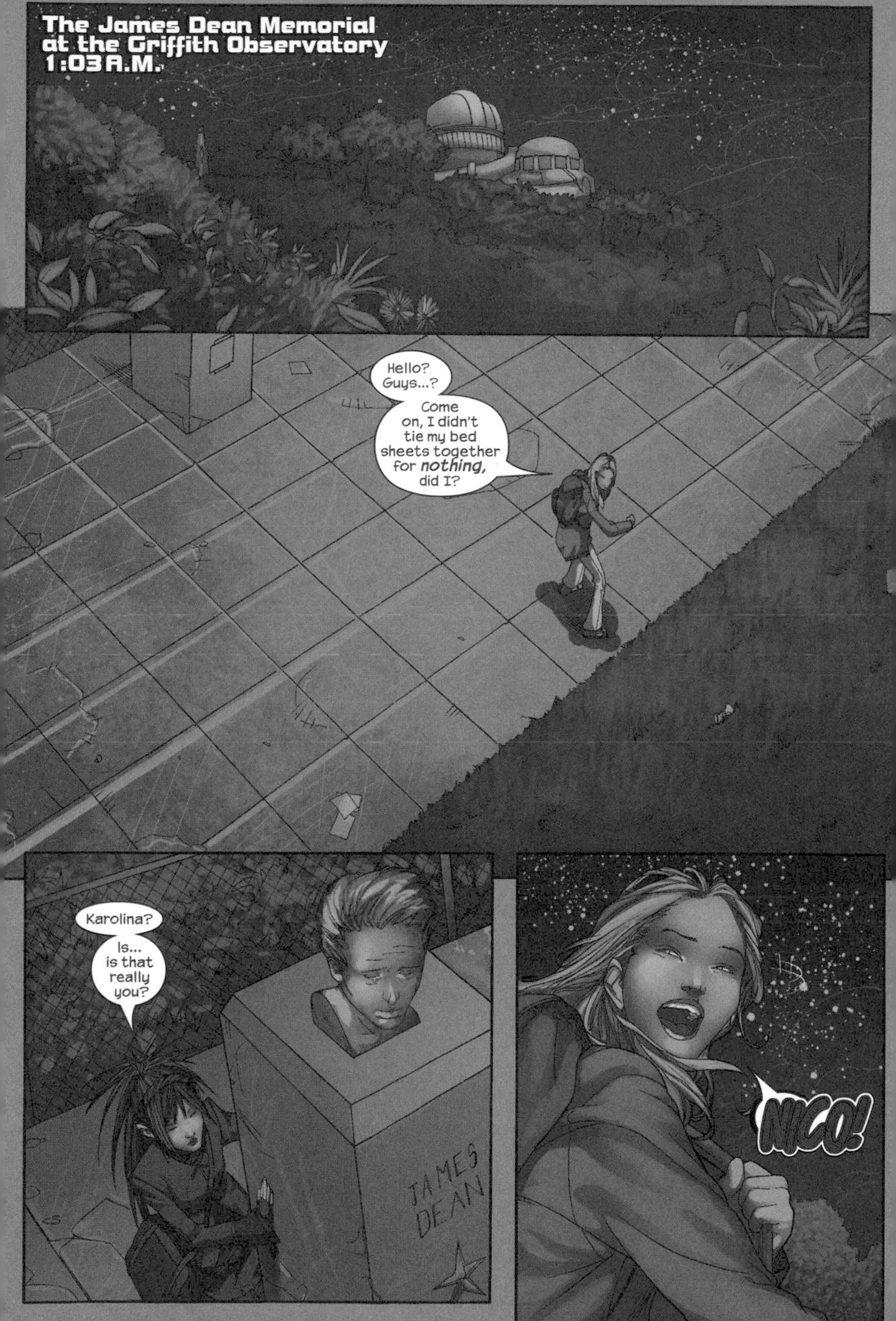
The James Dean Memorial at the Griffith Observatory 1:03 A.M.
Hello? Guys...?
Come on, I didn't tie my bed sheets together for *nothing,* did I?
Karolina?
Is... is that really you?
JAMES DEAN
NICO!

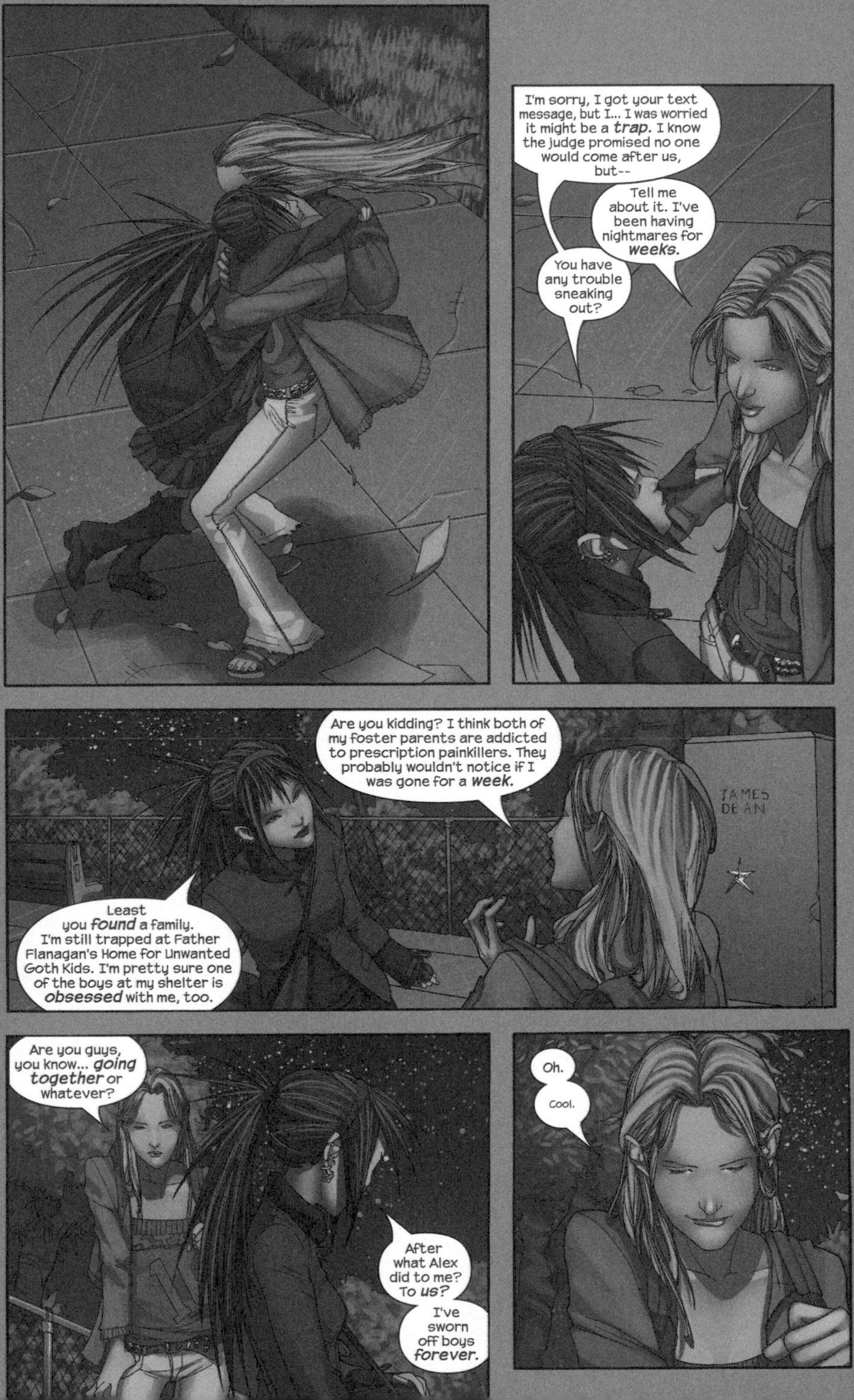

I'm sorry, I got your text message, but I... I was worried it might be a *trap*. I know the judge promised no one would come after us, but--
Tell me about it. I've been having nightmares for ***weeks***.
You have any trouble sneaking out?
Are you kidding? I think both of my foster parents are addicted to prescription painkillers. They probably wouldn't notice if I was gone for a ***week***.
JAMES DEAN
Least you ***found*** a family. I'm still trapped at Father Flanagan's Home for Unwanted Goth Kids. I'm pretty sure one of the boys at my shelter is ***obsessed*** with me, too.
Are you guys, you know... ***going together*** or whatever?
After what Alex did to me? To ***us?***
I've sworn off boys ***forever***.
Oh.
Cool.

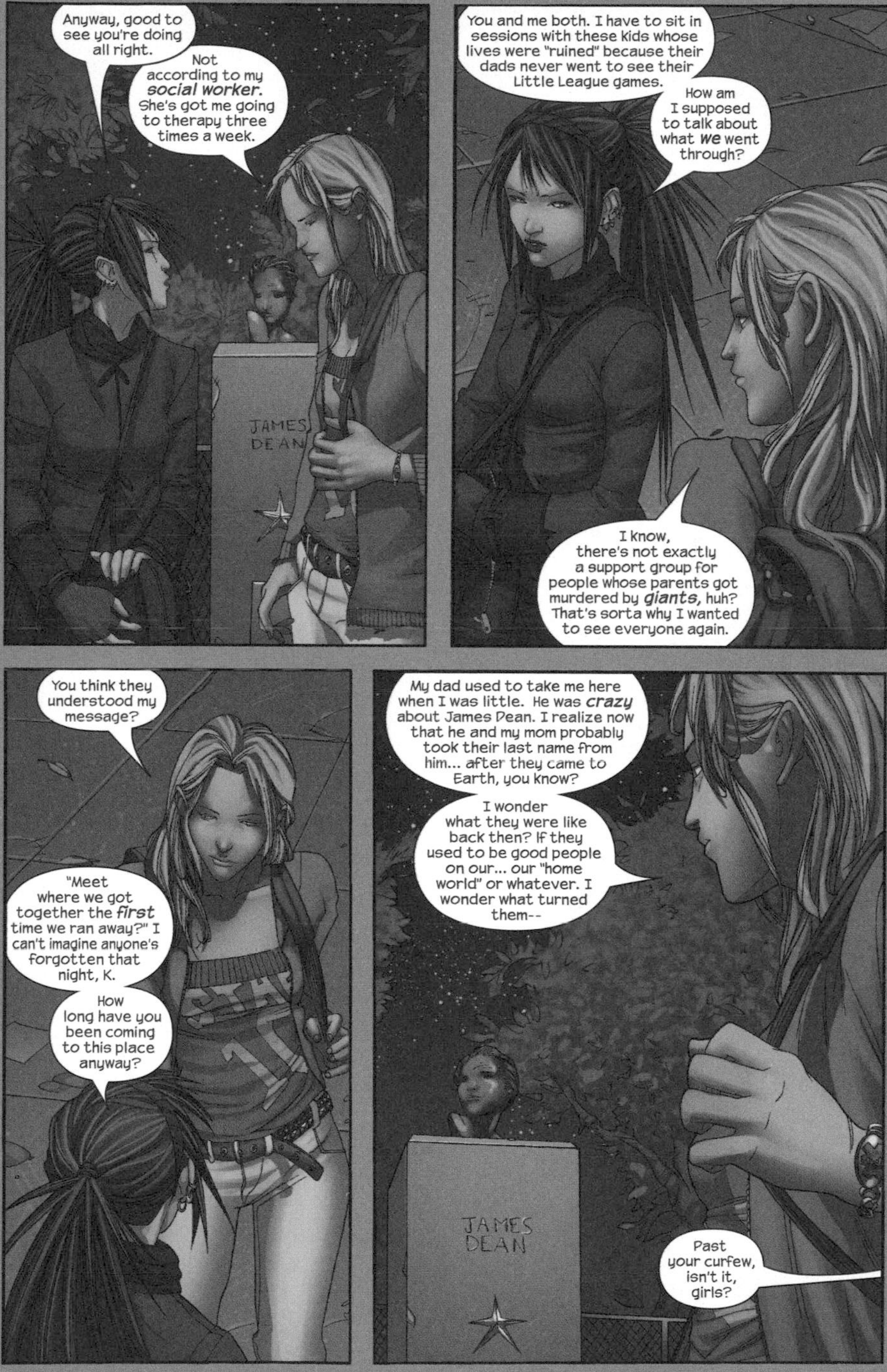
Anyway, good to see you're doing all right.
Not according to my *social worker*. She's got me going to therapy three times a week.
JAMES DEAN
You and me both. I have to sit in sessions with these kids whose lives were "ruined" because their dads never went to see their Little League games.
How am I supposed to talk about what *we* went through?
I know, there's not exactly a support group for people whose parents got murdered by *giants*, huh? That's sorta why I wanted to see everyone again.
You think they understood my message?
"Meet where we got together the *first* time we ran away?" I can't imagine anyone's forgotten that night, K.
How long have you been coming to this place anyway?
My dad used to take me here when I was little. He was *crazy* about James Dean. I realize now that he and my mom probably took their last name from him... after they came to Earth, you know?
I wonder what they were like back then? If they used to be good people on our... our "home world" or whatever. I wonder what turned them--
JAMES DEAN
Past your curfew, isn't it, girls?

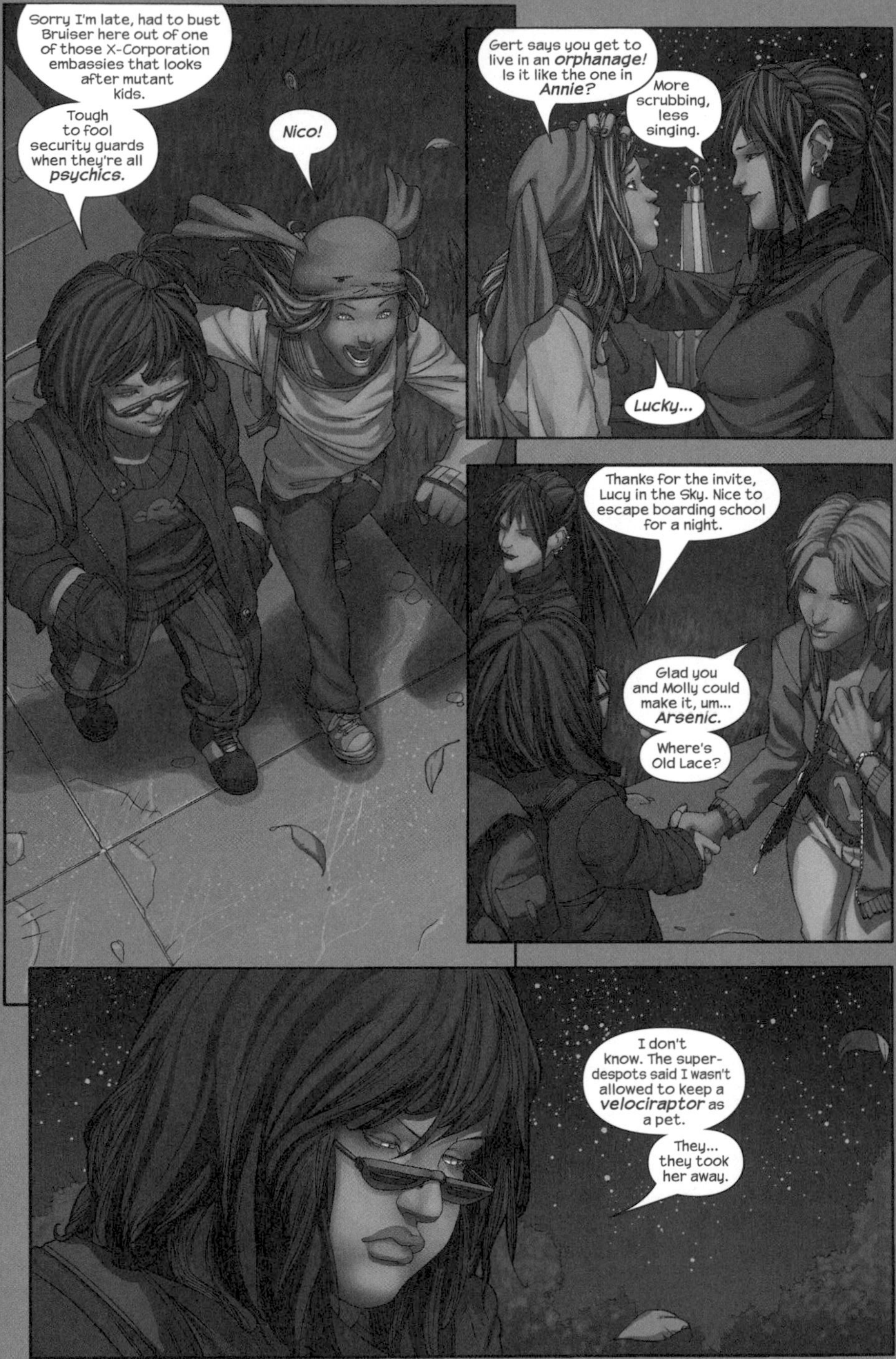
Sorry I'm late, had to bust Bruiser here out of one of those X-Corporation embassies that looks after mutant kids.
Tough to fool security guards when they're all *psychics.*
Nico!
Gert says you get to live in an *orphanage!* Is it like the one in *Annie?*
More scrubbing, less singing.
Lucky...
Thanks for the invite, Lucy in the Sky. Nice to escape boarding school for a night.
Glad you and Molly could make it, um... *Arsenic.*
Where's Old Lace?
I don't know. The super-despots said I wasn't allowed to keep a *velociraptor* as a pet.
They... they took her away.

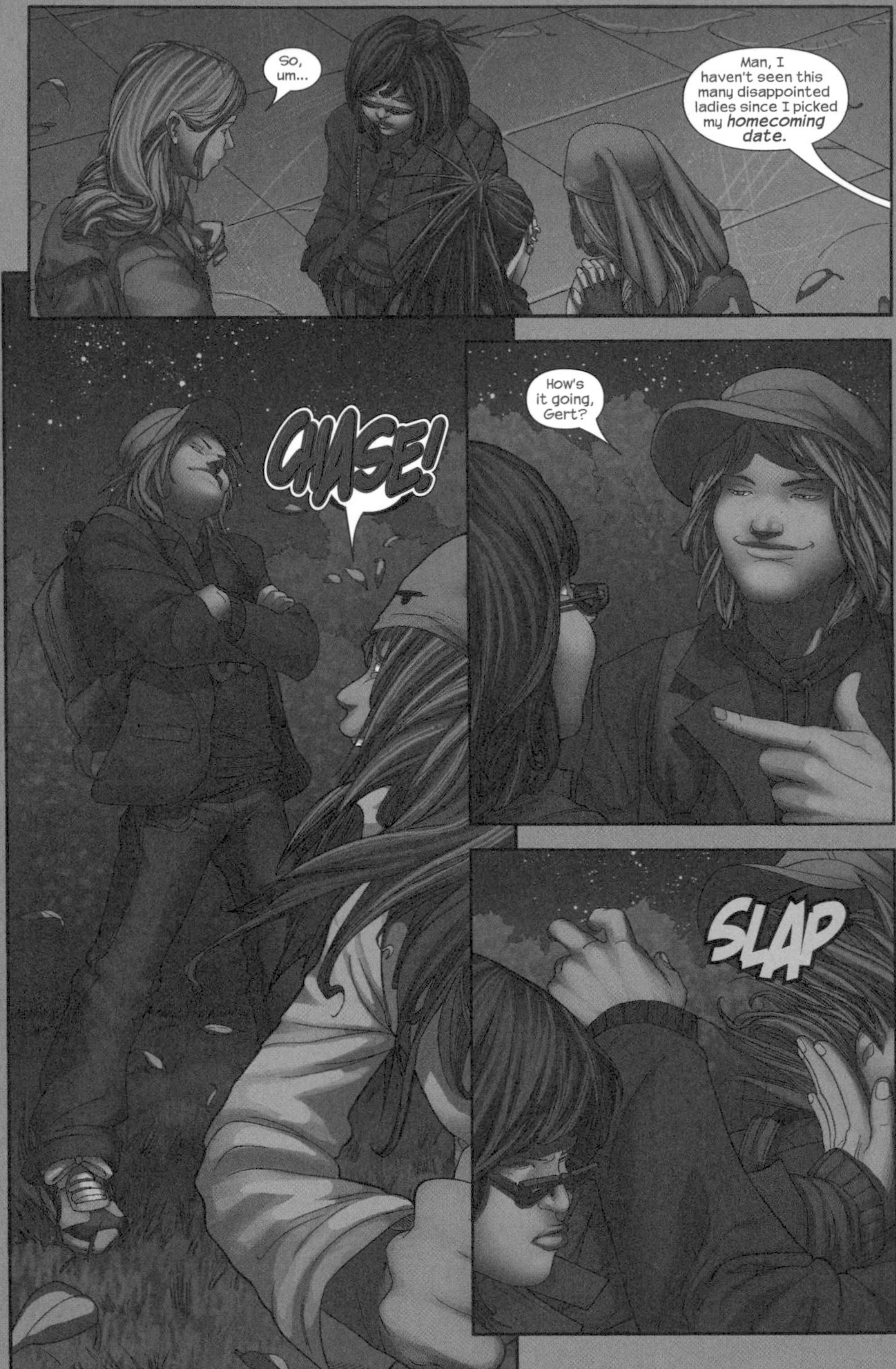
So, um...
Man, I haven't seen this many disappointed ladies since I picked my *homecoming date.*
CHASE!
How's it going, Gert?
SLAP

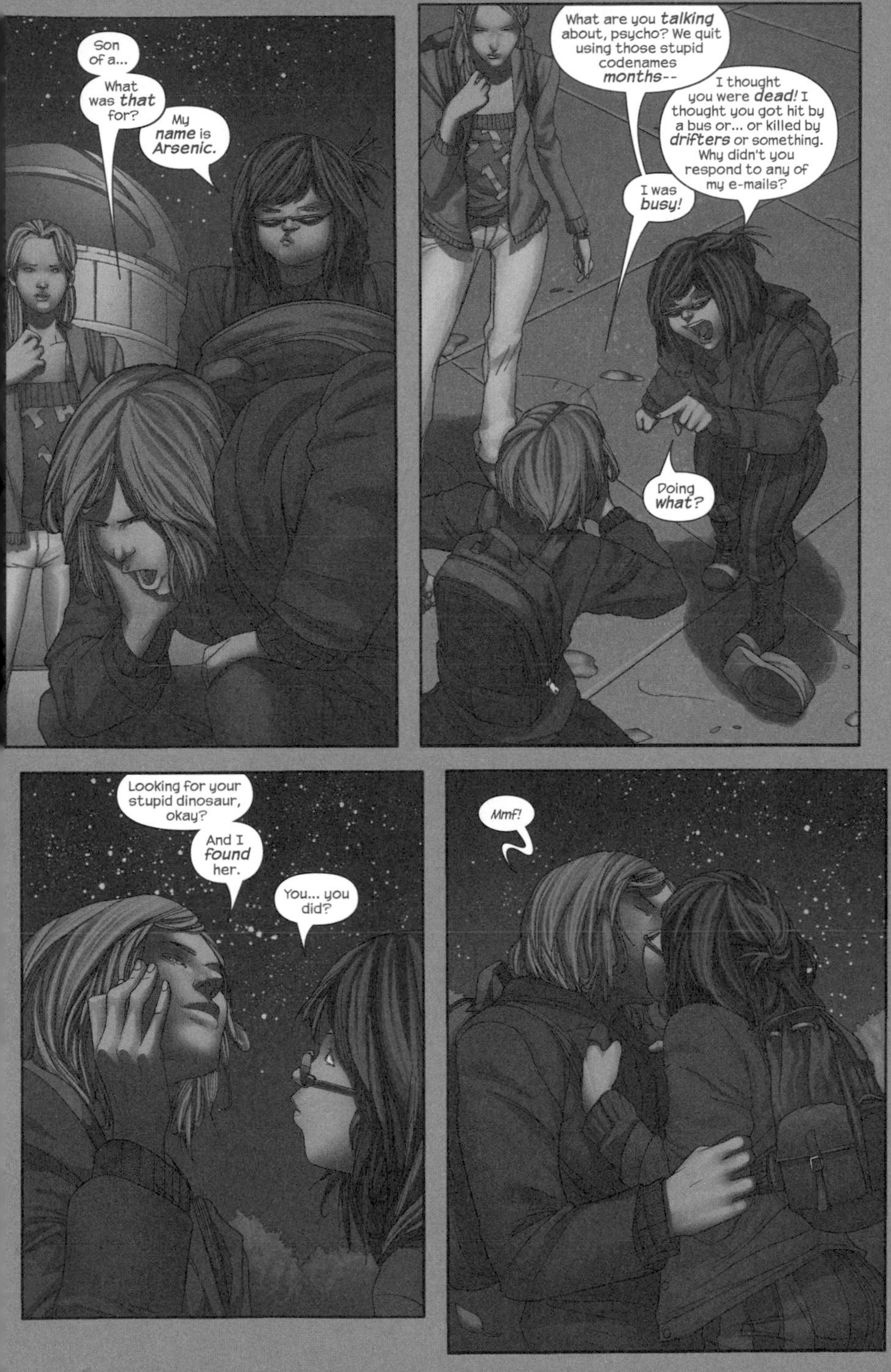

Son of a...
What was that for?
My name is Arsenic.
What are you talking about, psycho? We quit using those stupid codenames months--
I thought you were dead! I thought you got hit by a bus or... or killed by drifters or something. Why didn't you respond to any of my e-mails?
I was busy!
Doing what?
Looking for your stupid dinosaur, okay?
And I found her.
You... you did?
Mmf!

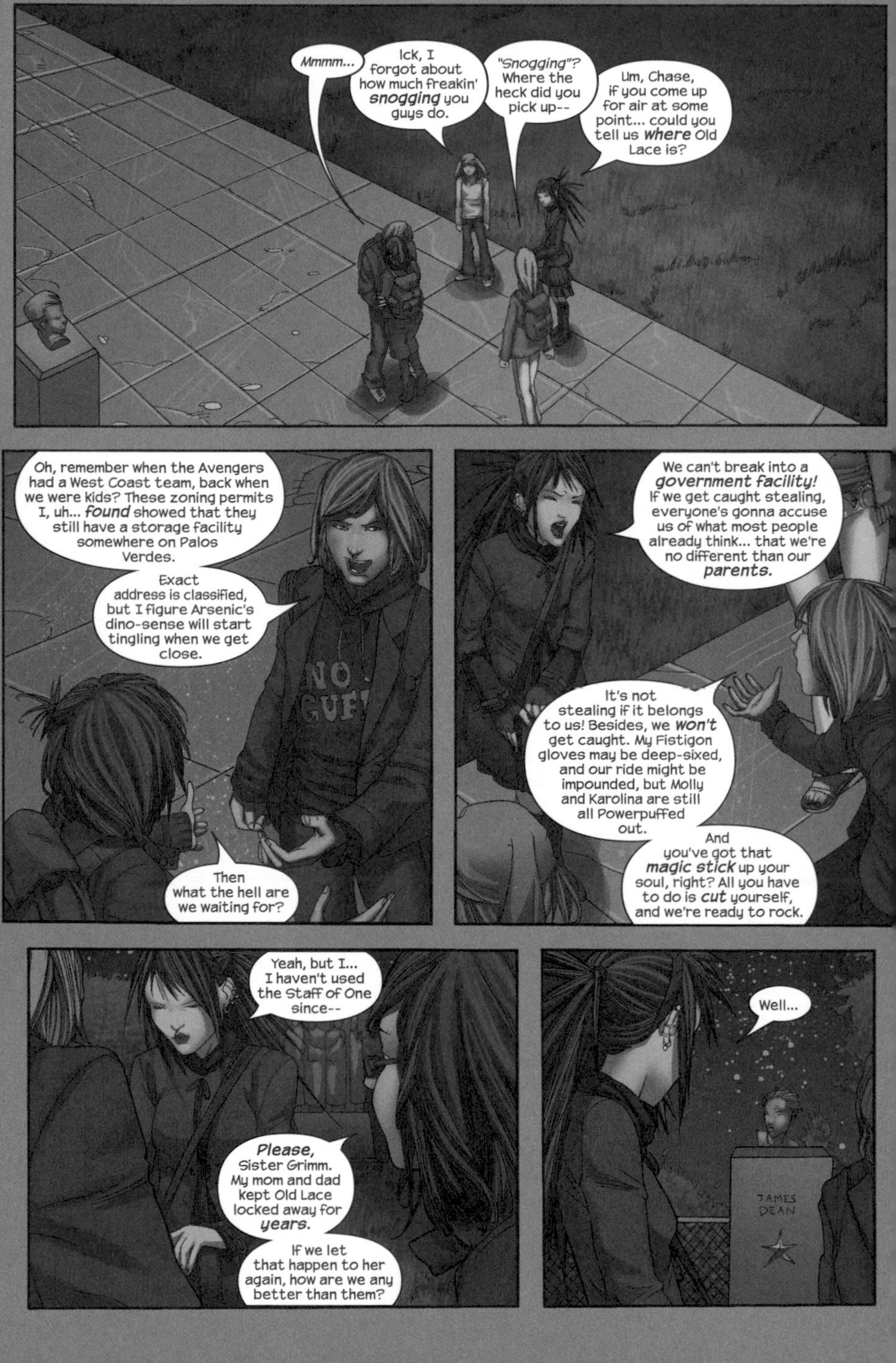
Mmmm...
Ick, I forgot about how much freakin' snogging you guys do.
"Snogging"? Where the heck did you pick up--
Um, Chase, if you come up for air at some point... could you tell us where Old Lace is?
Oh, remember when the Avengers had a West Coast team, back when we were kids? These zoning permits I, uh... found showed that they still have a storage facility somewhere on Palos Verdes.
Exact address is classified, but I figure Arsenic's dino-sense will start tingling when we get close.
NO GUFF
Then what the hell are we waiting for?
We can't break into a government facility! If we get caught stealing, everyone's gonna accuse us of what most people already think... that we're no different than our parents.
It's not stealing if it belongs to us! Besides, we won't get caught. My Fistigon gloves may be deep-sixed, and our ride might be impounded, but Molly and Karolina are still all Powerpuffed out.
And you've got that magic stick up your soul, right? All you have to do is cut yourself, and we're ready to rock.
Yeah, but I... I haven't used the Staff of One since--
Please, Sister Grimm. My mom and dad kept Old Lace locked away for years.
If we let that happen to her again, how are we any better than them?
Well...
JAMES DEAN

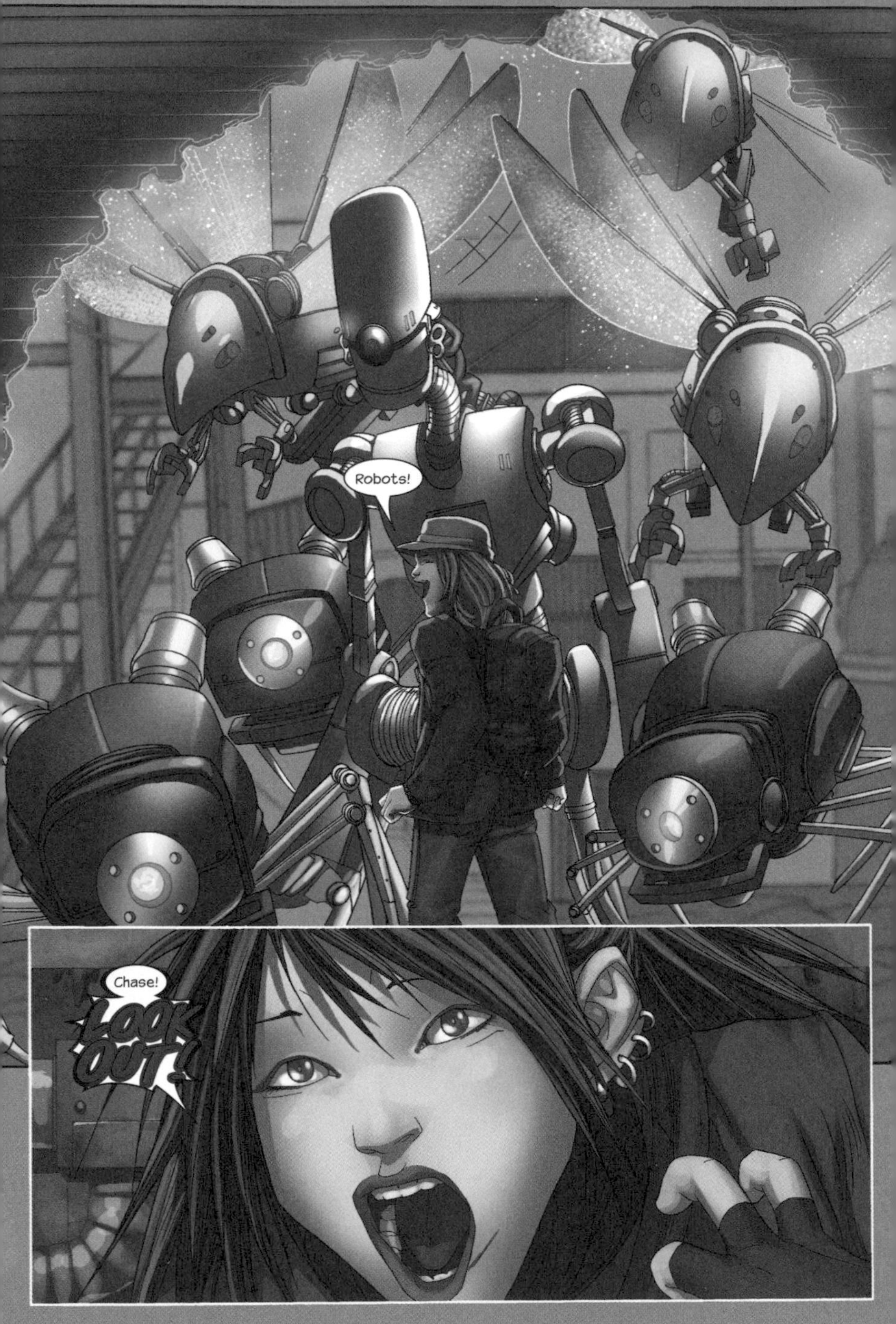

Robots!
Chase!
LOOK OUT!

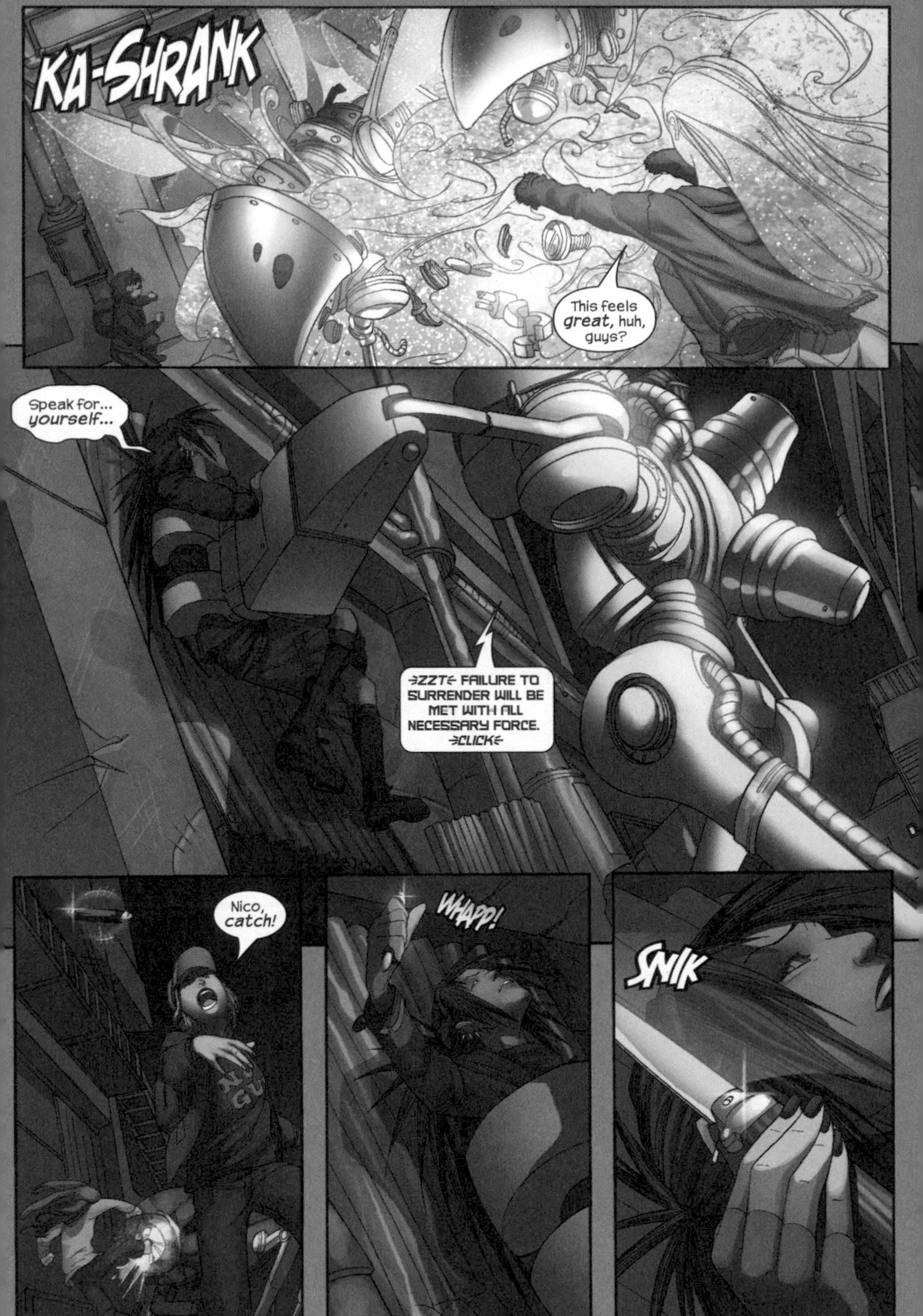

KA-SHRANK
This feels great, huh, guys?
Speak for... yourself...
ZZT FAILURE TO SURRENDER WILL BE MET WITH ALL NECESSARY FORCE. CLICK
Nico, catch!
WHAPP!
SNIK

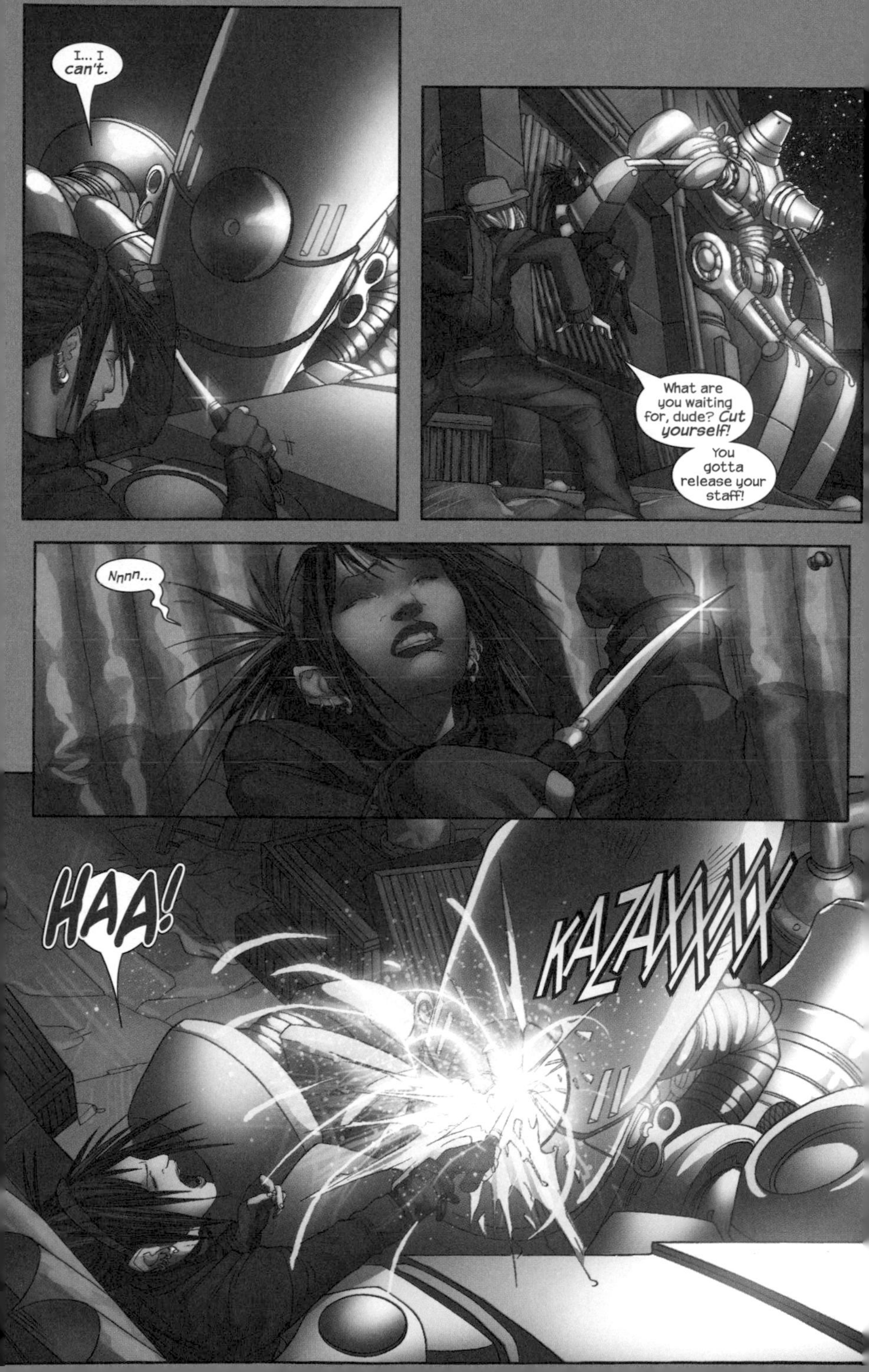
I... I can't.
What are you waiting for, dude? Cut yourself!
You gotta release your staff!
Nnnn...
HAA!
KAZAKKK

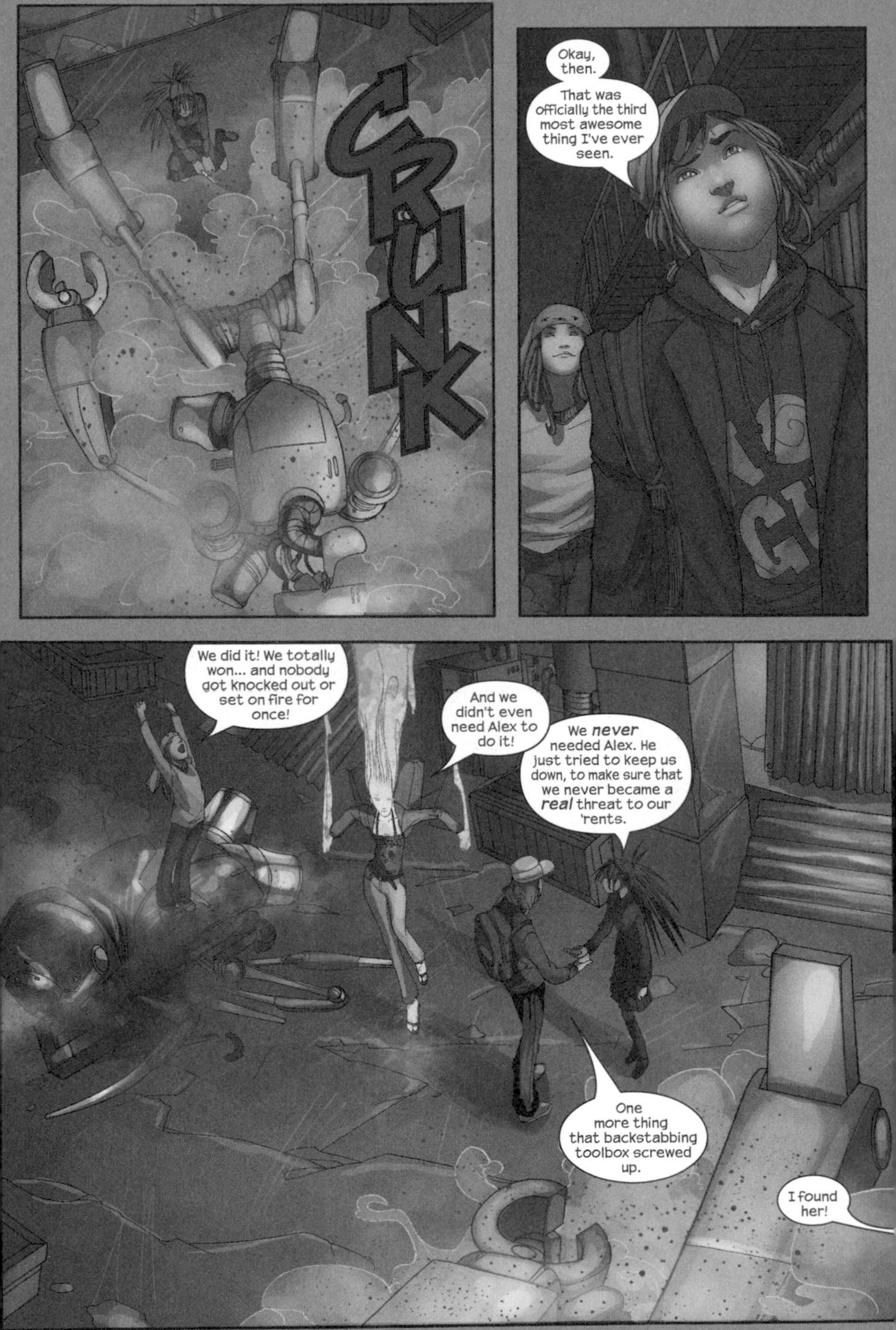

CRUNK
Okay, then.
That was officially the third most awesome thing I've ever seen.
We did it! We totally won... and nobody got knocked out or set on fire for once!
And we didn't even need Alex to do it!
We *never* needed Alex. He just tried to keep us down, to make sure that we never became a *real* threat to our 'rents.
One more thing that backstabbing toolbox screwed up.
I found her!

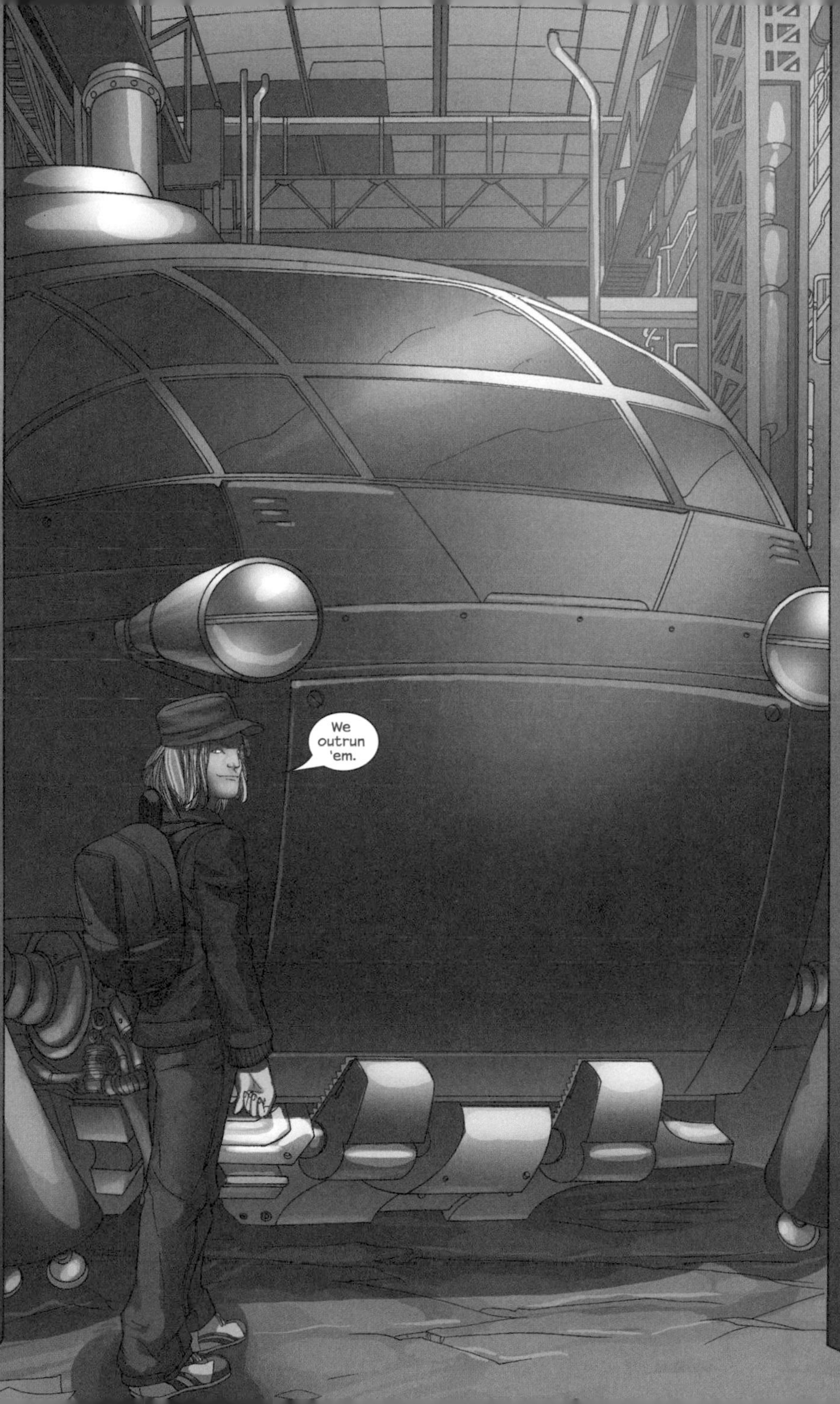
We outrun 'em.

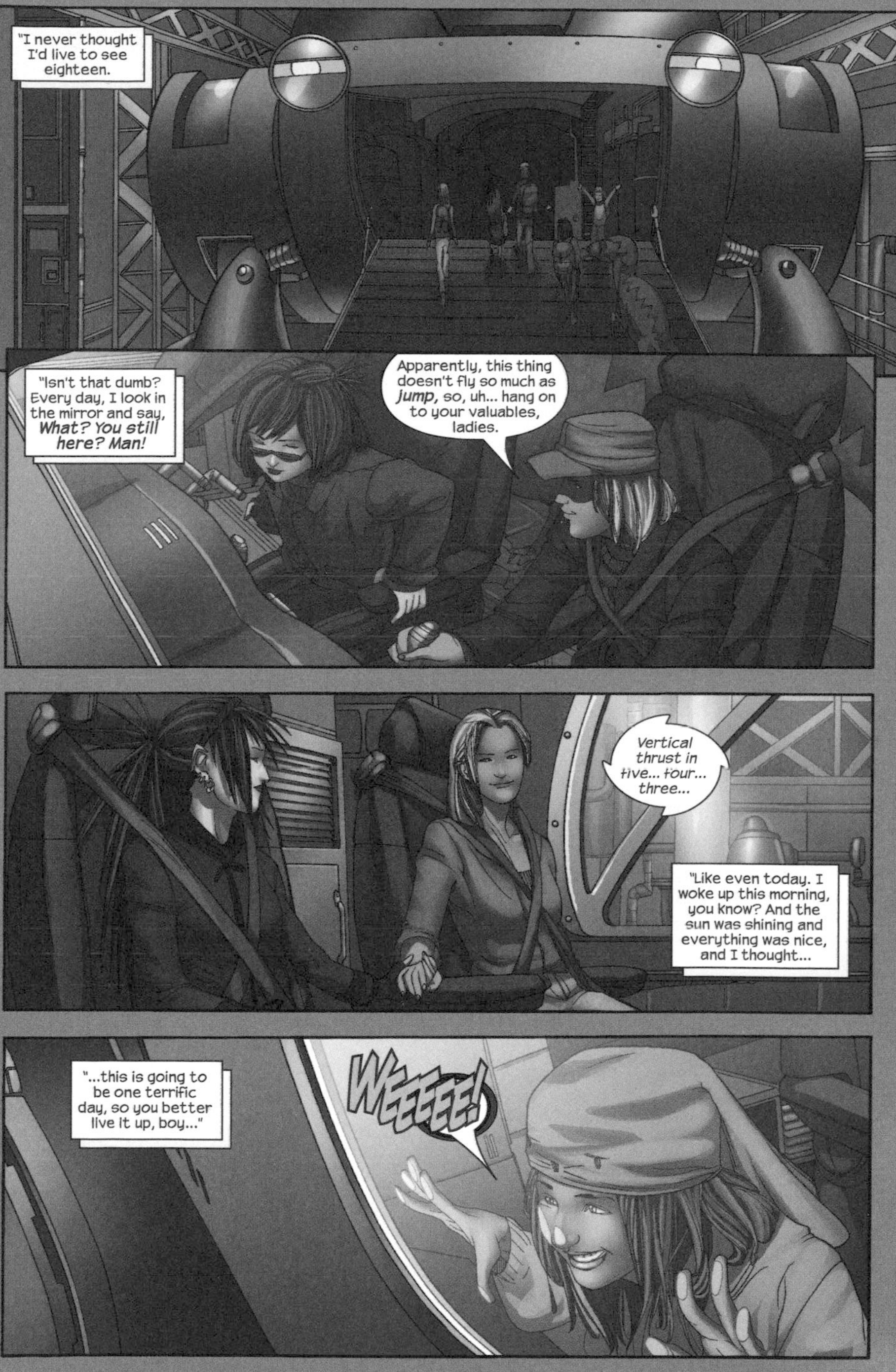

"I never thought I'd live to see eighteen.
"Isn't that dumb? Every day, I look in the mirror and say, *What? You still here? Man!*
Apparently, this thing doesn't fly so much as *jump*, so, uh... hang on to your valuables, ladies.
Vertical thrust in five... four... three...
"Like even today. I woke up this morning, you know? And the sun was shining and everything was nice, and I thought...
"...this is going to be one terrific day, so you better live it up, boy..."
WEEEEE!

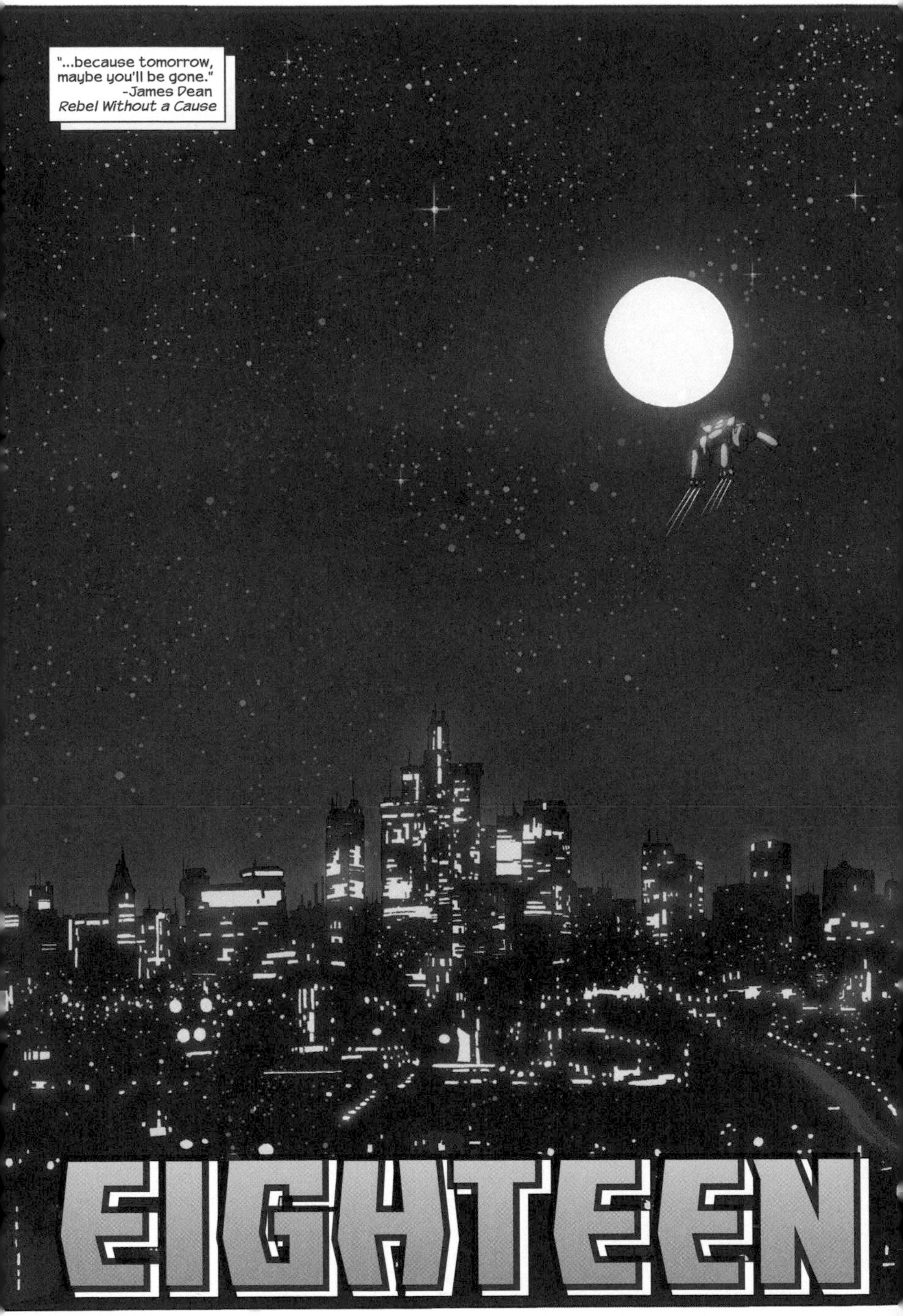
"...because tomorrow, maybe you'll be gone."
-James Dean
Rebel Without a Cause
EIGHTEEN

THIS LETTER APPEARED IN *RUNAWAYS #18*, FOLLOWED BY BRIAN K. VAUGHAN'S RESPONSE:

Team Runaways,

Last issue? What do you mean, LAST ISSUE? What the hell does that mean? Did you type it wrong? Were you thinking of something else, like maybe the Sub-Mariner or the Smurfs? How can there be a last issue when the story is obviously going to continue for years? You're some kind of wrong person. Have It looked Into.

Your fan,
Joss Whedon

Yep, that's the real Joss Whedon, of BUFFY, ASTONISHING X-MEN and, uh, ROSEANNE fame. Cool, huh? But thanks to the vocal support of loyal readers like you (and Joss), I am thrilled to announce that this is NOT the last issue of Runaways. Our kids are going on a well-deserved vacation for a few short months, but the entire creative team will be bringing them back in early 2005 for RUNAWAYS #1! One chapter in the lives of our young heroes has ended, but an all-new, all-different one is about to begin.

THANK YOU NOTE FROM CHRISTINA STRAIN

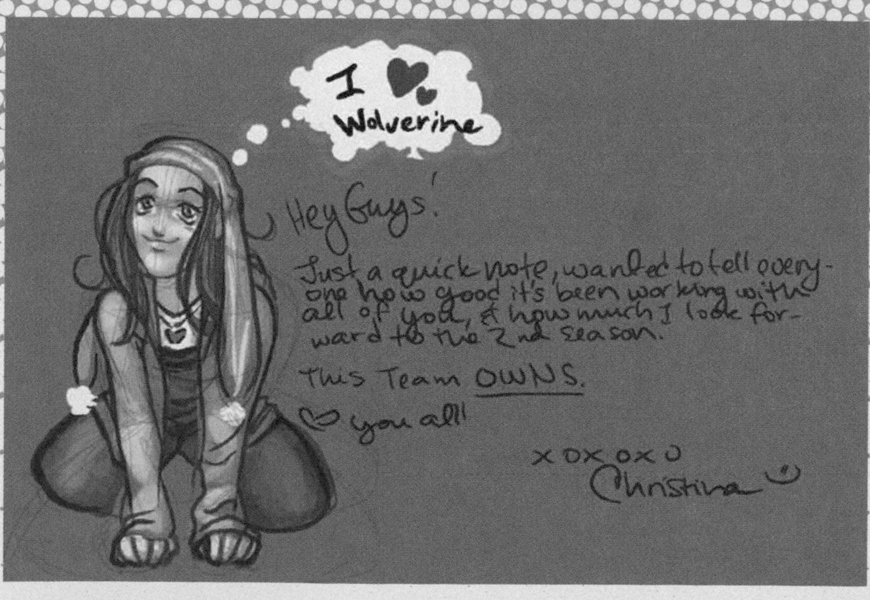
I ♥ Wolverine
Hey Guys!
Just a quick note, wanted to tell every-one how good it's been working with all of you, & how much I look for-ward to the 2nd season.
This Team OWNS.
♥ you all!
xoxoxo
Christina

ADRIAN ALPHONA SKETCHBOOK

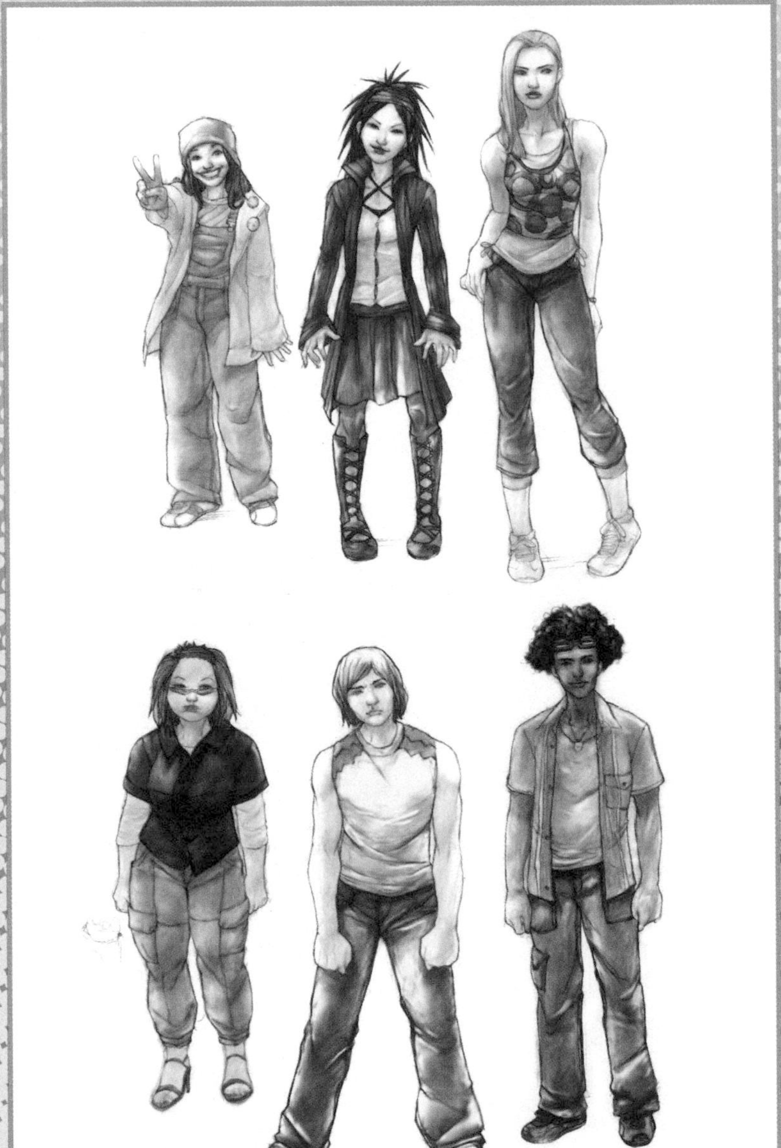

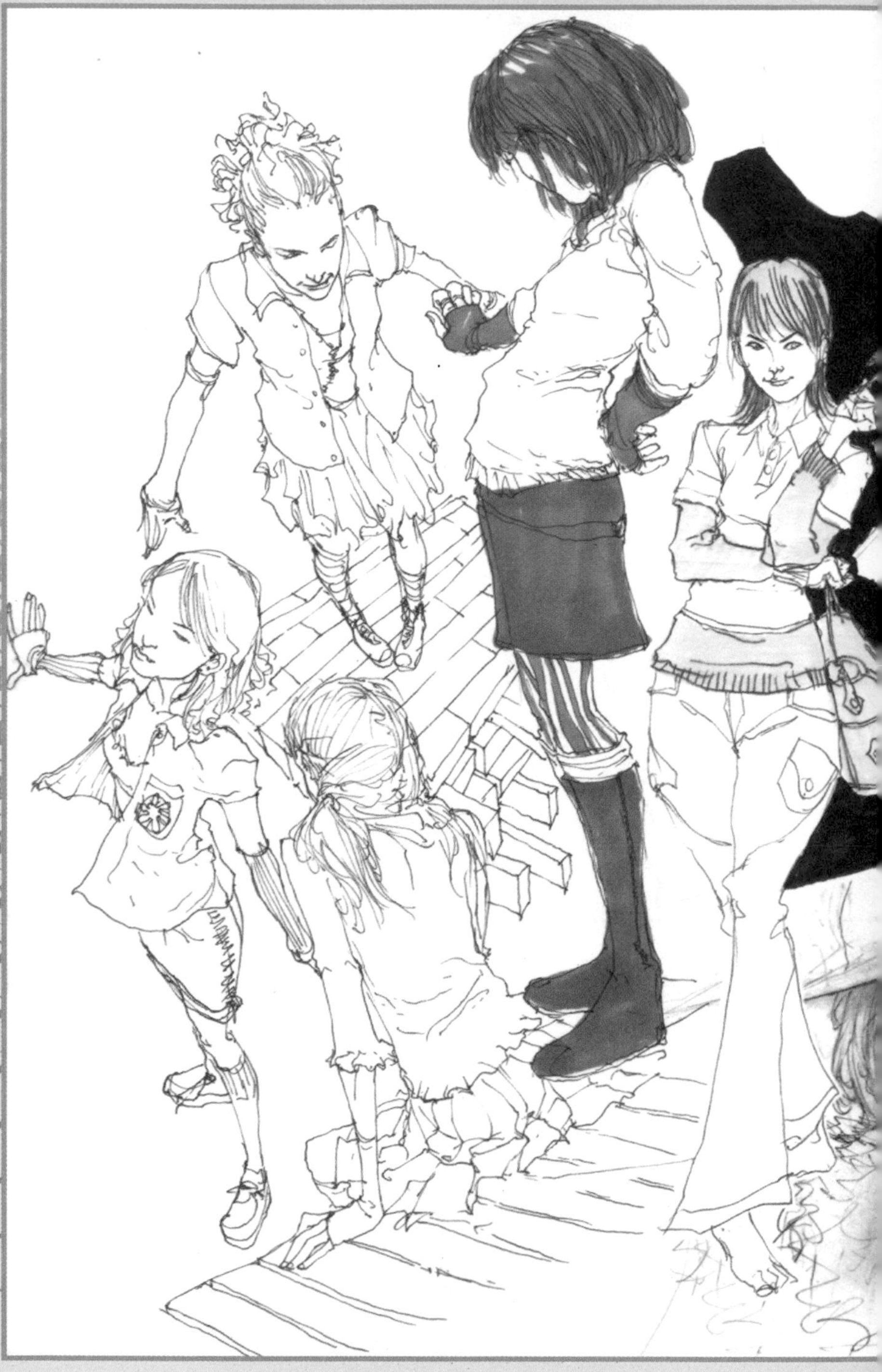

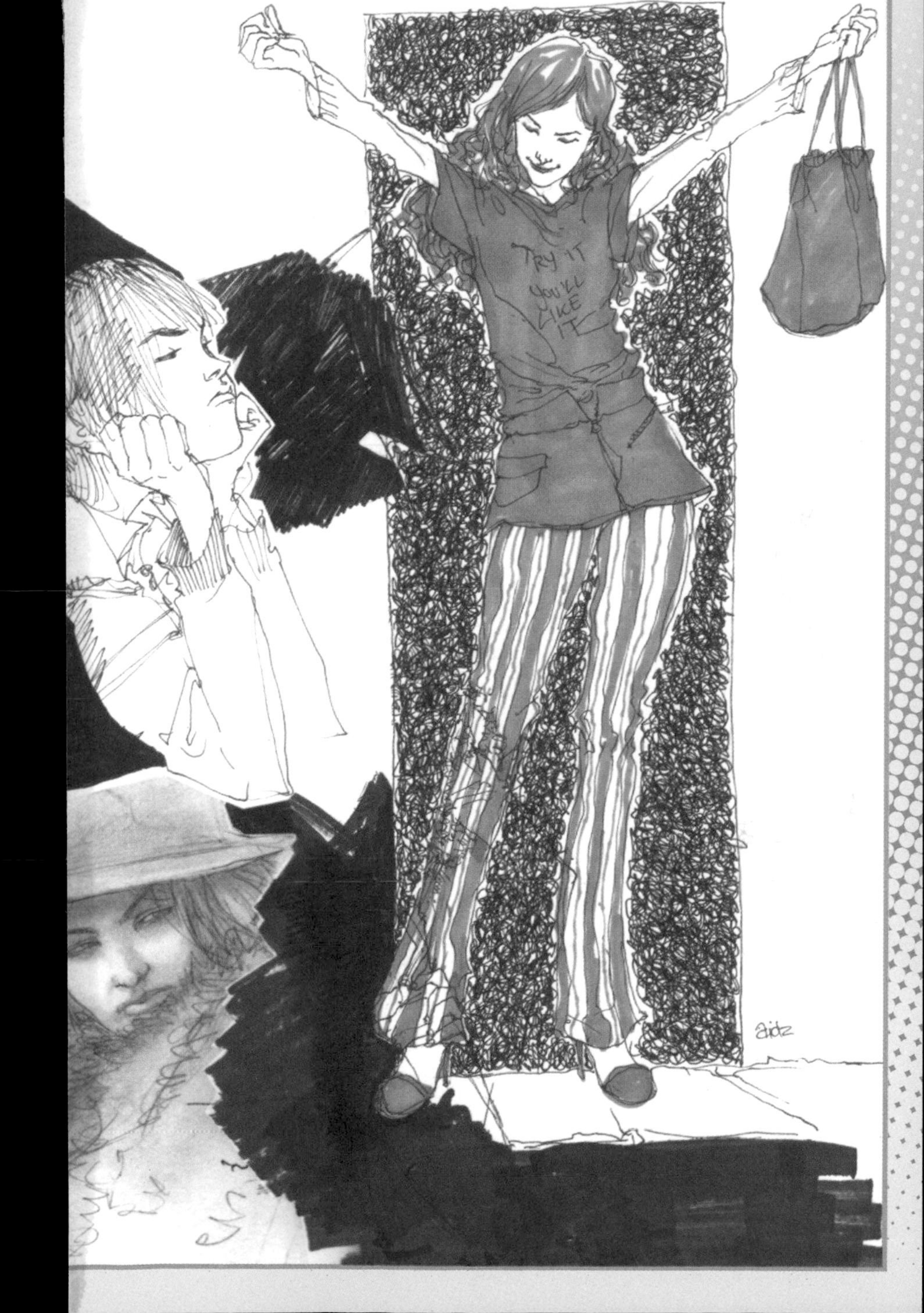
TRY IT YOU'LL LIKE IT
aidz

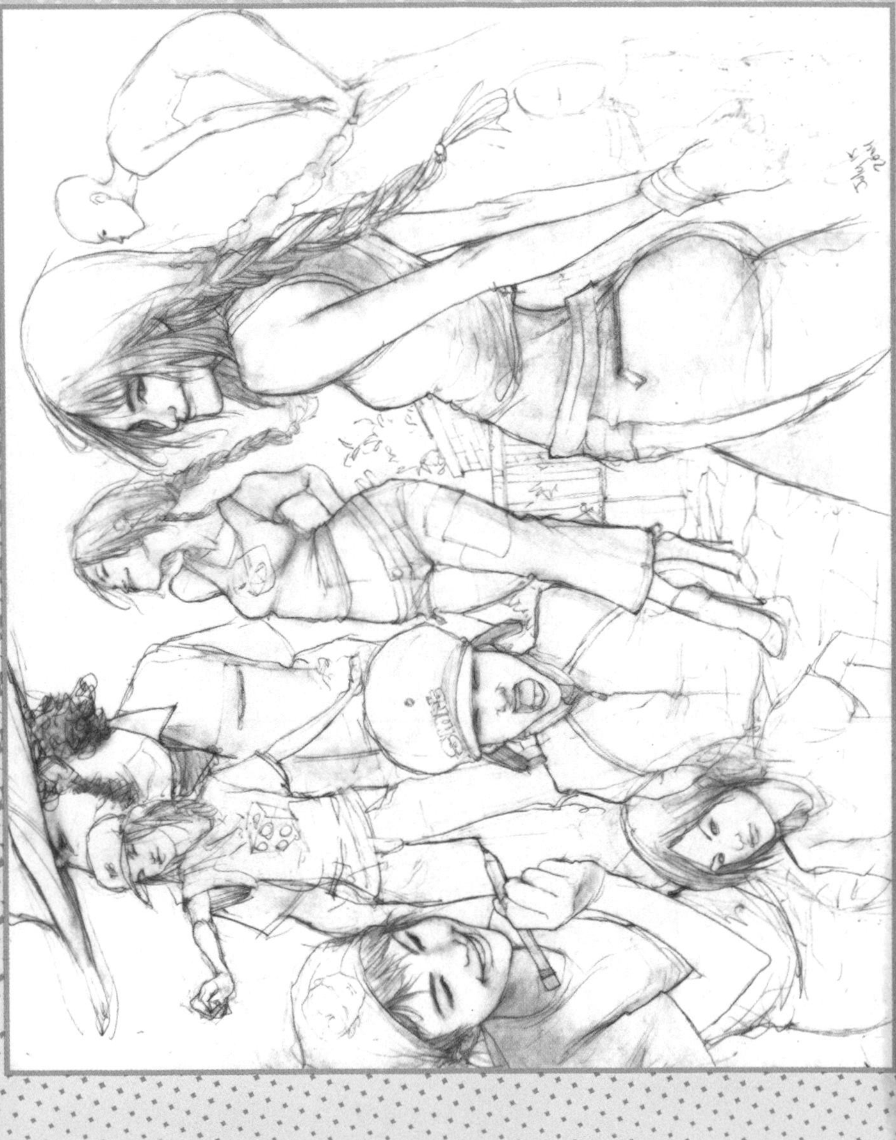